SUPERHEROES AND ECONOMICS

At first sight, superheroes and economics seem to occupy completely different dimensions – but a clash of dimensions is a classic comic book storyline! In this first-of-its-kind book, an economist and a business writer assemble an A-team of academic talent to explore the intersection of superhero mythology and economic theory in ten accessible chapters.

Superheroes and Economics uncovers basic economic truths that are integral to the comic stories from some of the genre's most famous names. The authors of the chapters look at ways that economic principles can add authenticity to imagined universes, and how familiar superhero stories can demonstrate concepts used by economists to forecast the behavior of markets and individuals. If Spider-Man is so smart, why isn't he rich? What are the economic implications of a tech entrepreneur like Tony Stark actually inventing Iron Man armor? What does the 80-year career of Wonder Woman tell us about the evolving role of women in the workplace?

This unique book extends the scope of comics studies to encompass social sciences. It offers a great way to introduce both fans and students to topics like opportunity cost, growth, inflation and cost benefit analysis, as well as more advanced concepts like moral hazard, utility functions and economic growth. This text can be used to supplement economics courses using colorful examples that any pop culture fan can relate to.

Brian O'Roark is a University Professor of Economics at Robert Morris University in Pittsburgh, USA. He is on the board of directors for the *Journal of Economics Teaching* and serves in the role of associate editor. In 2014, Brian was given the Undergraduate Teaching Innovation Award by the Middle Atlantic Association of Colleges of Business Administration and in 2016 he received the President's Award for Outstanding Teaching at RMU.

Rob Salkowitz is an author, consultant and educator focused on the impact of new technology on work, business and popular culture. He is author of four books as well as a contributor to FORBES and his work has appeared in Fast Company, Publishers Weekly, Entrepreneur, Bloomberg Business Week and ICv2, the trade publication of the comics and gaming industry. He teaches in the Communication Leadership Graduate Program at the University of Washington, USA and runs the consulting firm Fathom Fandom.

ROUTLEDGE ECONOMICS AND POPULAR CULTURE

Series Editor
Brian O'Roark, Robert Morris University, USA

Broadway and Economics
Economic Lessons from Show Tunes
Matthew C. Rousu

Dystopia and Economics
A Guide to Surviving Everything from the Apocalypse to Zombies
Edited by Charity-Joy Revere Acchiardo and Michelle Albert Vachris

Contemporary Film and Economics
Lights! Camera! Econ!
Samuel R. Staley

Superheroes and Economics
The Shadowy World of Capes, Masks and Invisible Hands
Edited by Brian O'Roark and Rob Salkowitz

For a full list of titles in this series, please visit www.routledge.com/Routledge-Economics-and-Popular-Culture-Series/book-series/REPC

SUPERHEROES AND ECONOMICS

The Shadowy World of Capes, Masks and Invisible Hands

Edited by Brian O'Roark and Rob Salkowitz

Routledge
Taylor & Francis Group
LONDON AND NEW YORK

First published 2019
by Routledge
2 Park Square, Milton Park, Abingdon, Oxon OX14 4RN

and by Routledge
711 Third Avenue, New York, NY 10017

Routledge is an imprint of the Taylor & Francis Group, an informa business

British Library Cataloguing in Publication Data
A catalogue record for this book is available from the British Library

Library of Congress Cataloging in Publication Data
A catalog record has been requested for this book

ISBN: 978-0-8153-6707-9 (hbk)
ISBN: 978-0-8153-6708-6 (pbk)
ISBN: 978-1-351-25816-6 (ebk)

Typeset in Bembo
by Taylor & Francis Books

To those two kids who were talking about Green Arrow before class, and the girls in my life who have been watching ever since. Brian

To my teachers, students and colleagues for an education that never ends. Rob.

CONTENTS

List of illustrations *ix*
List of contributors *x*
Preface *xiii*

1 Economic realism in the worlds of Alan Moore 1
Rob Salkowitz

PART I
Microeconomics **13**

2 The high cost of being Batman 15
Clair Smith

3 Wonder Woman: Feminist and economic icon 25
James Bryan

4 Poor Peter Parker: Spider sense doesn't apply to making a living 38
Patrick Holt

PART II
Macroeconomics **49**

5 From weakling to superhero: The economics of Captain America 51
John Robinson and William C. Wood

6 The political economy of Black Panther's Wakanda 65
J. Robert Subrick

7 Truth, justice and the economic way 80
Brian O'Roark

PART III
Advanced **95**

8 From the comic book to the real world: The principal-agent problem and moral hazards when Iron Man flies over your backyard 97
Deborah Kozdras and Antoinette Criss

9 The Shadow vs. Batman: Contrasting approaches to "producing" justice 111
John R. Swinton

10 The Avengers vs. the Incredible (but unpredictable) Hulk 124
Amanda Mandzik

Index *140*

ILLUSTRATIONS

Figures

9.1 Superhero isoquants 118
9.2 Superhero isoquant and isocost lines 121
10.1 An indifference curve 127
10.2 Preference map: a family of indifference curves 128
10.3 The Hulk's preference map 129
10.4 Bruce Banner's preference map 130
10.5 Banner and the Hulk's preferences mapped simultaneously 131
10.6 Violation of rationality: overlapping indifference curves 131
10.7 Decision tree for the Avengers: include the Hulk or not? 133
10.8 Utility functions: diminishing marginal utility and increasing marginal utility 135
10.9 Two hypothetical payoffs for the Avengers after the Hulk joins the team 136
10.10 The convex shape of the Avengers' utility function shows that they are risk-loving 137

Tables

5.1 Value of Rogers's 1943 investment of $1000 54
9.1 Hero production (five villains per night)* 120

CONTRIBUTORS

James Bryan is a late in life comic book fan and a novice economist. Having logged many hours in a cube as a financial representative, he is now enjoying a secluded retirement. He spends his days catching up with the exploits of caped crusaders, men of steel, and women of extraordinary abilities.

Antoinette (Toni) Criss is a Senior Instructor of Economics at the University of South Florida, Tampa. She received her PhD in Economics from the University of New Hampshire and has been teaching economics at various institutions for over 20 years. Her economics superheroes are Gary Becker and Steven Levitt whose work encourages her to boldly seek opportunities to find and apply economic concepts and reasoning in unique settings. In the classroom, she strives to do the same with her students.

Patrick Holt is a computer engineer and comic book fan. Introduced to comics by his older brother's collection in the early 1970s, he was hooked. He has read and collected thousands of comics, noticing details in the art and story lines that piqued his curiosity about the economic and financial repercussions in that world. He is currently working on his degree in Economics and Finance at the University of Texas, San Antonio. He and his wife volunteer with animal rescue and live on a small hobby farm with too many dogs, cats, and not enough chickens.

Deborah Kozdras is the Associate Director of the Gus A. Stavros Center for Free Enterprise and Economic Education in the College of Education at the University of South Florida, Tampa. With a PhD in Curriculum and Instruction, Deborah conducts workshops for K-12 educators that use an interdisciplinary approach to infuse economic decision-making and entrepreneurial thinking across the curriculum. Her entrepreneurial superheroes are Steve Jobs and Elon Musk and she encourages teachers to inspire students to invent ways to fly faster than a speeding bullet to make the world a better place.

Amanda Mandzik received her B.S. from Shepherd University in West Virginia in 2008, and her PhD in Economics from West Virginia University in 2014. She taught Statistics, Principles of Macroeconomics, and Principles of Microeconomics at West Virginia University, and then began teaching at Penn State University in 2014 where she has taught Introductory Macroeconomics, Statistical Foundations of Econometrics, and Introduction to Econometrics. Amanda lives in State College with her husband Philip and their sons Little Phil and Alek. They also have two dogs named Dartanian and Black Jack.

Brian O'Roark is a University Professor of Economics at Robert Morris University in Pittsburgh, and is a co-author of *Essentials of Economics* (with Lee Coppock and Dirk Mateer, W.W. Norton, 2016). He is on the board of directors for the *Journal of Economics Teaching* and serves in the role of associate editor. In 2014, Brian was presented the Undergraduate Teaching Innovation Award by the Middle Atlantic Association of Colleges of Business Administration and in 2016 he received the President's Award for Outstanding Teaching at RMU. A veteran of many marathons and many more half-marathons, he wishes he could run like the Flash.

John Robinson is a Lecturer in the College of Business at James Madison University. He received his PhD in Economics from George Mason University in 2016, with fields in Political Economy and History of Economic Thought. His primary research focuses on historical and conceptual approaches to ownership and argues that our modern perspective – relying on the "bundle of rights" metaphor – understates exclusivity as the primary attribute of property. His work on property theory has been published in the *Journal of Scottish Philosophy, Econ Journal Watch,* and *The Independent Review.*

Rob Salkowitz is an author, consultant and educator focused on the impact of new technology on work, business and popular culture. He is author of four books including *Comic-Con and the Business of Pop Culture* (2012), *Young World Rising: How Youth, Technology and Entrepreneurship are Changing the World from the Bottom Up* (2010) and *Generation Blend: Managing Across the Technology Age Gap* (2008), and *Listening to the Future: Why It's Everybody's Business* (2008). He is a contributor to FORBES and his work has appeared in Fast Company, Publishers Weekly, Entrepreneur, Bloomberg Business Week and ICv2, the trade publication of the comics and gaming industry. He teaches in the Communication Leadership Graduate Program at the University of Washington, is founding partner in MediaPlant, a digital communications firm, and serves as a consultant and strategist for companies worldwide. Rob earned a BA in Political Science at Columbia University. He and his wife Eunice Verstegen live and work in Seattle, WA. Follow him on Twitter @robsalk.

Clair Smith is an associate professor and chair of the Department of Economics at St. John Fisher College in Rochester, New York. He is passionate about the application of microeconomics to all areas of life – including superheroes. His academic areas of interest include economic education, law and economics, and public choice. He currently serves as president of the New York State Economics Association.

J. Robert Subrick is an Associate Professor of Economics and the Gilliam Professor of Free Enterprise at James Madison University. He holds a B.A. (history and international relations) and B.S. (economics) from the University of Delaware and a PhD (economics) from George Mason University. Before coming to JMU, he was a Research Associate at the Center for Institutional Reform and the Informal Sector at the University of Maryland and Associate Director of the Center for the Economic Study for Religion at George Mason University. His research and teaching focus on economic development, political economy, and the history of economic thought.

John R. Swinton is Professor of Economics and the Director for the Center for Economic Education at Georgia College. His areas of teaching and research are wide reaching. They span public finance, environmental economics and the economics of education. His work has been nationally recognized by groups such as the National Association of Economic Educators and the Freedoms Foundation at Valley Forge. He comes to a love of comic book characters from the ability of writers to embed discussions of important social issues within the context of fantastical characters. It is simply up to the reader to choose to contemplate the deeper messages.

William C. Wood is Professor of Economics and Director of the Center for Economic Education at James Madison University. Wood received his PhD in economics from the University of Virginia in 1980. His research awards include the Henry H. Villard Award from the National Association of Economic Educators (2016), the Best Paper award from the *Journal of Private Enterprise* (with David Kreutzer, 2001) and the Clifford D. Spangler Award from the American Risk and Insurance Association (1991). Wood was an inaugural winner of the Southern Economic Association's Kenneth G. Elzinga Teaching Award in 2002. His research interests include industrial organization, behavioral finance and economic education.

PREFACE

It would be difficult to imagine two subjects further apart than economics and superheroes. Superheroes speak to our imagination, our idealistic belief in justice and the prospect of becoming more than human. Economics traffics in the more obscure. Realists complain that economic ideas are reduced to equations and human behavior flattened into coarse abstractions. The impulses that guide behavior at both the micro and macro levels are credited to such mystic forces as invisible hands and animal spirits.

And yet these two worlds influence and inform one another to a remarkable degree. As superheroes have become staples of the entertainment world in the 21st century, reaching an audience of billions through the media of film, television and videogames in addition to their native format of comics, they require at least a toehold in the world of ordinary experience to achieve a suspension of disbelief. In other words, we need the worlds inhabited by superheroes to resemble our own in superficial aspects so we can buy into the fantasy, action and drama of the stories.

Economics can help. Everyone experiences the economic world at some level. We buy tickets to see the movies, after all. When we see characters on screen or on the page who struggle to pay the rent, who must grapple with the opportunity costs of forgoing a date or a job opportunity because of their sidelight as a costumed vigilante, or whose access to crime fighting equipment is funded by private or corporate wealth, it deepens our immersion in the storytelling world. It provides a veneer of plausibility to fantastic ideas, and grounds the motivations of the characters in forces we all recognize.

By the same token, superheroes can help demonstrate or explain economic concepts for which the ordinary student or citizen might not have a concrete frame of reference. The economic notion of "moral hazard" was interesting and important enough to win its exponents a Nobel Prize, but try explaining it without a relatable example. Superheroes have become a common language, a rare cultural touchpoint that everyone across our fragmented ideological landscape can recognize. By using their well-known stories as springboards, we can broaden understanding of economic principles and add a little panache to a discourse that could use a few colorful costumes and big explosions.

The two editors of this volume also come from contrasting backgrounds. Brian O'Roark is University Professor of Economics at Robert Morris University in Pennsylvania who has written extensively on the use of superheroes and popular culture tropes to teach economics.

Rob Salkowitz teaches in the Communication Leadership Graduate Program at the University of Washington, but is better known as a writer about the comics and entertainment industry for FORBES and other publications, and as the author of the 2012 book *Comic-Con and the Business of Pop Culture*. While Brian approaches the subject from within the discipline of economics, looking for ways that superhero texts can illuminate the theories, Rob views comics as a storytelling medium informed by economic discourse, and as a business influenced by economic factors.

In this book, we've curated a range of chapters from scholars across the country who offer different perspectives on the intersection between economic and superheroes. Rob's chapter, "Economic Realism in the Worlds of Alan Moore," kicks things off with an exploration of some of the seminal works in the comics-superhero canon to deal explicitly with economic issues as a text or subtext. The British comic writer Alan Moore (most famous for *Watchmen*) anticipated and demonstrated sophisticated techniques of economic modeling to give his story universes a rigorous internal logic that has elevated them into recognized classics, not just of the superhero genre, but of contemporary literature. That storytelling style brought a heightened sense of sophistication to superhero comics and laid the groundwork for today's shared universes.

Micro stories

The remaining chapters of the book are divided into sections to reflect the economic discipline. Economics is separated into two subsets: microeconomics and macroeconomics. In micro we examine the decision making at the individual or firm level. Micro does mean small, but it does not mean insignificant. As chapters two through four suggest, there are some substantial issues in the lives of individuals that are dealt with at the micro level, including how a hero deals with scarcity, how another hero deals with discrimination and how a third hero deal with poverty.

When the Flash asked Batman what his superpower was in the 2017 *Justice League* movie, the caped crusader replied, "I'm rich." Just how rich? Clair Smith of St. John Fisher College cracks open the ledger books of Wayne Enterprises to tally up the high costs of being a Dark Knight in "The High Cost of Being Batman."

Did you know that Wonder Woman, the mighty Amazon princess Diana, was once relegated to the role of "secretary" in the 1940s super group The Justice Society of America, because, by the logic of the time, that's what women did? She's come a long way, and her journey reflects the changing role of women in the workplace and society. James Bryan traces the evolution of the Amazon princess in "Wonder Woman: Feminist and Economic Icon".

Patrick Holt of the University of Texas at San Antonio explores one of the persistent questions in superhero fiction: if you're so super, why aren't you rich? His chapter, "Poor Peter Parker: Spider Sense Doesn't Apply to Making a Living," follows the long-suffering Peter Parker, aka Spider-Man, who swings freely from skyscrapers and wisecracks his way to victory over criminals, but constantly struggles to pay the rent and care for his dear Aunt May.

Macro stories

Macroeconomics involves economic analysis that focuses on larger decision making units. Activity that happens in the macro sphere is typically national or international in nature. The decision made at this level impacts far more people than those at the micro level. To that end, in chapters five through seven we examine three heroes whose stories are intertwined with the financial system, economic growth and economic institutions.

Since Captain America first appeared in the pages of comic books in 1941, he has commanded a lot of reader interest, but what about compound interest? James Madison University's John Robinson and William Wood inquire into Captain America's investment strategies to see how well his portfolio performed while he was frozen in ice for 80 years in "From Weakling to Superhero: The Economics of Captain America."

The Black Panther has a leg up on Batman in terms of wealth. Bruce Wayne may be a billionaire industrialist, but T'Challa is absolute monarch of a fabulously wealthy country. J. Robert Subrick of James Madison University shines a spotlight on "The Political Economy of Black Panther's Wakanda," contrasting the mythical African nation with the very real issues of economic development and political dynamics in post-colonial Africa.

Superman is a systems guy. He fights for what is right and upholds the ideals of the country in which he lives. That means he supports the institutions that make society work. James Bryan tackles the question of why we should be thankful that the Man of Steel lands in Kansas and not the Ukraine in "Truth, Justice and the Economic Way".

Graduate studies

The final three chapters move us beyond the basics to tackle a few more complicated subjects. Most people think that superhero stories are for kids, but the economics can be quite advanced as chapters eight through ten show us. Here we plunge into moral hazard, production optimization and risk tolerance.

In "From the Comic Book to the Real World: The Principal-Agent Problem and Moral Hazards When Iron Man Flies Over Your Backyard," Deborah Kozdras and Antoinette Criss, University of South Florida, use Iron Man, the armored alter-ego of entrepreneur and inventor Tony Stark, to explore a host of economic issues including the tricky matter of eminent domain and moral hazard. At the heart of their inquiry is the balance between privately driven innovation and responsibility to the public. What, if anything, should the government do when an individual invents something to give them superpowers?

John R. Swinton of Georgia College uses the techniques of an economist and the encyclopedic knowledge of a true fan to compare the crime fighting styles of two of the original costumed vigilantes from comics' Golden Age: Batman, and his pulp and radio inspiration, The Shadow, in "The Shadow vs. Batman: Contrasting Approaches to Producing Justice." These two non-powered super-sleuths take two very different approaches, based on the personas of the heroes, to achieve the same ends.

One overlapping theme between comics and economics is the role of uncertainty and "wild cards." Amanda Mandzik of Penn State University, in her chapter "The Avengers vs. The Incredible (but Unpredictable) Hulk," tallies the costs and benefits of having someone on your team capable of winning a battle with a single blow, but who could just as easily turn against his teammates if the mood strikes.

Up, up and away

Comics and economics definitely make for strange bedfellows. So, do our dual objectives of delighting comic fans with a new perspective on some of our favorite characters while breathing life into economic concepts that don't always light up the room. We hope the selections in this collection inform and entertain in equal measure, but we will, in the name of accessibility and better sales, resist the temptation to express that in the form of an equation.

Enjoy!

Rob Salkowitz and Brian O'Roark, January 2018

1

ECONOMIC REALISM IN THE WORLDS OF ALAN MOORE

Rob Salkowitz

We don't usually think of speculative fiction writers in genres like sci-fi and superhero comics as having much in common with economists, given their different audiences and objectives. In fact, both are engaged in a similar process: creating scenarios realistic enough to model outcomes when variables are introduced into the premise. Economists generally use their models to answer questions like "how will changes in government spending affect the unemployment rate?" Authors of speculative fiction in prose and comics tend toward more imaginative variations from current conditions: What if time travel were possible? What if humans colonized nearby planets? What if a nascent technology like robotics or virtual reality became pervasive through the ordinary processes of commercialization and consumerization?

Just as good economic models need to plausibly resemble real world conditions and behaviors, so too does good speculative fiction need to evoke a willing suspension of disbelief in which the reader accepts the premise and underlying world logic so the story can establish an emotional connection. A "magic asterisk" meant to wave away inconvenient inconsistencies is no more welcome in a good work of fiction than it is in a forecast of economic growth. Even in genres less dependent on scientific realism than science fiction, such as fantasy and horror, authors strive to create, if not realism, then *consistency* in the settings of their stories so as not to distract from the drama and conflict taking place in the foreground. As the superhero genre has evolved from its simple roots into a more sophisticated storytelling platform, it has grappled with these same issues.

Alan Moore, who burst onto the comics scene in the 1980s, is the pivotal figure in the evolution of comics toward greater economic realism in multiple dimensions. His influential early work like *V for Vendetta* (1982), *Miracleman* (1982) and *Watchmen* (1986) fleshed out the motivations of super-powered characters in greater detail than had been previously attempted, and set those characters loose in worlds that more closely resembled our own.

Moore's concerns were primarily social, political, psychological and philosophical. The realism he brought to comics raised questions about the nature of power, the deeper motives of vigilantes and villains, the relationship between individuals and institutions, and the heretofore unexamined issues of sexuality and sexual violence in the context of super-powered individuals. However, his approach to storytelling and his personal background required him to ask and answer important micro- and macro-economic questions as a way of fleshing out the worlds he built.

Even when Moore moved beyond superheroes later in his career, he never neglected the role of economics, sometimes giving issues like globalization and gentrification a pivotal role in the plot (as in *Big Numbers* from 1988–1989) or using behaviors associated with economic class as a crucial element of characterization (as in *From Hell*, 1989–1997). By the mid-1990s, his innovations had been internalized by other comic storytellers whose work laid the foundations for the 21st century boom in superhero stories in mass media.

Another interesting feature of Moore's innovations from an economics perspective is how closely his creative process mirrored more systematic approaches to forecasting that were evolving in the business world around the same time. The setting of Moore's stories aren't just backdrops to conflict and action; they are *scenarios* that carefully reflect the logical outcome of their underlying assumptions.

Economic realism in superhero comics

The subject of economic realism in fictional works can be approached several ways. Traditionally, critics would say a work is economically realistic if the actions and settings accurately reflect the economic conditions of the real world: People worry about money; they don't inexplicably have access to things beyond their economic means; the economic class origins of characters influence their attitudes and behavior; and so on.

In genres where the premise or setting departs from ordinary reality in important ways – science fiction, fantasy, superheroes – our expectations of realism are both more modest and more extravagant. It may be beside the point for the protagonist to sweat certain dollars and cents details. However, we expect the creator(s) to have thought through the logic of the entire story world so we are not confused or distracted by inconsistencies. We expect them to *construct a world* where economic relationships are consistent, even if the conditions of that world depart dramatically from what we are used to.

Today, world-building is an important element in superhero stories, arguably more important than any individual character or story set in that world. Superhero properties are taken into other media not one at a time, but as entire universes that can be embroidered and extended infinitely across different products and different media. Because superhero character arcs so often develop along predictable patterns and use many stock story tropes, the richness and integrity of the universe becomes the selling point that keeps readers emotionally invested in outcomes over and over again.

That was not always the case. For the first 30 or so years of comic book superheroes in the United States, from the 1930s to the 1960s, the storytelling was straightforward and unsophisticated in many ways, including the depiction of economics.

Influenced by science fiction from the pulp magazines of the 1920s and 1930s, creators of superhero stories often felt the need to ground their fantasies in some kind of more or less scientific explanation. Superman came from another planet and got his powers because of Earth's lower gravity and more intense solar radiation. The Flash, Captain America and others were the products of scientific experiments that created changes in human biology. Non-powered crimefighters often used advanced technology to give them an advantage.

But while science fiction soon evolved to encompass broader social and economic themes in an effort to make their story-worlds more convincing, comics were slower to do so.[1] Comic publishers assumed their audience to be children with a low critical threshold, who would not notice or question the lack of realism. The superheroes themselves were archetypes, not fully realized characters. They didn't need motives beyond altruism; they didn't need rich social and economic lives. They just needed good costumes and cool powers.

As superheroes started reaching an older audience in the mid-1960s, the genre began to strive for greater realism in its characterizations, including introducing economic considerations. Spider-Man's alter-ego, Peter Parker, struggled to make ends meet; the Fantastic Four sometimes had trouble paying the rent on their Manhattan skyscraper headquarters. Ill-advised stock market speculation cost Oliver Queen (The Green Arrow) his fortune, and the experience transformed him from a cutout, wealthy playboy to a crusader for social justice (O'Neill and Dillin, 1969).

These details made the stories richer and the characters more believable at the margins, but they rarely addressed the larger question of how extraordinary characters and events might influence the world(s) in which they took place. Technology innovations like Iron Man's suit, for example, were deemed unique and impossible to replicate, except by assorted super-villains. Near-omnipotent characters like Superman occasionally tackled natural disasters, but rarely interfered in world events in a transformative way. Super-powered characters who struggled with their finances hardly ever used their abilities for personal enrichment; that was the mark of a villain, not a hero.

That began to change in the late 1970s and early 1980s, as the more rigorous world-building logics of New Wave science fiction authors like Brian Aldiss, John Brunner and J.G. Ballard began influencing an up and coming generation of comic book writers who had greater literary ambitions for themselves and the superhero genre. Foremost among them was a young English writer named Alan Moore.

Working class (super) hero

Alan Moore was born in 1953 in Northampton, an industrial city in the middle of England. He grew up reading first British and then American comics that made their way to the UK in the 1960s, and was making his own comics by his teenage years. Though his parents were working class, the precocious Moore placed into a grammar (preparatory) school over the objections of its elitist headmaster, but got expelled at age 17 for dealing LSD. From that point on, he read widely and scraped out a living for himself and his young family doing a variety of odd jobs (Millidge, 2011, pp. 18–41).

Moore soon found work writing and drawing strips for British underground comix in the mid-1970s. Like their American equivalents, these short-run, independently published titles primarily featured sex, drugs, music and left-wing politics. Punk rock arrived on the scene in the late 1970s, adding to the general sense of mayhem and rebellion.

By the early 1980s, Moore had moved higher in the industry, writing science fiction stories for the groundbreaking British weekly *2000 AD* and working on characters like Doctor Who and Captain Britain, published by Marvel UK. He also still wrote and drew a couple of weekly strips for the undergrounds.

These experiences shaped Moore's sensibilities as a writer and made him a unique voice when he rose to mainstream prominence later in the 1980s. In particular, Moore's British working class background made him far more attuned to economic issues and their relationship to politics and sociology than his contemporaries in American comics, who were largely the product of post-war suburban affluence. He was also more thoroughly steeped in the radicalism of the underground movement relative to others in the superhero side of the business.

V for Vendetta: economic inequality and political violence

Moore's political and economic concerns soon manifested in his work, culminating in his first masterpiece, *V for Vendetta,* serialized in *Warrior*, a new publication spotlighting the rising generation of British creators, starting in 1982. It was eventually completed and collected by DC Comics in 1988, then issued as a collected trade edition graphic novel shortly afterwards.

V for Vendetta, atmospherically drawn by artist David Lloyd, is contemporary dystopic science fiction rather than a superhero story. It's set in a near-future Britain ruled by a fascist regime that maintains its grip through surveillance, secret police and propaganda. The protagonist, known only as V, who hides his face behind a sinister Guy Fawkes mask, stages a series of acts of resistance as he is pursued by the forces of the state.

Though well plotted and gripping, the foreground action of *V for Vendetta* is just window-dressing for the political themes that were very much in the air in the early 1980s. The world of *Vendetta* specifically reflected concerns about Margaret Thatcher's Tory government, which profoundly disrupted the lives of hundreds of thousands of workers in bringing deregulation, privatization and the animal spirits of free market capitalism to British shores. Moore, hailing from the Midlands, saw the impact of those policies all around him. He grasped the relationship between wealth, political power, control of the narrative and economic policymaking, and used the medium of comics to conjure a vision of one possible outcome of right-wing policies and attitudes taken to their logical conclusion.

Totalitarian dystopias are a dime a dozen in the speculative fiction genre, and the dissident rebel protagonist can easily veer into cliché. What distinguishes *Vendetta* is how methodically Moore extrapolated from the current economic and political environment of early-1980s Britain to create a future in which the citizenry would plausibly hand over their liberty to a despotic regime.

The dictatorship in *Vendetta* more closely resembles Chile under Pinochet – a regime that used police-state violence to safeguard market-driven economic inequality – than other types of fascism motivated by ideology such as Nazism. The Leader isn't a charismatic madman or crackpot; he's a deft manipulator of the levers of power who rose gradually as panic set in around a crisis. He governs behind the rhetoric of nationalism: "the duty of every citizen is to seize the day and make Britain great again" (Moore and Lloyd, 1990, p. 10). To perpetuate his rule he maintains institutions that legitimize his government like Parliament and the Crown while hollowing them out, and projects force under the guise of maintaining law and order.

The repressive politics in *Vendetta* lead to a society in which the corrupt and incompetent prosper, the favored class of elites and professionals enjoy every privilege, and arrogant brutes perpetrate injustices on ordinary people with impunity. V, the dissident anarchist in the Guy Fawkes mask, responds to the covert violence of this social order with overt violence. It makes for an exciting, emotionally engaging and cathartic story, treading on terrain that had, until that time, rarely been explored in mainstream comics.

Miracleman: the economics of a superhero utopia

At the same time Moore was sharpening his political critique in *V for Vendetta*, he launched a different kind of storytelling revolution in *Marvelman*, also serialized in the pages of *Warrior*. Marvelman was a character created for the British market by Mick Angelo in the 1950s, modeled heavily on Captain Marvel, a popular character from the 1940s published by Fawcett (later purchased by DC and rebranded "Shazam!"). Like American comics from the same era, Marvelman's original adventures were innocent and unsophisticated, even corny, but Moore's generation remembered them with nostalgic affection.

Dez Skinn, publisher of *Warrior*, believed he had acquired the rights to the character[2] and wanted to relaunch an updated version. Alan Moore, in the midst of a highly successful run on the "other" native British superhero, Marvel's Captain Britain, was recommended for the job, paired with Gary Leach, an artist with a realistic style to complement Moore's reimagining of the character. For legal reasons, when Eclipse Comics began publishing the series in the United States in 1984, the title and character were renamed Miracleman.

From the first page of the new series, it was clear that Moore's ambitions extended beyond anything previously attempted in mainstream superhero comics.[3]

He began poking at the familiar tropes of the genre inherited from the first generation of creators: tropes that anchored superheroes in a world of simplistic morality, juvenile concepts and inconsistencies that no longer rang true to more mature readers. He addressed a number of questions that had inhibited fans' suspension of disbelief as superheroes had struggled over the preceding two decades toward greater sophistication, for example:

- If every story in a character's 40+ year history is considered part of a canonical continuity, how can more complex present-day interpretations of the character be reconciled with some of the sillier concepts and behaviors from bygone decades?
- How do superheroes maintain adult romantic relationships with ordinary humans?
- Why don't governments take more of an official interest in superpowered people?
- Considering how much death and destruction supervillains cause, and the fact that they always manage to escape from prison, why don't the heroes just kill them and be done with it?
- Why don't superpowered people use their powers to get rich through ordinary means (as opposed to robbing banks or demanding ransoms), considering the advantages they have over others?
- Why don't superheroes use their extraordinary powers to solve the world's big problems, rather than just fighting with bad guys and aliens all the time?

Moore tackled each one of these topics through the course of Miracleman's run from 1982 to 1989. He provided a backstory that plausibly incorporated the fanciful 1950s and 1960s Marvelman stories into his more sophisticated narrative; answered the question of government involvement in a typically sinister fashion that has subsequently become a genre cliché; created a complex and troubling relationship between Miracleman, his married alter ego (ordinary, middle-aged mortal Mike Moran) and Moran's wife Liz; and had his protagonist mete out a more permanent and unforgiving brand of justice when it was called for (Miracleman literally disposed of his arch-enemy by throwing him at a planet.)

The two final questions point the way toward Moore's more realistic treatment of economic issues within the superhero story framework. In the first story arc, for instance, we learn that, though Miracleman/Mike Moran had lost his memory in a disaster that destroyed his team, his former protégé Jonathan Bates (Kid Miracleman) survived, maintaining his super identity even though disguised as a civilian.

Moran, unconscious of his true superhuman nature, struggled as a freelance journalist, but Bates used his near omnipotence to become the head of a vast multinational corporation. Along the way, the wealth and power corrupted his altruistic morals – or his corrupt nature led him to seek personal enrichment. Either way, his character arc ran contrary to decades of expectations of good-guy behavior in superhero comics and arguably reflected a more realistic scenario of how a superpowered individual would deal with matters of personal finance. Moore would return to this device again in *Watchmen*.

Moore saved the answer to the biggest question – how a real superman would solve Earth's biggest problems – for his final issue, *Miracleman* #16, which was published in the US in 1989. Having vanquished his foes and made peace with the aliens who had been observing his development, Miracleman and his team, possessed of godlike powers, decide to solve all the world's problems and injustices by taking over and remaking society according to their vision of justice. They destroy all the nuclear weapons on Earth by depositing them into the sun. They undo the damage of greenhouse gasses by altering the chemistry of the atmosphere. They use psychic powers to rehabilitate habitual criminals and violent individuals.

They also undertake an ambitious economic agenda. In an extraordinary passage that might be the most intensive exposition of economic issues yet attempted in superhero comics, Miracleman explains his policy to the public.

> A lack of money causes deforestation in Brazil, and the extinction of whales. These resources cannot be protected while people starve. But money is a fiction. It is a false promise. If we all, at the same time, try to redeem the paper for the gold or goods that back it we would run, full force, into the reality that money is an illusion. Rich countries sustain that illusion with guns, and make everyone adhere to it.
>
> From this time forward, this fiction will no longer exist. Everything will now be free.
>
> National surplus teleported to those nations most in need until they master self-sufficiency. Each soul shall have free clothing, food and shelter, entertainment, education, all requirements for a worthwhile life …
>
> … with greater luxuries for those who wish to work providing the above.
>
> Come summer, money won't exist …
>
> … But then, it never did.
>
> *(Moore and Totleben, 2015, p. 103)*

Is this economic realism? Perhaps not in any sense that an economist would recognize, although it does touch on important economic concepts like fiat currency and trade imbalances. But it does reflect a sincere attempt to address how an omnipotent being with human morality might approach the question of distributive justice. In a way, it is easier to see this as the outcome of living in a world with a helpful superman determined to solve all our problems, as opposed to all preceding attempts at worldbuilding that suggested that having super powered characters flying around would just be business as usual.

Moore appeared to recognize the contradiction between utopian rhetoric and reality. In the end, the world Miracleman wrought out of his best intentions seems as oppressive in its way as the fascist dystopia of *V for Vendetta*.[4]

From today's vantage point, it is easy to see *Miracleman* as a fundamental turning point in the superhero genre, but in the 1980s, its impact was blunted by an infrequent publication schedule, spotty distribution and inconsistencies of five different artists drawing the feature over the course of 16 issues.

Fortunately, Moore soon had a larger platform than the independent publishers Warrior and Eclipse could provide. In 1982, Len Wein, an editor at DC Comics, approached Moore to take up scripting duties on *Swamp Thing,* a second-tier horror comic struggling creatively and in danger of cancelation due to poor sales. Writer Moore joined the art team of Steve Bissette and Jon Totlebein (who also drew Miracleman's later issues) and caused an instant sensation with his reimagining of the character. Moore also scripted a handful of filler issues on DC's top titles including Superman, Batman and Green Lantern that met with rapturous fan approval.

In 1985, DC acquired the intellectual property of Charlton Comics, a low-rent publisher of costumed characters dating from the 1950s and 1960s, including The Question, Blue Beetle, Peacemaker and Captain Atom. Moore proposed using the characters in a limited series that explored the issues of superheroes in the modern world in greater depth. Because Moore's story ended with the deaths of many of the characters DC had just purchased, they suggested he create his own pantheon of original characters for the series instead. Moore agreed, and alongside artist Dave Gibbons, proceeded to develop a completely new story that would be published in 12 monthly issues from June 1986 through June 1987, called *Watchmen.*

Watchmen: economic modeling as a super-power

The story of *Watchmen* is set in an alternative version of the 1980s where the presence of Doctor Manhattan, an omnipotent superhero created in a nuclear accident, has tilted the balance of power toward America. Though non-powered masked vigilantes had been a feature of the world since the 1930s, they had been driven to the sidelines by political controversy over their roles and methods. Some retired, some worked for the government and one, the obsessive loner Rorschach, continued to fight crime outside the law. When someone starts killing the old heroes, Rorschach's investigation exposes the sordid conflicts and dark secrets behind the masks.

As many critics have observed, *Watchmen* bubbles over with striking innovations in aesthetics, character development, philosophy and politics.[5] Every detail of the story, from the plot, to references to comics history, to the end matter in each issue, to the page design (down to the visual details within each panel), serve Moore's singular vision.

Moore constructs an elaborate political and social scenario that builds logically on the foundations of his premise. Civilians have mixed reactions to the presence of costumed crusaders; some see them as heroes, others as unaccountable vigilantes. Politicians like Richard Nixon, who is serving his fourth term as president of the United States in the world of *Watchmen,* use them as vehicles for personal power and geopolitical advantage. The media incorporate the fundamental strangeness of superheroes seamlessly into their existing narratives of celebrity, alarmism and partisan squabbling.

The wealth of detail, beautifully rendered by Gibbons, gives the setting of *Watchmen* an air of verisimilitude never before seen in superhero comics. Because the world-building logic is integral and consistent, the world itself is immersive and intriguing. The more readers search for clues in the details of each panel, the more they are rewarded. That lays the groundwork for the foreground action: an exploration of the psychological nature of superheroes even more profound and penetrating that he undertook with *Miracleman*.

Like *Miracleman, Watchmen* sets aside the idealistic moral universe that superheroes had occupied for the preceding 40 years and presents us with characters motivated by ordinary human emotions: obsession, greed, lust, arrogance, insecurity. They are less heroic, but their behavior rings true to anyone with life experience, and makes it possible to read the story as a work of literature rather than a fable or fairytale.

The realistic motivations of the characters also extend to economic behavior. When the world's smartest man, Adrian Veidt, was forced to retire his superhero identity Ozymandias, he went into business, parleying his extraordinary gifts into a fortune, just as Kid Miracleman/Jonathan Bates did. In one extraordinary scene, we see Veidt watching a screen full of monitors tuned to random channels, trying to pick out patterns in the stream of media images. Veidt's observation is that the flow of pictures portend war. His suggestion is to begin buying stock in companies that are part of the military industrial complex. His assistant claims that this is a tactic they have never adopted, and Veidt agrees, but chastises the assistant for missing an opportunity. He discerns that there is "increased sexual imagery, even in the candy ads. It implies an undercurrent not uncommon in times of war. Remember the baby boom." The one-sided conversation continues:

MINION: So we should buy into … uh …?

VEIDT: Into the major erotic video companies. That's short term. Also, we should negotiate controlling shares in selected baby food and maternity goods manufacturers.

(Moore and Gibbons, 1987, pp. 7–8)

This vignette demonstrates Veidt's preternatural powers of intuition and is also a key bit of foreshadowing. It turns out that Veidt's machinations, based on a very complicated set of if-then contingencies, set the entire plot of *Watchmen* in motion and trigger its cataclysmic finale.

By making the arrogant, too-clever-by-half, capitalist pretty boy superhero the villain of the story, Moore was again reminding his readers how economic elites use their power to manipulate the masses to forward their own wealth, power and political agenda. But whether he knew it or not, he was also pulling back the curtain on a sophisticated technique of strategic forecasting that was being developed just 70 miles to the south at the offices of Royal Dutch Petroleum (Shell Oil) in London.

The methodology is known as Scenario Planning, and it was created in the late 1970s by a team within Shell to address failures in traditional economic forecasting that had left the oil industry flatfooted in the face of a collapse in global prices.[6] Rather than relying on consensus expert estimates, which produced a constrained range of possibilities because of implicit assumptions and biases within the community of experts, Scenario Planning embraced a wider set of uncertainties, and thus a wider range of outcomes, including black swan events ordinarily judged too unlikely to consider. The planning group looked to a wide range of influences, including science fiction, for ways that narratives could be used to explore speculative topics with depth and logical rigor.

In the methodology, planners identify critical uncertainties to serve as foundational premises, then construct detailed narratives to flesh out how economic, political, social, technological and business issues might play out under different sets of conditions. These coherent narratives are known as scenarios, and planners use them to test the validity of different approaches such as investment strategies, technology implementation, workforce development and multinational expansion against divergent sets of global conditions.

Organizational leaders can then use the scenarios as both a map and a compass. They can survey the landscape – including media and other cultural megatrends – for clues as to where things are heading, then start applying the scenario logic to identify which pre-planned tactics might work best in the emerging set of conditions … which is exactly what Adrian Veidt was doing in the scene above.

Evidence of deep, scenario-based modeling is present in the background of *Watchmen* as well, as Moore once again addresses the question of how the presence of a genuine metahuman would affect the global economy. Doctor Manhattan's impact on the world is less obvious and agenda-driven than Miracleman's, but it is profound, and Moore illustrates it by the inclusion of subtle details throughout the story.

For example, in the first issue, as two characters dine in a fancy restaurant, a chicken being served on a tray appears to have four drumsticks (Moore and Gibbons, 1986, p. 25). Why? Presumably because Adrian Veidt managed to commercialize the genetic engineering breakthroughs made possible by Doctor Manhattan to create new species. This detail was curious enough to merit inclusion in Zack Snyder's 2009 film adaptation as a line of dialogue ("I'm glad I ordered the four-legged chicken") – a tip of the hat to Moore and Gibbons' unprecedented thoroughness in their world-building efforts.

After Moore: superhero worlds as scenarios

The late 1970s–early 1980s era when Moore began his career in comics was a moment of historical consequence. The postwar era of economic stability was unraveling. The institutions on both sides of the Atlantic that supported it, such state-run and corporate monopolies on essential services, a vibrant labor movement and a general center-left political consensus, were crumbling. We were about to enter into an era of rapid change and displacement driven by technological innovation, globalization and deregulation.

As change became less predictable and more consequential, stories that could point the way forward became more compelling and more essential. We wanted fictional worlds that made sense to replace a real world that seemed to be spinning out of control.

In the world of business and economics, practices like scenario planning gained traction because they helped organizations plan for uncertainty. They used stories to visualize radically different conditions, and thrust decision makers into a new mindset where they could embrace unforeseen possibilities.

Alan Moore did not run in those exclusive circles of strategy and business, but, as a creative artist destined to have a generationally transformative impact on his medium, he was uncommonly tuned to the zeitgeist. His radar was picking up the same signals as thought-leaders in other fields, and his instincts were leading him to the same conclusions. Audiences needed stories that explained how everything seemed to go from familiar to strange overnight; that emphasized how ordinary people lived their lives in the midst of extraordinary and outlandish developments. Moore was there to tell them.

The rigor and logic that Moore brought to the creation of fictional worlds in comics in the 1980s pushed the superhero genre in a new direction. In the 1970s, the rising generation of creators was obsessed with internal consistency and continuity within the self-created mythology, establishing a canon in which the fictional universe had rules, a timeline and consequential moments that endured from story to story, character to character.

Moore revised and extended this project, not only attempting to rationalize some of the more farfetched foundational tenets of the genre for a more mature readership, but also aligning the political, social, psychological and economic worlds of superheroes more closely with ordinary experience. The worlds he created were not necessarily more realistic, but certainly more convincing in how they operated.

By the 1990s, mainstream comics had internalized his innovations, if not his political sensibilities and his craft. Creators like Kurt Busiek (*Marvels, Astro City*), Warren Ellis (*The Authority, Transmetropolitan*), Grant Morrison (*The Invisibles*) and others incorporated elements of economic realism deeply into the settings of their stories. Eventually the corporate-managed superhero universes of DC and Marvel embraced similar techniques that made their stories and the all-important story universes more compelling and realistic, particularly to audiences that weren't marinated in decades of lore and continuity.

Today, superhero mythology is one of the few points of common reference in a culture divided by ideological fault lines. It transcended its niche as juvenilia, and then as the object of cultish affection, to become the center of 21st century popular culture by adopting richer story structures that can satisfy more sophisticated readers, address deeper themes, and even become fodder for academic exploration.

Alan Moore built the genre a better model to carry that weight.

Notes

1 As seen in *The Brave and the Bold* #85 (Haney and Adams, 1969).

2 He didn't in fact acquire the rights, as many parties, including Moore, later discovered to their consternation. For further details, see Pádraig Ó Méalóid (2013), "The Poisoned Chalice."

3 The prose novel *Superfolks* by Robert Meyer (1977) took a similar realistic approach to the inner lives of superheroes, but Moore was the first to bring this perspective to the comics medium.
4 Having said his piece, Moore departed and left the character in the hands of a young writer named Neil Gaiman, who, along with artist Mark Buckingham, took the concept to its logical conclusion. Decades later, fans are still waiting for them to produce more of the story.
5 Several good explorations of this topic include *Considering Watchmen: Poetics, Prosperity, Politics* by Andrew Hoberek (2014), *Watchmen as Literature: A Critical Study of the Graphic Novel* by Sara J. Van Ness (2010) and *Watchmen as Philosophy: A Rorschach Test,* edited by Mark D. White (2009).
6 For a good discussion of the technique, its history and its applications, see *The Art of the Long View* by Peter Schwartz (1991).

References

Haney, B. and N. Adams. (1969). *The Brave and the Bold* #85. DC Comics.

Hoberek, A. (2014). *Considering Watchmen: Poetics, Prosperity, Politics.* New Brunswick, New Jersey: Rutgers University Press.

Meyer, R. (1977). *Superfolks.* New York: Dial Press.

Millidge, G. S. (2011). *Alan Moore Storyteller.* New York: Universe Publishing.

Moore, A. and D. Gibbons. (1986). *Watchmen* #1. New York: DC Comics.

Moore, A. and D. Gibbons. (1987). *Watchmen* #10. New York: DC Comics.

Moore, A. and D. Lloyd. (1990). *V for Vendetta.* New York: Vertigo Books/DC.

Moore, A. and J. Totleben. (2015). Olympus. In C. Sedlmeier (Ed.) *Miracleman Book Three: Olympus.* New York: Marvel Comics. (Original work published 1989).

Ó Méalóid, P. (2013, February 10). The Poisoned Chalice: The Extremely Long and Incredibly Complex Story of Marvelman. *Comics Beat.* Retrieved from www.comicsbeat.com/poisoned-chalice-the-extremely-long-and-incredibly-complex-story-of-marvelman-introduction/.

O'Neill, D. and D. Dillin. (1969). *Justice League of America* #75. DC Comics.

Schwartz, P. (1991). *The Art of the Long View.* New York: Doubleday Business.

Snyder, Z. (Director). (2009). *Watchmen* [Motion Picture].

Van Ness, S. J. (2010). *Watchmen as Literature: A Critical Study of the Graphic Novel.* Jefferson, North Carolina: McFarland.

White, M. D. (Ed.). (2009). *Watchmen as Philosophy: A Rorschach Test.* Hoboken, New Jersey: John Wiley and Sons.

PART I
Microeconomics

2

THE HIGH COST OF BEING BATMAN

Clair Smith

Batman is a powerhouse, physically, mentally, and economically. He is strong, smart, and determined. His work ethic and devotion to his mission are without comparison. Financially, he is the keeper of the Wayne family fortune and the owner of Wayne Enterprises. Within the storyline itself, Batman is an economic force. Outside of Gotham – in this "real world" in which we live – the Batman storyline earns billions and billions of dollars through comics, movies, TV, video games, and other licensed products. USA Today reports that Warner Brothers has grossed $3.8 billion in Batman movie revenue alone (Ausick, 2015). The Batman character has evolved over time and through different media, but whether in traditional comic books or stories on screens large and small, fans have been paying for the Batman experience since his 1939 introduction in Detective Comics.

While the Batman money-making machine is interesting, this chapter is concerned primarily with the world within the Batman narrative. Batman makes billions of dollars for Time Warner and DC Comics in the real world, but in Gotham City, Wayne Enterprises is an equally impressive economic powerhouse. According to a Forbes estimate, 2007 revenue for Wayne Enterprises was $31.3 billion (Noer, 2011). As a result of the income from Wayne Enterprises, in which he has a controlling interest, and the fortune he inherited from his parents, Forbes estimated in 2013 that fictional character Bruce Wayne was worth $9.2 billion, making him the 6th richest fictional character in their list (Noer and Ewalt, 2013).

Perhaps his wealth would be much greater if he was not such a spendthrift. Bruce Wayne, the man behind Batman, is continually, though secretly, spending to maintain and augment his arsenal of new technological gizmos, gadgets, and crime-fighting tools. This impressive collection of bad guy-blasting technology is housed in the similarly impressive Batcave deep beneath Wayne Manor. This large ancestral family home is complete with military grade security and defenses, though none of it is visible to casual observer.

The massive collection of crime-fighting tech that he has assembled is just the beginning of his expenses. His extensive physical training and knowledge of martial arts stems from the years he spent abroad at university and training both body and mind with talented mentors. His personal payroll is mostly limited to his loyal butler Alfred Pennyworth, but his considerable charitable endeavors extend throughout the Gotham community.

Yet Bruce Wayne maintains these many enabling aspects of his Batman character without a reference to any limitations on resources or tradeoffs in his purchases. This is peculiar to an economist, who finds most all resources to be limited in nature. Curiously, it seems at first glance that scarcity, the fundamental principle in economics, applies everywhere and to everyone *except* Batman.

This chapter will explore this question by beginning with a review of Batman's origins. Then I will proceed to examine the concept of scarcity more closely. This is the real reason economics exists, so to understand the discrepancies between Batman and the real world, we need to know more about this economic condition. Next, I will take a look at Bruce Wayne's seemingly uncontrolled spending, followed up by an answer to the question: does Batman face scarcity? Finally, I will introduce the importance of Robin. Beyond selling more comics, Robin plays an instrumental, economic role in Batman's battle against scarcity. It is safe to say, that without Robin, Batman might be less believable because the specter of scarcity would be too far removed from the story.

Batman's origin

Many readers are familiar with the Caped Crusader's origin story. Bruce Wayne was born to a wealthy and socially elite family. His family has lived for centuries on the same hillside on Gotham's north side. The current expansive mansion on the site forms a "W" when viewed from above. His family grew rich through enterprise, starting with a merchant house and lucrative shipping business. While overseeing the family businesses, his forebears also served their community in other ways. His great-great grandfather was a judge, and Bruce's father was a physician (Wallace, 2012).

While just a child, Bruce witnessed his parents' gruesome deaths when they were mugged while returning from a family trip to the movies. The police could never crack the case, but young Bruce vowed to do whatever was necessary to make the streets of Gotham safe again, and for over 75 years we have been reading and watching as he strives to do just that.

Bruce inherited Wayne Manor and his family's considerable wealth, which he now uses in his training and ultimate crusade against evil in Gotham City. Batman is among a small cadre of superheroes who have no supernatural powers. He must train his body and mind to be in peak condition at all times. He spends years learning languages and psychology at top universities like Cambridge and the Sorbonne. He studied martial arts in Korea and lived in Africa and Tibet. He trained with top criminologists. His elite physical conditioning and intellectual prowess make him a worthy foe even without the many gadgets he employs fighting crime and evil in Gotham.

His technical knowledge and skill is also extensive. He outfits a large cave under Wayne Manor with the latest technology and security and makes this his base of operations. His family enterprises include technology and defense contractors from which he can acquire much of the technology he uses in his crusade against evil. With these resources at his disposal, he dons the cape and cowl essential to the role of his dominating alter ego Batman.

Despite all of these advantages though, his ability to avoid the demon of scarcity isn't unique. The most notable exception to this is Oliver Queen (the Green Arrow). Queen has lost his family fortune multiple times (*Justice League of America* #75 (O'Neil, Dillin and Giella, 1969), and *Green Arrow* #2 (Percy and Schmidt, 2016)) meaning he has had to fight crime without the unlimited resources he was used to. The loss helped him to see the world from the perspective of the poor, and the character became an advocate for the downtrodden. In other story arcs, the loss of wealth is temporary. Danny Rand (Iron Fist) has to fight to regain his role at Rand Enterprises after his father is killed. Thus, for a time, he is without the family business. Similarly, in the *Iron Man* films, Tony Stark loses his company for a time. Even Bruce Wayne experiences this hiccup in the movie *Batman Begins*, we hear that while he is out searching for himself, Bruce is declared legally dead. Wayne Enterprises is being taken public, and Bruce has to scrape up the billions of dollars necessary to buy a controlling stake in the company, which of course he does.

The economic condition

Scarcity has been called the economic condition. Who among us has not wished for more money or more time? Everyone, even the very richest men and women on Forbes' annual list, face resource constraints. They simply cannot have as much of everything as they would like. Sure, they might be able to buy a car for every day of the week, but they might value the eradication of AIDS just as much; however, because of the immense expense of eliminating the disease world-wide, even the richest men and women on the planet cannot achieve what they would like. Economics teaches us that absolutely no one has all the time, money, gold, oil, or technology that they might want. Nearly every resource is available only in limited quantities. Even things like air, water, and sunlight are acquired at a cost – the time and resources it takes to harness or enjoy them. And though their plights may be very different, both billionaires and beach bums are constrained by scarcity.

In this world of scarce resources, individuals are compelled to make choices. Unable to do all the things we want, we must choose the things we most wish to do. Will I go to the movies to watch *The Dark Knight*, or should I run some errands? Will I buy a new car or remodel the bathroom? Should I spend a week at the beach or relax close to home and augment my retirement savings? The economic concept of scarcity demands that we make choices. When I cannot do or buy everything I want, I am compelled to choose that option that I value most.

As a result of being forced to choose, individuals necessarily leave options on the table. The best options given up are what economists call opportunity costs. In choosing, I leave a potential action untaken. As Robert Frost poignantly observed long ago, when I am hiking and I come upon the fork in the road, I must choose one path to continue hiking and forgo the present exploration of the other. The opportunity cost of choosing one fork in the road is the second trail that I cannot currently explore. So it is with all choices. Any option taken means an alternative option given up.

Scarcity, choice, and opportunity cost are fundamental tenets of economics. Economists take scarcity very seriously, and believe the concept to be universal. But is it? Does scarcity apply to the Dark Knight? If it did, there should be an example where Batman decides that the price tag on the resources used to fight crime in some way is just too high. The Bat Plane cannot be used until the dividend check arrives next week, or the newest version of his costume will have to be made without the bullet proof cape. Yet, one is hard-pressed to find the story where Batman chooses not to spend money on a particular item because the opportunity cost is too high.

Batman's spending

While we rarely see Batman in the act of spending, the evidence of his consumption is everywhere. Wayne Manor is a large, extravagant, and old house. Built during the 19th century, the Gothic mansion houses paintings and antiques, and its grounds are home to garages, stables, and gardens as well as the residence itself (Wallace, 2012). The Huffington Post used a map of Wayne Manor from a board game to estimate the size and value of the Batman's home in 2012. They suggest the home is about 42,500 square feet and worth over $32 million, excluding the technology-laden Batcave below (Cross, 2012). That is not a huge issue though, because the mortgage is almost certainly paid off, based on how long the Wayne family has lived there. Nevertheless, Gotham City is reported to be located in New Jersey[1], a state with some of the highest property taxes in the United States with an average property tax of 2.2%. On a $32 million property, the annual tax burden is $704,000. If you can afford the property taxes you must be doing OK.

Not only are the property taxes high, but a mansion of this size and historical character requires extensive maintenance and care. Think of the utility bills to heat and cool this monstrosity. And that is without considering the special features Bruce Wayne has incorporated, like foundations reinforced against tectonic shocks, hidden radar and biometric sensors around the exterior, nausea-inducing sonic projectors, and the voice-activated taser lawn (Wallace, 2012). The visible mansion, however, is only the beginning of Batman's property expense. Turn the hands on the grandfather clock to 10:47 and enter the secret passage to the subterranean Batcave: seven levels of secret bunker infrastructure and technology below the basement of Wayne Manor. How Batman could initially have this constructed in secret is a mystery in itself. Bruce provides just a glimpse of the construction when he invites his new girlfriend, Jezebel Jet, to visit the cave. He acknowledges that it was not all glitz and glamour. Not only did the Batcave take a while to build, but early on he and Alfred would huddle around a computer covered in bat guano. Now though, it is humming along brilliantly. Jet declares that her country's debt could be erased with what it costs to run the Batcave (Morrison and Daniel, 2010). In fact, the resource cost of this marvel is likely rivaled by only a few things (maybe the Fantastic Four's Baxter Building, the Avenger's Tower, or the Justice League's satellite headquarters the Watchtower), in the superhero world.

The expansive underground lair has security even more extensive than the manor above. It houses the nerve center of the Dark Knight's operations, the Batcomputer. It also has room for a combat training chamber, a trophy room, and easy-access storage for his entire wardrobe of Batsuits. Within the garage area of the Batcave the Caped Crusader keeps his fleet of vehicles, and chief among is the iconic Batmobile. But it is not just one Batmobile for all time, but a series of ever evolving technological driving machines sit fueled and ready on a rotating platform that can position any vehicle for use (Wallace, 2012). The Batmobiles gets regular updates both because of Batman's penchant for the latest technology and because they are regularly destroyed in his altercations with evil-doers. For evaluating new updates to the Batmobile, the Batcave includes a wind tunnel that can assess not only the aerodynamics of the vehicle but can also test the bulletproof glass and armor on each car (Wallace, 2012). Protected within this armored skin each of these vehicles contains mobile communication and weapons repositories, equipped with every imaginable gizmo and gadget that Batman might need.

If the versatile Batmobile is not the right vehicle for the mission, he can simply jump in the Batplane, Batboat, Batcycle, Batsubmarine, or any number of other specialized crime-fighting apparatuses also stored in the sizable Batcave. Ports in the ceiling provide quick-launch capability for the Batplane (Wallace, 2012). Other areas in the Batcave provide storage and quick access to other important tools and weapons, like his utility belts, various styles of Batarangs, Bat-cuffs, darts, mobile computers, grapnels, darts, tools, masks, and more. Batman surely has the best-equipped garage in the superhero world.

Installed throughout Wayne Manor, the Batcave, and his many vehicles is an endless assortment of technology and gadgets. These are the kinds of things we could not imagine we would even want or need until we see Batman use them. Proprietary, custom Batman technology from Batman's own creative ability and the engineering prowess of Wayne Industries is pervasive.

Notwithstanding the array of advanced technologies, before Bruce Wayne ever donned his Batsuit to fight crime on Gotham's streets, he spent years in training to prepare for the physical and mental challenges he would face. This important preparation for his self-appointed role was attained at prestigious universities and remote communities around the world. He invested years of his life and a considerable fortune in developing the physical and mental strength necessary for his crime-fighting endeavors.

And so, we end this section where we began: Though we do not see Batman actively spending money, evidence of his expenditures are everywhere. Our brief tour of the infrastructure of Wayne Manor and the Batcave considers only the most obvious expenditures. Additional and unmentioned security, weapons, and gadgets augment the spending we have considered. His travel and training as well as the maintenance and replacement of his fleets of high-tech vehicles add significantly more to the bill. If we were discussing anyone other than Bruce Wayne, we might be planning an intervention to address his spending problem.

On the contrary, Bruce Wayne is heralded as one of the benefactors of his city. On top of his spending to maintain his crusade against the "superstitious and cowardly lot" (Finger and Kane, 1939), Wayne is exceedingly generous with his personal wealth. He regularly hosts galas and events at the manor that benefit the arts and the poor of Gotham City. These events may welcome hundreds of people to his home in an effort to raise awareness and resources for his charitable endeavors. His philanthropy, like his personal spending, appears to have no limits.

Wayne Enterprises

While his expenditures are extreme, he does have a stream of income to support, at least in part, his endeavors, which should not be overlooked. The family company, Wayne Enterprises, has subsidiaries in shipping, chemicals, biotech, aerospace, and technology. The firm is well diversified and apparently highly profitable. It is engaged in many areas of cutting edge research and engineering, and while some of these areas involve significant risk, there is certainly the possibility of significant reward.

As mentioned above, efforts to estimate the annual revenue of Wayne Enterprises place it north of $30 billion per year in 2007 dollars (Noer, 2011). Yet, revenues do not equal profits. Profits are revenues *minus* costs. Many an enterprise has failed because they ignore the cost side of the equation. Wayne's industries surely have significant costs as well, and so annual profit is only a fraction of these estimated revenues. Bruce Wayne then benefits from the profits in proportion to his ownership share in the company. Nevertheless, if for no other reason than it began in the 17th century and has survived turbulent economic times through the centuries, one can expect that in most years the business lines of Wayne Enterprises generates significant income for Batman.

The benefits of Wayne Enterprises extend beyond the healthy profits it generates for its largest shareholder. Several of the divisions within Wayne Enterprises are particularly useful and pertinent to Batman's crime-fighting endeavors. Through the company's work in aerospace, chemicals, biotech, and general defense contracting, Batman can procure military grade machinery and technology even as prototypes. So, while he often has to confront foes with superhuman powers, he is always equipped with the best technology to address the situation. His ownership of these businesses provides him direct and secret access to the research and experimental kit on the cutting edge of military technology.

Does Batman face scarcity?

And so, we arrive at the anticipated question: Does Batman face the economic condition of scarcity? In a nutshell, yes. Even Batman faces scarcity.

It is true that in the fictional world created by the writers we never see a binding income constraint. We might know the names of some of Batman's associates like Alfred Pennyworth, Lucius Fox (the gadget master from Wayne Enterprises), and Harold Allnut (hired by Batman personally to help develop his technology), who helped him develop the tools of his trade, but we never learn the name of his accountant. The storyline never reveals that Wayne cannot afford to host a particular charity gala or that the Batmobile cannot be upgraded with the latest technology. He never has to choose between a needed historic repair to Wayne Manor or a new Kevlar-coated Batglider. And perhaps most importantly, Wayne is never unable to meet payroll for his trusted butler, Alfred. His significant family wealth and high income from Wayne Enterprises allow the writers to portray Bruce Wayne and Batman as if they are exempt from these economic forces. Or perhaps they find it simply impolite to talk about money. Either way, to some extent we see a world where an economic principle is suspended, at least for the sake of a good storyline. There are no examples of the tradeoffs caused by scarcity. We never see Batman reflect on opportunity costs. These are the liberties one can take as author.

But even in the fictional world of Gotham, Bruce Wayne is subject to the same limitations on his time as the rest of us. Batman, mortal that he is, simply cannot be in multiple places simultaneously. The significant time he spends training cannot also be spent fighting crime. When he visits Wayne Enterprises in his role as CEO, he is not in the Batcave testing the latest technological addition to his fleet of Bat vehicles. While he is dealing with Joker, he cannot simultaneously be apprehending the Penguin. Even Wayne's cunning intelligence, physical prowess, and stash of technology cannot defeat the economic condition. The physical limitation of his humanity implies that Batman does, in fact, live in a world of scarcity.

This is one of the common tropes of superhero comics in general, and Batman in particular. Perhaps the most dramatic example of this occurs in the movie *Dark Knight*, where the Joker, utilizing a network of corrupt cops, gives Batman a choice: in one building, the intrepid district attorney Harvey Dent. In another building, the love of his life Rachel Dawes. Batman needs to choose one to save. The other will die in a violent explosion. Here scarcity rears its head and bites Batman in the face because, even with the help of the police commissioner, there is no way to save both people. Batman must choose, and that is the essence of economics. All the money in the world is not going to get Bats out of this conundrum. There is no dollar price on Rachel or Harvey, but there is a cost to the choice, one that Batman cannot pay with his seemingly endless pile of money.

Did he choose wisely? SPOILER ALERT! Unbeknownst to Batman, Joker has added a sadistic twist to the choice. The information about the location of the two victims is faulty. While he wants to save Rachel more than Harvey, Batman ends up at Harvey's location because Joker lied about who was where. It seems that even though he thinks the decision is easy, he is sadly mistaken.

Batman and Robin

Batman's humanity is central to the essence of his character, because it is precisely what makes him appealing to his many fans. While other superheroes have specific supernatural powers, any one of us could be Batman. Or so we think (Weldon, 2016). In reality, most all of us lack the discipline Bruce Wayne displays in developing his mind and body to the peak level required of Batman. Few of us have the ability, intuition, or strong jawline of Batman. Furthermore, we lack the ostensibly endless Wayne family fortune that funds the infrastructure, gadgets, and technology that empower Batman to fight against the criminal elements of Gotham. Nevertheless, Batman still faces some of the same quandaries we do. Batman's time is scarce, and he is limited in what and how much he can accomplish. The writers can pretend his monetary resources have no end, but there is no way to maintain his human condition and allow him to suspend the limits of time.

Further evidence of the limitation of scarcity is demonstrated in his partnership with a series of Robin characters. Over the course of the Batman series, he has engaged with sidekicks playing the role of Robin. The Dynamic Duo is one of the great teams of all time. The original Robin, Dick Grayson, was part of a family of circus performers when his parents were murdered by a Gotham City mobster. He was followed by Jason Todd, a rebellious character who tried to steal the Batmobile's tires. Tim Drake discerned the real identities of Batman and Robin and served in the role of Robin upon the death of Jason Todd. Stephanie Brown, daughter of a crook named Cluemaster, served as Robin for a period before being fired. With the taste of crime fighting on her tongue, she returned to her previous role as the Spoiler, specifically targeting her father's criminal plans. Lastly, Damian Wayne, a son Bruce didn't know he had until the boy was ten years old, assumed the role of Robin (Wallace, 2012).[2]

The evolution of the Robin character allows Batman to battle on multiple fronts or in multiple places simultaneously, a proposition not possible with a single mortally-constrained Batman. Batman simply cannot address multiple threats, especially, in multiple places, at the same time. The Robin sidekick doubles Batman's ability to confront evil.[3] Batman and Robin may sometimes engage the enemy together and provide dramatic last-minute rescues, but many times they work separately to confront multiple threats or tasks simultaneously. The very existence of a sidekick like Robin suggests that Batman alone faces limitations in his crime-fighting ability. Batman faces scarcity. This is also true of the Batfamily. Over time, there are others, in addition to the Robins who enter the fray to assist the Dark Knight: Batgirl, Batwoman, the Huntress, Jean-Paul Valley, Bluebird, Duke Thomas, and Gotham Girl to name just a few.

To a lesser extent, the loyal butler Alfred Pennyworth further evidences the constraint of scarcity on Batman. When Bruce Wayne was a boy, Alfred acted as his guardian and surrogate father upon the death of his parents. Now that Bruce

Wayne is grown and independent, he does not need a butler, except for the formal household duties a servant might perform for a man of his wealth and social stature. But Alfred's role goes well beyond that of traditional butler. Alfred has full access to the Batcave and all its elements. He operates the Batcomputer. He functions as a skilled mechanic and makes repairs to the Batmobile. He restocks utility belts and mends Batsuits. He performs surgery on Batman's injuries. His formal role is butler, but he functions as advisor and friend.

Batman could also perform the specialized tasks Alfred undertakes in the Batcave, but because he faces scarcity, the time Bruce Wayne spends working on the Batmobile is time he is not actively engaging the evil underbelly of Gotham. A trusted assistant like Alfred Pennyworth allows Batman to spend more time engaging in what he is uniquely skilled in accomplishing: the good fight against crime. Reliance on Alfred allows Batman to exploit what economists call comparative advantage – the action that one can accomplish at a lower opportunity cost than someone else. This kind of specialization, where Batman engages in active crime-fighting and Alfred refuels the vehicles, only makes sense in a world of limited resources. With the help he enlists, though not always enthusiastically, we see that Batman becomes much more proficient (even if this means he has to engage in more rescue operations than he might when working on his own). Because the help makes him a better crime fighter, we have more evidence that yes, Batman does in fact face scarcity.

Conclusion

The Wayne family fortune is massive. The income-earning potential of Wayne Industries is equally stunning. Between the pile of old money and incredible profits from the current business, the Batman storyline never confronts tradeoffs in how to allocate resources. Batman never frets about tradeoffs in spending; no hospital gala need be given up in order to update the Batmobile. When looking at monetary spending alone, one could begin to think that Batman is not subject to the primary economic condition that confronts the rest of us. Yet, no matter how large the pecuniary fortune, the writers are unable to avoid the fact that Batman still faces scarcity. In preserving the humanity of our beloved Batman, the writers cannot suspend the space-time continuum. He might be rich, but he still only has 24 hours in a day, just like the rest of us. As a result of his inability to be everywhere at once, we can clearly see that Batman lives in a world of scarcity. The usefulness of a sidekick like Robin and a servant like Alfred further evidences the limitations that Bruce Wayne faces as a result of scarcity. Just because you have billions of dollars at your beck and call, does not mean you can escape the ubiquitous economic condition of scarcity.

Notes

1 This comes from the *Atlas of the DC Universe* (Kupperberg, 1990).
2 There was one other, somewhat controversial, Robin. Carrie Kelley appeared as Robin in the graphic novel *The Dark Knight Returns* (Miller, 2016) but is not considered part of

the actual DC continuity. Her only appearance as Robin was in this graphic novel by Frank Miller.

3 Ok, maybe doubling Batman's ability is a stretch, after all, even Nightwing – the moniker Dick Grayson adopts when he splits from Bruce Wayne's tutelage – isn't as good a Batman. But, at least Batman is able to do more than he can on his own.

References

Ausick, P. (2015, May 3). "Most Valuable Comic Book Movie Franchises." *USA Today*, online. Retrieved from: www.usatoday.com/story/money/business/2015/05/03/24-7-wall-st-comic-book-movies/26567645/.

Cross, D. (2012, July 19 (updated Dec 6, 2017)). "Batman's Crib: The Real Value of Wayne Manor." *Huffington Post*, online. Retrieved from: https://www.huffingtonpost.com/david-j-cross/wayne-manor-price_b_1687535.html.

Finger, B. and B. Kane. (1939). *Detective Comics*, #33. DC Comics.

Kupperberg, P. (1990). *Atlas of the DC Universe*. Mayfair Games.

Miller, F. (2016). *Batman: The Dark Knight Returns, 30th Anniversary Edition*. DC Comics.

Morrison, G. and T. Daniel. (2010). *Batman R.I.P.* DC Comics.

Noer, M. (2011, March 11). "The 25 Largest Fictional Companies." *Forbes*, online. Retrieved from: https://www.forbes.com/sites/michaelnoer/2011/03/11/the-25-largest-fictional-companies/#5b6630f45d81

Noer, M. and D. Ewalt. (2013, July 31). "The Forbes Fictional 15." *Forbes*, online. Retrieved from: https://www.forbes.com/special-report/2013/fictional-15/bruce-wayne.html.

O'Neil, D., D. Dillin and J. Giella. (1969). *Justice League of America*, #75. DC Comics.

Percy, B. and O. Schmidt. (2016). *Green Arrow*, #2. DC Comics.

Wallace, D. (2012). *Batman: The World of the Dark Knight*. New York: DK Publishing.

Weldon, G. (2016). *The Caped Crusader: Batman and the Rise of Nerd Culture*. New York: Simon & Schuster.

3

WONDER WOMAN

Feminist and economic icon

James Bryan

In 1972, a first of its kind magazine appeared on newsstands. It had been a struggle finding a publisher, and the first issue was expected to be available for a few months. The subject matter was questioned, the editorial staff had little to no experience running a magazine, and the model for the cover of the inaugural issue was a cartoon character. To everyone's surprise, the initial 300,000 copies sold out in eight days. *Ms.* magazine, the first national, serial, publication to take on women's issues was born, and the cartoon cover model, chosen expressly by magazine founder Gloria Steinem to represent the feminist movement, was Wonder Woman.

For Steinem, Wonder Woman was the perfect candidate to grace the cover of a magazine devoted to feminism. In her formative years, Steinem had followed Wonder Woman in the comics.[1] The Amazonian's strength, wisdom, and speed, granted by Demeter, Athena, and Hermes, were combined with more feminine attributes of communion with animals, a sisterhood with fire and a loving heart granted by Artemis, Hestia, and Aphrodite. What better representative for the feminist movement could there be? Wonder Woman, Steinem hoped, would bridge the gap between the feminism of the 1910s and that of the 1970s (Lepore, 2014, p. 285).

Curiously however, the Wonder Woman of Steinem's youth was no longer the Wonder Woman of the comics in 1972. In a fit of madness, DC Comics had rebooted Wonder Woman in 1968. No longer was she a superhero in the traditional sense, instead she renounced her powers, became a spy, learned some kung-fu, and opened a fashion boutique.[2] Perhaps Steinem hadn't been keeping up with her comic reading, but when this was brought to her attention, she began poking at DC in her new outlet, and in 1973, Wonder Woman got her powers back. Steinem remembers that:

> the person in charge of Wonder Woman call[ed] me up from DC Comics. He said: "OK. She has her magical powers back, her lasso, her bracelets, she has

Paradise Island back, and she has a black African Amazon sister named Nubia. Now will you leave me alone!"

(Kilkenny, 2017)

Wonder Woman was born in the trying times of World War II, and during a dearth of feminism. The War was not a time for social movements. Nevertheless, she became, and has continued to be, an icon for women's rights despite retconning, old-fashioned writers, and short-sighted editors. While to many she has been the beacon of a social movement, the message of Wonder Woman, especially early on, is couched in an equally powerful assertion that women deserved economic liberation.

This chapter will explore how Wonder Woman can be viewed as the vehicle for breaking the chains of economic subjugation. In this book, the authors have provided an origin story for the hero represented in the respective chapters, and while that will also be addressed, it is perhaps more important that we add some perspective on the characters who dreamt up the princess of Themescarya.[3] We will therefore begin with the curious story of Wonder Woman's creator, followed by the comic origin of our heroine. Next, we'll introduce feminist economics, a way of looking at the economic world through a more inclusive prism. While feminist economics as a subset of economics began in the late 1960s, some of the principle tenets can be found in the Wonder Woman comics of the early 1940s.

Noted psychologist revealed as author of best-selling "Wonder Woman"[4]

The history of Wonder Woman is almost as bizarre as the twists and turns the character has taken over the years. The ring-leader who brought Wonder Woman to life was called William Moulton Marston. For his entire life, Marston was surrounded by strong women. Raised by his mother and her four sisters, his father was somewhat disengaged. He married a childhood sweetheart Elizabeth who was at least his intellectual equal. She ended up as the primary breadwinner as Marston's career, first as an academic, then as a businessman, deteriorated. His path crossed many of the feminist luminaries of the early twentieth century and his work was most certainly impacted by them. At an early point in his life, he reached the conclusion that female rule of the world, both politically and economically was nigh, and he confidently declared that an American matriarchy would happen in the next 100 years [from 1937] (Hanley, 2014, p. 16).

Marston's educational pursuits coincided with the advent of psychology, and he became obsessed with promoting himself as a detector of truth. He invented an early version of the lie-detector test which was based on determining variations in systolic blood pressure. Despite his failure to get lie-detector results admitted in courts, his shameless self-promotion as an expert psychologist landed him in Hollywood as an assistant to screen writers looking to ensure new talking pictures would be attractive to paying audiences. When that career ended, he returned east where he was able to get himself hired as a consulting psychologist for DC Comics.

More than the meteoric rise and fall of his employment status,[5] his personal life was, if not bizarre, at least, unorthodox.

In addition to his wife, Marston also kept a mistress. That may not be wholly unusual, except that the mistress, Olive Byrne, lived with the Marstons. Byrne was a student of Marston's at Tufts University and would assist him with his research for a good deal of Marston's life. Elizabeth made the money, Olive raised the four children sired by Marston, two by each woman, and Marston wrote and gave interviews. After his death, Elizabeth and Olive continued to live together until Olive died in 1990. According to Hanley, Olive and Elizabeth "embodied the feminism of the day" (p. 12).

Olive provided two particularly important contributions to the Wonder Woman story. First, she always wore a pair of bracelets. Second, she was the niece of Margaret Sanger, the mother of birth control in America. Sanger's writing had an enormous influence on the threesome. Not only was she tacitly in favor of the relationship, giving them some degree of cover, but the philosophy of Sanger's *Woman and the New Race* would turn out to be the philosophy of Wonder Woman (Lepore, 2014, p. 102).

Marston noted that his brand of feminist thinking drove story development. "Frankly, Wonder Woman is psychological propaganda for the new type of woman who, I believe, should rule the world" (Lepore, 2014, p. vii). Marston's editor at DC Comics, Sheldon Mayer, concluded that Marston was writing feminism, but not for women. "The vast popularity of comic books offered a way to reach the malleable minds of America's male youth. Wonder Woman comics were essentially Marston's psychological theories masquerading as superhero adventures" (Hanley, 2014, p. 16). Because Wonder Woman sold, Marston's thinly veiled agenda was permitted to be part of the story line.

In summary, the creation of Wonder Woman was to advance Marston's feminist leanings. The influences of his wife, mistress, and contemporary feminist writers, particularly Margaret Sanger, were dominant in the initial stories. But even while Marston was alive, there was an attempt to shunt Wonder Woman to the background, especially when she was paired with male heroes. In *All-Star Comics* #13 (Fox and Burnley, 1942), she is named secretary of the Justice Society, a point that is confirmed in subsequent issues where the list of the male members is given followed by "and as secretary to the Justice-Society: Wonder Woman." In *All-Star Comics* #14 (Fox and Gallagher, 1943) she is left out of the action despite being far more powerful than other members of the Society, but the secretary and honorary member must remain behind. When Marston died, the writers who took over, specifically Robert Kanigher, did not have the same devotion to feminist doctrines. In fact, Kanigher hated Marston's Wonder Woman calling her "the grotesque inhuman original Wonder Woman" (Lepore, 2014, p. 271). More than any of the subsequent writers, Kanigher changed the tenor of Wonder Woman from a powerful, women's rights advocate, to something entirely unrecognizable. It took a long time to overcome the bias against Wonder Women. Nearly twenty years later in *Justice League of America*, #9, Aquaman notes that while there might not be a chairman for the League, "when it comes to cleaning time, we all agree Wonder Woman is boss" (Fox and Sekowsky, 1962).

Who she is or whence she came?

Wonder Woman's backstory has changed a bit over time. Originally, she was a child, formed from clay by Hippolyta, queen of the Amazons, and named Diana.[6] The child is raised on the island and when a man, Steve Trevor, crashes in the ocean near the island, Diana dives in and saves him. Hippolyta is told by the gods that someone needs to take Steve back to America and act as the Amazons' emissary to the world of men. A great tournament is to be held to choose the champion. Diana is banned from competing, so she dons a mask and enters the competition anyway. When she wins, Hippolyta has no choice but to send her. Bestowed with a magic lasso that will make anyone bound by it tell the truth (think a lie-detector), a dazzling costume, and an invisible jet, Diana takes Steve back to the United States and back to World War II.

In the other, current, version of Wonder Woman's origin, she is the daughter of Hippolyta and Zeus. This endows her with god-like powers, including the ability to fly. No need for the invisible jet anymore (and who could remember where that was parked anyway?). She has been graced with the gifts from the gods mentioned earlier and is a serious threat as the most powerful superhero in the Justice League.

Marston wanted a strong woman influencing the young, male readers of comics. To this end, Marston explained the rationality undergirding Wonder Woman to Mayer:

> Men (Greeks) were captured by predatory lover-seeking females until they got sick of it and made the women captive by force. But they were afraid of them (masculine inferiority complex) and kept them heavily chained lest the women put one over as they always had before. The Goddess of Love comes along and helps women break their chains by giving them the greater force of real altruism. Whereupon men turned about face and actually helped the women get away from domestic slavery – as men are doing now. The NEW WOMEN thus freed and strengthened by supporting themselves (on Paradise Island) developed enormous physical and mental power. But they have to use it for other people's benefit or they go back to chains, and weakness.
>
> *(Lepore, 2014, pp. 188–189)*

Marston was preparing his readers for the takeover of women. He felt that women were less inclined to resort to violence to settle disputes and as such female rule would lead to a more peaceful society. It was a natural direction for the evolution of all mankind. Interspersed within the pages of the early Wonder Woman stories though, was an economic message, one consistent with another form of feminism.

A job is better for me[7]

Economics is the study of how people deal with scarcity, but people are not homogenous. They are going to deal with scarcity in unique ways. How best to allocate your time, talents, and financial resources will be impacted not only by necessity, but also by individual preferences, and social norms, among many, many other things. In the process of understanding economics and the behaviors of people as they face the specter of scarcity, economists have brought their own sets of biases to the mix.

Feminist economics is a sub-field of economic study that attempts to alter the narrative of how economists conduct their work. The field gained prominence in the late 1980s with Marilyn Waring's (1988) book *If Women Counted*. Because economics is a field dominated by men feminist economists maintain the history, modeling, and empirical analysis that are presumed to apply to all of economic behavior are inherently biased.[8] The natural result of this is that research questions miss important details. Essentially, they claim that there is a lack of objectivity in the overall analysis due to the focus on masculine centric ideas. This has policy implications as well. Not only are policies flawed because they discount issues of concern to women like family economics and emotional responses, the data upon which policy decisions are made are defective. By ignoring productive activity like the work done at the household level, engaged in primarily by women, measures of national output, most prominently gross domestic product (GDP), are vastly undercounted. In so doing, the economic science is missing substantial portions of vital, productive activity. Consequently, public policies are not designed to promote the interests of women, because their activities are deemed to be irrelevant to national income.

Feminist economist writings are thus focused on issues that impact woman such as gender inequality, pay inequality, work force participation, domestic violence, and property rights for women. These issues have direct economic significance not only for the women impacted by them, but also for the economy as a whole. Policies provide incentives for people to engage in particular activities. If property rights do not transfer to women, there will be fewer women starting businesses. If women's work is not counted in the computation of GDP there will be an understatement of production in a country.

The advocacy of feminist economics has a great degree of merit and according to Amartya Sen, a Nobel Prize winning economist, the spread of it is "vastly enriching the understanding of important economic issues."[9] However, we need to pause at this point to bring the discussion back around to the real focus of this chapter: Wonder Woman. She may be a feminist icon, but "Merciful Minerva!" how in the world does this relate to feminist economics?

Counting women's work

Let's begin with data. It may not be the most exciting subject matter (ok, it would scarcely move the interest meter), but how we measure the economy is instrumental to getting policy right. If you are measuring things incorrectly and basing policy on that, you are likely not going to properly address problems. Again, for many economists, the most important measure of economic health is GDP. To define the term, GDP is the total output of final goods and services produced within the borders of a country over a given period of time. The definition has a few components to it that should be addressed to fully grasp the problems feminist economists see, and the role of Wonder Woman in GDP.

First, GDP is a measure of final goods and services. This means that we only count the good in GDP if it is the last time it is purchased. For example, if a company based in the United States is selling cell phones, but buys the software that runs the phone from another company, it is the dollar value of the cell phone that counts in GDP, not the dollar value of the software. If you counted both of these, you would be double counting, since the software is part of the phone.

Second, GDP is measured by production within geographic borders. It doesn't matter where you sell the product, what matters is where the product is made. Additionally, it doesn't matter where the company's headquarters is located, only where the production takes place. If, for instance, Toyota sets up a factory to manufacture cars in Georgetown, Kentucky, then the value of the cars sold is counted as GDP for the United States because of where the production takes place. The fact that Toyota is a Japanese company is irrelevant. Toyota also produces parts in the United States. They manufacture engines at a plant in Buffalo, West Virginia, but since the engines are part of the final product, the engines are only counted inasmuch as they are part of the vehicle.

Finally, GDP is a measure of a flow. Usually, GDP is counted over the course of a year, although estimates are provided every three months. The problem, of course, is that production of many goods doesn't occur in the course of a day, and even if it did, some days are more productive than others. If we were to count GDP on a particular day, which day would it be? Mondays and Fridays are probably bad choices because people are just getting back from the weekend, or looking forward to it. The Tuesday after the college football championship might not be a great choice, nor would Thanksgiving Thursday. What if on the day we were to count GDP a snowstorm hit Boston, or a hurricane hit south Florida, or an earthquake devastates the San Francisco Bay Area? There are just too many random variables that can affect production on a particular day so we measure GDP over time.

There is one more thing we need to discuss before we bring Wonder Woman into the arcane arithmetic of GDP, and that involves the incredible shortcomings of the system. Feminist economists aren't the only ones who see the problems inherent with the way GDP is counted. Diane Coyle's (2014) book on GDP provides an interesting history of where this number came from, but it also discusses the problems for measuring it. Similarly, Zachary Karabell (2014) notes there are some mighty big flaws in the biggest of macroeconomic numbers. Both authors, and any economics textbook worth its salt, will explain that GDP suffers from a few big problems. One of these, we've already noted. There is a lot of activity that isn't counted as productive.[10] This is one of the big feminist complaints against GDP. Any work you do for yourself at home is not counted, even though it is most certainly productive. The catch is that, if you pay someone to do the same work for you, it is counted. Suffering Sappho! What chicanery is afoot here?

First, an example. Let's say that at the end of a long day you decide that cooking dinner is for the birds. Instead, you stop off at your favorite local eatery to grab a salad, a sandwich, and a piece of cake for the road. You happily pay the fare and head home to luxuriate. Because you paid the restaurant for your meal it is counted as productive activity and thus is part of GDP. The next day, on your way home you pick up some food at a market and head home to make your specialty: chicken stir-fry. Here's where the GDP calculation gets a bit tricky. The food you pay for is part of GDP, but your cooking of the food is not. Before we get to why, let's consider one more scenario. It's been a bumper crop for you this year. Your backyard garden has yielded food by the bushel full. You decide to make a wonderful meal of fresh salad, fruit, and eggplant parmigiana. You cook it up, and think that this is the life. However, none of what you have done in this situation is counted in GDP, but what do you care. It is possibly the best meal you have ever prepared!

All these situations involve you eating, but not all of them are part of the measure of national production. Why? Basically, measuring production that happens in your home is far too difficult. Would you want an employee of the government hovering around you all the time trying to determine what work you did around the house is worthy of being included in GDP? They would be there when you picked the eggplant and when you chop the vegetables, and add the oil to the pans. They would also be with you when you wash your car, take out the trash, shovel the driveway, darn your socks, or change a lightbulb. This is all productive activity that you could pay someone else to do, and if you did, it would be counted as GDP. Household production is actually quite difficult to measure, not because of what the good is, but because of how intrusive the measurement process would be. And don't forget, there has to be a price tag associated with the activity. How much would you pay someone to cook for you? Are there people you know who you would pay more or less? How should this be determined?[11]

This is where the feminist economist's argument comes to the fore, and where we will bring Wonder Woman into the picture. Women have traditionally done the household production. Women have done most of the cooking, cleaning, and washing throughout history. Because that is household production, it doesn't get counted in GDP. It isn't that there is no value to the work, it is incredibly valuable. It is just too difficult to measure. Feminist economists say that because it isn't counted society is vastly undercounting the productive activity of half of the population. They are, of course, correct, but it doesn't mean that there is an easy solution.

What does Wonder Woman have to say about this? In Wonder Woman #5 (Moulton and Peter, 1943), the story begins with the god of war, Mars, freaking out about the number of women participating in the war effort in the U.S., Britain and Russia.[12] He is upset that by achieving power in war, women might escape the domination of men. Those fears are magnified by the thought that if women get too powerful they will put an end to war.

In reaction, Mars sends one of his minions to earth, to visit Dr. Psycho, a man whose fiancé, Marva, had set him up for a burglary he didn't commit. He goes to jail for robbery, and Marva marries someone else. During his time in prison, Dr. Psycho becomes determined to destroy any progress made by women. When he gets out he kills Marva's husband, and forces her to marry him. He then uses an occult method to project George Washington to a crowd using the hypnotized Marva. Washington tells the crowd not to allow women to work in the war effort, particularly in the munitions factory. He foretells the destruction of the plant due to women's carelessness, and it comes to pass. Psycho's war on women continues as he frames three army secretaries for stealing secret documents. The women are summarily arrested.

What's going on here? Economically, it doesn't make sense at all. Because so many men were on the front during World War II, women were vital to supporting the U.S. efforts at home. Without women to fill the employment ranks the war could not be successfully prosecuted. This reality makes for a socially relevant story line. Dr. Psycho tried to keep women out of the workforce for purely sexist reasons. Apparently, he would have them return to housework, even if there were no men at home to work for. Mars, and by proxy Dr. Psycho, wanted to keep women subservient. We see in the opening panel of the comic that Mars has a female slave acting as his secretary. That picture is a common one in early Wonder Woman comics.[13] The economic message in *Wonder Woman* #5 is that by enslaving women, you are only harming yourself. Without women, the workforce would be inadequate. Even if there were enough men to fill the available jobs by shunting women back to housework, by mismeasuring production as GDP measures do, output would not be as high as it could be. And only sexist villains like Mars and Dr. Psycho would do that.

There is another angle to the attack on women in the workforce. The economic freedom that results from being employed erodes the male dominance that Mars wants to maintain. This is highlighted once Dr. Psycho is finally apprehended and Marva is freed from his influence. She says "submitting to a cruel husband's domination has ruined my life! But what can a weak girl do?" Wonder Woman replies "get strong! Earn your own living – … and fight for your country!" (Moulton and Peter, 1943). Wonder Woman is advocating, as she often does, that employment should be a woman's first priority in gaining independence (Hanley, 2014, p. 21). She makes the same argument in *Sensation Comics* #8 where Wonder Woman helps her woefully underpaid friends working at the Bullfinch Department Stores. Alerted to the problem, she goes undercover in her secret identity as Diana Prince to get the story. She finds the girls protesting their treatment and asking for a "living wage and healthy working conditions" (Moulton and Peter, 1942a). In response, manager Googins fires them all. When confronted by Diana Prince, who asks him about being fair, Googins replies that it isn't his job to be fair, it is to make the company money.

Getting nowhere with the manager, Diana confronts the store's owner, Gloria Bullfinch. Using her magic lasso (early on the lasso would not just make you tell the truth but also compel you to submit to Wonder Woman's will), Wonder

Woman makes Gloria believe she is someone else so she can learn what it is like to work on the Bullfinch floor. Gloria realizes how difficult the job is and in reaction doubles everyone's salaries and improves the working conditions because Wonder Woman "made me work like you and now I understand."

Wonder Woman's fight in favor of higher wages is taken up in feminist economists' concerns over income inequality. In *Wonder Woman* #203 (Delany and Giordano, 1972), one of the post Marston writers finally gets the women's lib tone right. This issue, titled "The Women's Lib Issue," was set to kick off at least a two-issue story arc about women's lib issues of the day. This story takes place in the mod-Wonder Woman days preceding *Ms.* magazine. A fashionably attired Diana Prince is looking for a job and a place to stay when she runs into a group of brutish men. While she is never in any real trouble, because, although she no longer has her powers, her martial arts training would be more than a match for these thugs, out of the shadows dashes a woman, wildly kicking and throwing punches. It turns out to be a friend of Diana's, Cathy Perkins. Together, they beat back the men and after she explains her situation, Cathy invites Diana to crash at her place.

Cathy has been taking karate lessons with a woman she met at the local women's liberation meetings. Diana isn't convinced that the movement has anything to offer, but wonders if the woman living in the apartment above Cathy, who is constantly arguing with her husband, and who clearly wants to get a job, might benefit from the group.

The next day, Diana has a job interview. She is offered a great job by the owner of a department store, Mr. Grandee, who knows Diana used to be Wonder Woman. He convinces her that he wants Diana Prince to be the poster child for the new liberated woman to whom his store is catering. When she returns to Cathy's apartment, Cathy recounts some accusations against Grandee to Diana who at first doesn't believe them. Nevertheless, Cathy's passion moves her to attend a women's lib meeting, where it is revealed that Grandee is paying below the minimum wage. Grandee dodges the law in some ingenious ways. His staff is all female so there is no wage disparity between men and women, and the low wages are legal because he is buying cheap goods made in-state so there is no inter-state commerce. Eventually, Grandee's operation is shut down, and in celebration the women's lib group meets to pat themselves on the back. Unfortunately, their meeting is disrupted by a different group of women who accuse them of costing 250 jobs at Grandee's.

The issue concludes with a promised resolution to the dispute between the two groups of women, but inexplicably the next issue never ran. Perhaps in response to Gloria Steinem's demands, the next issue brings a return of Wonder Woman's powers, her costume and the Amazons, but we never hear from Cathy or the newly unemployed women again.

Milk and technology

There are other parts of the Wonder Woman story that deal with economics. In some cases, these coincide with the women's liberation agenda. The most decisive example of this is found in *Sensation Comics* #7 (Moulton and Peter, 1942b). A nefarious Nazi plot is afoot designed to weaken American children. Leading the scheme is one of Wonder Woman's earliest foes, the Baroness Paula Von Gunther. The baroness has bought up the country's entire milk supply. As a result, prices are rising and poor women cannot buy milk for their children. Here is the attack on women. It is their responsibility to care for the family. For single mothers, the higher prices for milk are particularly burdensome because they aren't making much. We are told of a woman who tragically has lost one of her children because of the sky-high price of milk. In this basic demand and supply story, the baroness purposefully holds back the supply of milk in an attempt to raise prices. Her agent, Alphonso de Gyppo, claims that he is paying dairy farmers a fair price, but to cover the costs of operation he must charge a high price to the end consumer – again, primarily women. When milk doesn't sell, they dump it, causing supplies to drop further and prices to rise precipitously.

Another thread, one that is consistent throughout the Wonder Woman oeuvre, is that Themescara is more technologically advanced than the man's world. Depending on which origin story you read the origin of Paradise Island varies. In all cases the home of the Amazons is devoid of men, but originally, Paradise Island was provided by Aphrodite as a haven for the Amazons to escape the treachery of men (Moulton and Peter, 1942c). Shortly thereafter, the story was altered and Paradise Island became a punishment for Hippolyta and the Amazons for allowing themselves to be tricked by Hercules (Moulton and Peter, 1942d). In the 1987 Wonder Woman reboot, Paradise Island was set aside for the reincarnated souls of women who had been killed by men (Perez and Potter, 1987). Regardless of how the island was established, the implication is that because women were left to their own devices, and being uninhibited by the wars of men, they used their minds to develop technologies for good rather than for war (Dini and Ross, 2001). This is evident in the inaugural issue of Wonder Woman. When Steve Trevor crashes, Diana saves him from the ocean and delivers him to the medical laboratory where she develops a healing ray which, against all odds, saves his life (Moulton and Peter, 1942b). Because Wonder Woman was able to spend time studying science rather than fighting, she had the knowledge necessary, somewhat ironically, to save Steve, the soldier. The message is that while war-time economies, like the ones that existed when Wonder Woman debuted, create things that are used to destroy other things and kill people, the peace-loving Amazons devote their resources to improving themselves and the world around them.

In explaining the origin of Paradise Island to Diana, Hippolyta says that their peaceful and prosperous existence will continue as long as they never let themselves be enthralled by men. She notes that "we Amazons have been able to far surpass the inventions of the so-called man-made civilization! We are not only stronger and wiser than men – but our weapons are better – our flying machines are further advanced!" (Moulton and Peter, 1942d).

Moulston's message was not only that women's intellect was equal to men's, but when put to use in a world that was not governed by the passions of men, that intellect would guide the human species. Prosperity would exist in perpetuity. However, a later arc finds Diana rethinking this position. When her mother is cursed into a clay statue, Diana must become queen in her place (Azzarello and Chiang, 2012). One of the early changes she tries to make is to integrate men into the Amazons' world. She claims that Amazonian society is stagnating. By cutting itself off from the rest of the world, it is bad for development. Perhaps she is right, but her Amazonian sisters don't take the news well. They are very resistant to such a change in their culture (Finch and Finch, 2014). Wonder Woman has been out in the world of men for a long time now, and perhaps she has found that men aren't all like Hercules, Mars, and the conniving Greek gods that comprise the Amazons' experience. While they may not be as adept as the women of Paradise Island, there is certainly something they can offer.

The economic significance of Wonder Woman

Wonder Woman is a feminist comic. At least that was the intention of the creator. Despite the mass appeal of Wonder Woman in the early days – they were selling upwards of 10 million copies by 1944 (Lepore, 2014, p. 246) – DC has retconned the book so many times the heroine is sometimes unrecognizable. In those early years, the feminist message was more than equal voting rights for women, it includes a significant dose of economics. The economic angle is always from a feminist perspective, which makes sense considering the thinly veiled cultural message of the story. The economics in Wonder Woman predates the formal study of feminist economics by nearly 40 years. While she has not yet appeared on the cover of the journal *Feminist Economics* perhaps she should.[14] As *Ms*. magazine recognized the importance of the social message of Wonder Woman, the economic world might want to consider the economic significance of the great heroine as well.

Notes

1 Steinem not only read the comics, she actually worked in comics early in her career, as assistant editor for *Help Magazine* produced by Harvey Kurtzman (creator of MAD). She also edited a collection of Golden Age Wonder Woman stories, with feminist commentary, in 1972. It was one of the first trade collections of comic book stories to reach bookstores.
2 Wonder Woman officially gives up her powers in issue #179 (O'Neil and Sekowsky, 1968).
3 This is the home of Wonder Woman and her Amazonian sisters. Of course, these are the Amazons of Greek mythology. They have nothing to do with Jeff Bezos or the company he founded.
4 This title of a press release authored by the psychologist himself (Lepore, 2014, p. 231).
5 Marston followed a most unorthodox path in academics progressing backward from a tenure track position at Harvard, to adjunct teaching at a variety of colleges. He also started a number of businesses that all failed, some in a matter of days.
6 There seems to be very little consistency with the use of the names Paradise Island and Themescara in the comics. The clearest distinction is that Themescara is the name of the

capital city of the Amazons, while Paradise Island refers to the entire island, or chain of islands, making up the home land of the Amazons.

7 This is part of a quote from Princess Diana of Wales (not Wonder Woman). The full quote states "People think at the end of the day that a man is the only answer [to fulfillment]. Actually a job is better for me" (retrieved from www.feminist.com/resources/quotes/).

8 According to the *Wall Street Journal*, there is approximately a three to one male to female ratio in undergraduate economics majors (Cronin, 2014).

9 This quote can be found on the website for the Feminist Economics journal: www.feministeconomics.org/.

10 A few other problems with counting GDP include the exemption of black market and illegal activity. Sure, such activity may be against the law, but that doesn't mean it isn't productive. Additionally, as a measure of overall well-being – economists typically say more GDP is preferred to less – this number ignores the value people place on leisure and a clean environment.

11 I know that if I had to pay my wife to cook for me, I would pay her a lot because she's really good at it. If I had to pay my youngest daughter to do the same thing I wouldn't pay her nearly as much. The quality would be far less and after two or three weeks of grilled cheese sandwiches and cold cereal, I would be willing to pay other people a lot of money to put me out of my culinary misery.

12 There is no discrepancy here. William Moulton Marston used the pen name Charles Moulton when writing Wonder Woman. I will therefore be referencing Moulton as the author of comics starring Wonder Woman, even though it was Marston who wrote them.

13 There is a psychological component of enslaving woman and the bondage scenes in Wonder Woman that is beyond the scope of this paper, but Hanley (2014) covers it in detail.

14 This journal doesn't actually have people on the cover.

References

Azzarello, B. and C. Chiang. (2012). *Wonder Woman*, #4. DC Comics.

Coyle, D. (2014). *GDP: A Brief but Affectionate History*. Princeton, N.J.: Princeton University Press.

Cronin, B. (2014, January 8). Despite Rising Profile in Economics, Women Still Trail Men in Academia. *Wall Street Journal*. Retrieved from https://www.wsj.com/articles/despite-rising-profile-in-economics-women-still-trail-men-in-academia-1389052829

Delany, S. and D. Giordano. (1972). *Wonder Woman*, #203. DC Comics.

Dini, P. and A. Ross. (2001). *Spirit of Truth*. New York: DC Comics.

Finch, M. and D. Finch. (2014). *Wonder Woman*, #36. DC Comics.

Fox, G. and J. Burnley. (1942). *All-Star Comics*, #13. DC Comics.

Fox, G. and J. Gallagher. (1943). *All-Star Comics*, #14. DC Comics.

Fox, G. and M. Sekowsky. (1962). *Justice League of America*, #9. DC Comics.

Hanley, T. (2014). *Wonder Woman Unbound: The Curious History of the World's Most Famous Heroine*. Chicago: Chicago Review Press.

Karabell, Z. (2014). *The Leading Indicators: A Short History of the Numbers That Rule Our World*. New York: Simon and Shuster.

Kilkenny, K. (2017, June 21). How a Magazine Cover From the 1970s Helped Wonder Woman Win Over Feminists. *Pacific Standard*. Retrieved from https://psmag.com/social-justice/ms-magazine-helped-make-wonder-woman-a-feminist-icon.

Lepore, J. (2014). *The Secret History of Wonder Woman*. New York: Alfred A. Knopf.

Moulton, C. and H. Peter. (1942a). *Sensation Comics*, #8. DC Comics.

Moulton, C. and H. Peter. (1942b). *Sensation Comics*, #7. DC Comics.

Moulton, C. and H. Peter. (1942c). *Wonder Woman*, #1. DC Comics.
Moulton, C. and H. Peter. (1942d). *All-Star Comics*, #8. DC Comics.
Moulton, C. and H. Peter. (1943). *Wonder Woman*, #5. DC Comics.
O'Neil, D. and M. Sekowsky. (1968). *Wonder Woman*, #179. DC Comics.
Perez, G. and G. Potter. (1987). *Wonder Woman*, #1. DC Comics.
Waring, M. (1988). *If Women Counted*. San Francisco: Harper Row.

4

POOR PETER PARKER

Spider sense doesn't apply to making a living

Patrick Holt

As one of the most recognizable heroes in the comic world, Spider-Man has been entertaining readers and viewers since 1962. There have been many versions of the Web-Slinger in comics, in movies and in television series, and throughout the adventures of the friendly, neighborhood Spider-Man, there is one overriding tension, even beyond whether he should ask out Mary Jane or Gwen Stacey: Peter Parker is poor. Living paycheck to paycheck – or in the case of Aunt May, social security check to social security check – takes its toll on Peter, but when he is surreptitiously bitten by a spider and gains his super powers, it looks like things are going to change. But they don't. Peter remains poor, yet he is reluctant to use his powers for personal gain. This is really the mystery of the Spider-Man story, at least from an economic perspective. Why has Peter Parker failed to utilize his skill set in a way that makes him better off? Surely it isn't just as homage to his deceased uncle. Answering this question isn't that complicated, but does require an understanding of some basic economic concepts. Peter stays poor because, well, he's a bad economist.

Peter Parker's origin story is familiar to most comic fans, but just in case you've forgotten the main players, and before we get to the economics, this chapter will begin by exploring the genesis of Spider-Man. Next, we'll explore Peter's primary problem: he isn't using his brain. Peter is smart, which means he has the first economic topic, what economists call human capital. Even without his Spider skills, he should be able to make something of his life, yet he fails to do so. This failure is driven in part by the second economic topic in our analysis: utility. Peter likes being Spider-Man. He is happy swinging through New York on a gossamer strand, even though he must forego opportunities to maximize his utility. Which raises a third point. This happiness in avocation necessitates giving up potential vocations, and relations. Being a hero involves costs, what economists call opportunity costs, because there are some things you have to give up when you put on the mask.

Finally, we need to consider the impact being a hero has on other people. In this case, we don't just mean those closest to you. As a hero, your actions have the potential for destroying city blocks or saving the universe; however, those people you harm or help are not part of the decisions you or your antagonist make and are thus third party players. The benefits or costs you impose upon them are called externalities. These externalities can be positive or negative, but they exist nonetheless. No matter how much happiness being a hero yields you, there are others who might be impacted by your actions. If you don't take that into consideration, then you might be doing too much, or even too little, web slinging.

So, let's take a look at the world of Spider-Man. He can spin a web any size, and catch thieves just like flies, but that might not bring home the bacon.

Spider-Man vs. Peter Parker

Peter Parker first appeared in the comic *Amazing Fantasy* #15 in 1962. The creation of Stan Lee and Steve Ditko, Peter Parker was a character aimed at a younger, poorer generation of comic book reader. Peter was originally a teenage high school student being raised by his Uncle Ben and Aunt May after his parents were killed in an airplane crash overseas when Peter was very young (Gruenwald and Frenz, 1986). Growing up in the New York borough of Queens, Peter was the stereotypical nerd. Highly intelligent but socially and physically awkward, he was ridiculed by his classmates but praised by his teachers, especially the ones in the science department. During a trip to a science demonstration on controlling radioactivity in the laboratory, Peter's life would be dramatically changed when, during the demonstration, an irradiated spider drops onto Peter's hand and promptly bites him. The spider dies, and Peter begins feeling ill. Leaving the demonstration, he notices that his body now feels different. Distracted by this new sensation he walks into the middle of the street and is nearly run down by a car. Leaping out of the way, farther out of the way than a normal human could, he finds himself sticking to the wall of a nearby building. Thus, begins Peter's new life. From the bite of that spider he acquired the powers of a spider with increased strength, reflexes, durability and a sort of "Spidey Sense" that warns him of danger. Peter now has brawn to go with his brain.

Excited to test his newfound abilities, the perpetually poor Peter takes a chance to win some money in a wrestling match, in which one only had to stay in the ring a few minutes with a huge, carnival, strong-man style wrestler by the name of Crusher Hogan. Fearing he could potentially lose the match and become the laughing stock of the neighborhood, Peter disguises himself and proceeds to easily win the prize money with his enhanced abilities. Catching the eye of a television producer who feels the mask creates a great angle for television, Peter is offered the chance to make more money by being on television dressed as a mysterious masked character. Peter goes home and creates a costume, artificial webbing and web shooters, assuming the character Spider-Man. Spider-Man becomes an overnight sensation on television with New Yorkers as we the reader are treated to a montage of newspaper headlines around all the buzz this character has created after his on-screen appearance. However, while backstage after the end of this first appearance, he has the chance to stop a thief who had robbed the producer and is being chased by a police officer. He selfishly feels that is the job of the police and goes on his way allowing the robber to run by him unaccosted while pursued by the officer. A few weeks later he arrives home to find police cars at the house. The police inform him that his Uncle Ben had been killed by a burglar. The police have the criminal holed up in a building downtown. Distraught, Peter dons his costume and swings to the building to confront his uncle's killer, only to find that the burglar was the man he had the opportunity to stop backstage. He captures the burglar leaving him tangled in webbing for the police. As he walks off into the night, the narrator informs the reader that Peter has learned a hard lesson, the lesson that with great power comes great responsibility (Lee and Ditko, 1962).

With great power comes great economics

So, what does all of this have to with the subject of economics? Economics is often described as the study of how people deal with scarcity of resources such as money or time. A re-occurring theme across the Spider-Man comics is that Peter Parker is poor. He is barely scraping by most of the time. The comic never specifically elaborates on how much Uncle Ben made or what his occupation was, but it does tell us in *Spider-Man* issue #1 that after his death, his widow, Aunt May, has a hard time making ends meet. Peter witnesses her having to tell the landlord that she needs another week in order to be able to pay the rent. Peter is owed money by the television producer but due to fact that he has to keep his identity a secret and that the check is made out to Spider-Man, he can't cash his paycheck. He sees Aunt May going to a pawnshop to pawn her jewelry just to get enough money to pay rent, and he vows to find a way to make money. After approaching the Fantastic Four for a job, he is disappointed to learn they are a non-profit organization and don't pay their members (Lee and Ditko, 1963a). In *Amazing Spider-Man* #2 he is able to sell photos to the newspaper *The Daily Bugle* which provides for a steady, if not spectacular, stream of income (Lee and Ditko, 1963b). He is able to do this because, as Spider-Man, he was able to capture photos that no one else could, and this allows him to earn enough money to pre-pay a year's worth of rent. Later on, Aunt May faces health issues and requires either expensive medication or surgery and Peter struggles to find a way to come up the funds (Lee and Ditko, 1964). If Peter were not such a good person he could use his powers to turn to a life of crime, or even become a Robin Hood style vigilante and rob the criminals he captures à la the Punisher.[1] But Peter Parker has a moral code that won't allow him to do that in good conscience and, so he must turn to other means to make ends meet. He seems reluctant to use his super-powers to earn money, but in reality, he has many other options.

Putting the "man" in Spider-Man

This is a good time to segue into the economic concept of "human capital". The term has been around for some time but gained prominence through the work of economist Gary Becker (1964). Simply put, human capital is what you bring to the table by being you. It might be a strong back and work ethic in the case of jobs involving manual labor, or intelligence, education or organizational skills needed for desk jobs. In Peter Parker's case, a new term must be added to the human capital lexicon: super-human capital. There is the capital he had before he was bitten by the radioactive spider and the additional "super-human" capital that the bite gave him. In the course of the Spider-Man series, Peter relies more on his super-human capital while his normal, human capital, his skills and abilities that he had before he was bitten, is underutilized.

Peter's aunt and uncle instilled in him an ethic that barred him from using his super-powers to make money as a criminal and learned the hard way with the death of his uncle that he has responsibilities to the greater good. But Peter lives in New York City and if you look at the costume and gadgets he created to become Spider-Man it's clear that Peter did not have to settle on becoming a freelance photographer just to help makes ends meet. Let's look at the human and super-human capital Peter Parker has at his disposal. On the super-human capital side, he has enhanced strength, the ability to stick to surfaces, extraordinary reflexes and agility, and the sixth "Spidey" sense. Contrast this with the pre-spider bite human capital which he maintains even when his powers are lost or negated. He obviously has an eye for photography, but more germane to income generation, he possesses a genius level intellect, and is a talented inventor, not to mention he is "probably the world's greatest authority on the subject of webs and their creation" (Lee and Ditko, 2014). And keep in mind, he is still in high school at this point.

Peter could try and capitalize on his super-human capital but that could make his life more complicated. For instance, he could use his super strength and wall crawling ability to become a super construction worker, or he could start a superhero for hire business à la Power Man and Iron Fist of Heroes for Hire. He could also easily use his powers to become a performer without the mask, so that he could be paid, but I think we can assume that the events that led to his Uncle Ben's death would cause him to shy away from the entertainment spotlight. He could also have elected to work for the U.S. government or S.H.I.E.L.D.[2] but he is too young to enlist when he first gains his powers, and too far into his superhero career by the time he is old enough to join. It is notable that early on he does try a few times to join the Avengers[3] only to be rebuffed.[4]

Perhaps the most important aspect of Peter's normal human capital is that he is a genius, and an inventor as well. It is one thing to have an idea for an invention, and quite another to be able to single-handedly build and market a creation. This, in some ways, puts Peter on par with Tony Stark or Reed Richards.[5] Consider that at the beginning of the series Peter is just in high school. Yet being a high school student with access to presumably only the school's science department's lab (which does appear very well stocked for a public school), his allowance and a Radio Shack,[6] he is able to invent his webbing, his web shooters with all the micro-mechanization and machining that required, as well as a miniature spider tracer used to track unsuspecting people, both good and bad (Hudlin, Tan and Buckingham, 2005).[7]

Peter comes close to using his inventions for economic gain. Recall that Peter needed to quickly raise money to help his Aunt May. He is so desperate to come up with money to pay for her medication that he visits some scientists as Spider-Man and offers to sell them the formula for his webbing. The creation of Spider-Man's webbing might have been inspired by the abilities he received from the radioactive spider bite, but it is something that Peter could have designed with or without being bitten. The webbing is by itself an amazing invention. A one-inch strand of it is strong enough to hold the Thing, a member of the Fantastic Four whose body is made of rock and is believed to weigh 500 pounds. It is 90% fireproof and can withstand the Human Torch's heat at normal output levels. Furthermore, it can stretch and is bullet proof as well as lightweight and waterproof, and it dissolves or evaporates after 1–2 hours, which is why there aren't web-lines hanging all over New York City (Lee and Ditko, 2014). It is, in short, a miracle invention. It is initially formulated with the chemicals Peter could acquire from his high school's chemistry lab. On top of that, Peter also designed the web-shooters, which are themselves a miracle of micro mechanization. Steve Jobs had nothing on Peter Parker. One of the previously mentioned advantages of the webbing is that it dissolves after a few hours. Unfortunately for Peter Parker, the fact that the webbing didn't last made the scientists pass (Lee and Ditko, 2017). Curiously though, we find out later, in the same storyline, that Peter can and does re-formulate the web fluid and could manufacture variations of it. In a fit of short-sightedness, the scientists passed up a potentially lucrative invention.

All these inventions also have marketable value. It is given that it might be unrealistic to expect a teenager to know how to cash in on these inventions, but certainly as Peter grows older and goes to college the opportunities his inventions afford should become more obvious. Again, it is important to realize Peter's brain was not enhanced by the radioactive spider bite. He was always capable of these inventions; it was just the bite and powers he gained from it, that inspired their creation. These ideas are part of his human capital, not his super-human capital.

What makes a spider happy?

Peter Parker lives in New York City, a city full of opportunity, and while he makes a living as a photo-journalist, Peter gives up a lot to be Spider-Man. In economics, "utility" is a measure of happiness or satisfaction (Mankiw, 2015). It is not unreasonable to assume that a person will try to maximize utility. Economists assume that given the constraint of income and other resources, individuals will use or spend their scarce resources to bring them the most utility/happiness. Peter's decisions both as Peter Parker and as Spider-Man are driven by the utility he derives from being the masked Spider-Man and the sense of duty and moral obligation he feels to use his powers for the greater good.

It is natural to want to maximize the utility you get from something. As your utility from consuming that thing diminishes, you then reallocate your resources to something else that has more utility. For the most part, Peter receives significant utility from being Spider-Man. Peter Parker is a genius; he could be studying or inventing things and selling them, but he chooses to put on his costume and fight crime. Additionally, Peter Parker has fun playing the role of Spider-Man. Being Spider-Man is its own utility to Peter. Regardless of his age or circumstance, Peter is shown in the various Spider-Man titles as happy-go-lucky. He swings through the city, cracking jokes and having fun while capturing criminals. It would seem he derives utility out of just being Spider-Man and stopping bad guys. Putting a spin on Spider-Man's most famous saying, Layman (2008) says, "With great power comes great personal satisfaction" (p. 195).

However, the fact that Peter keeps a secret identity shows that he also derives utility from being plain old Peter Parker. Specifically, as Peter Parker, he can access a "normal" life that he cannot as Spider-Man, focused around personal relationships. Peter obviously loves his Aunt May. Peter also revels in the dating life, a benefit of his newfound confidence from his powers. As an adult, Peter's calling is science. But his other life will never allow that, so how else might he get the maximum utility from being Peter Parker and not Spider-Man?

As Peter Parker, he additionally gains utility by earning a steady income that Spider Man cannot. The magic of comic timelines is they tend to reset themselves to bring in new readers. So while Peter Parker was originally a child of the 1960s, newer comics have him growing up the 1980 or 1990s so that the character will still be relatable to new or younger readers. Along with the timeline changes came shifts in the utility Peter could access from being a "normal" person. What did the late 1990s have that the 1960s didn't have? The internet and much more powerful computers and software. Now Peter could pursue a sort of independent academic and teaching career through the magic of the internet (we know he uses it as Spider-Man because he tweets to Squirrel Girl (North and Chabot, 2016)). In fact, as we slide Peter into the 1990s and 2000s, the internet and other contemporary inventions would make it even more clear that Peter could easily be a millionaire or better,[8] without ever compromising his life as Spider-Man or having to show up regularly to a job. Considering the fate of newspapers in the 2000s would also mean his life as a photo-journalist would be in jeopardy. If *The Daily Bugle*'s is like every other newspaper, readership would be in decline. In some ways the information age could make it easier or harder to for heroes to make a living.

Hero life isn't all it's cracked up to be

Living the life of a superhero isn't easy. Pressures on your time and relationships are magnified ten-fold when at any moment you might be called into service. As a result, being a hero means you will have to abandon some things you want to do.

In economics, we refer to the next best option that you do not choose as an opportunity cost. These forfeitures can be a physical something or an action. If for example, Peter decides to save Mary Jane from falling to her death after being tossed off Green Goblin's glider, allowing the Green Goblin to escape, then the opportunity cost for saving his girlfriend/wife is getting to capture one of his greatest foes.

More directly, we get a glimpse of the opportunities Peter gives up when he occasionally tries to quit being Spider-Man to lead a so-called normal life.

A re-occurring example for Peter Parker that demonstrates the opportunity costs of being Spider-Man is not being able to have a normal job. Peter's desired career path was that of an academic and teacher, but because of his duties as Spider-Man he cannot meet the obligations that go along with being a teacher, or even a teaching assistant. Regardless of whether we look at him as a teenager or an adult, we can see that he can be called away at a moment's notice and gone for weeks at a time as Spider-Man. He may be called to go into space with the Avengers or be captured for some undetermined length of time by one of the many villains in his rogues gallery.

Being Spider-Man also represents a financial opportunity cost for Peter. Peter's failed attempt to sell his webbing stemmed from his chagrin that Aunt May doesn't have enough money to make ends meet. The failure to pursue the sale of the webbing represents a huge opportunity cost to Peter Parker. He could have patented any number of derivatives of the web-fluid and sold the patents to make his life easier. We know this is not unheard of in the Marvel universe simply by looking at other heroes such as Hank Pym (Ant-Man), Tony Stark (Iron Man) and Reed Richards (Mr. Fantastic). All of these characters make a living from marketing their research or inventions. Given that we know Peter Parker is a genius, it is safe to assume that paperwork involved with patenting an invention would give him no trouble, and in fact as we watch Peter grow up and go to college we know that he would have access to the needed advice to market his inventions as well. The problem for Peter is that being Spider-Man takes up a great deal of time leaving him little opportunity to improve on his creations.

The opportunity cost of not being able to earn a living is something of a theme in Peter's life. Often, he is desperate for money (but never to the point of committing crime) and even if he briefly seems to get to a place of stability such as when he joined the Avengers, (who provide members with a $1000 dollar a week stipend, free medical, and free room and board in the Avengers mansion) those things are taken from him in one way or another, and he returns to the "poor" Peter Parker baseline. As such, poverty could be viewed as one of the opportunity costs that Peter pays for being Spider-Man and one of the factors that force him to make some of the choices he makes.

In *Amazing Spider-Man* #551 we get an idea of not only Peter's money woes, but some of the practical costs of being Spider-Man as well. For instance, we learn that the ingredients for web fluid cost around 2000 dollars per batch and if he is out of fluid and doesn't have the funding to make more, then his life as a superhero becomes much more difficult (Guggenheim and Larroca, 2011). The whole story arc this issue follows is Peter's quest to get a job as his Aunt May is tired of him moping about the house. Remember that Peter has been a professional photo-journalist, and a teacher and lab assistant in his past. However, he faces rejection again and again as his dual life leads him to being disqualified for employment that requires he keep a schedule. His photography style is judged not that great for being a model photographer because his photography style is to stick a camera on something with his webbing and let it auto snap photos as he fights.

Consider though all the incredible technology in his web-shooter, which he developed while still in high school on a high schooler's budget. How much easier could his life be if he had only taken some of these early, basic inventions, patented them and sold that patent to the world. Perhaps a competitor of Tony Stark (Iron Man) would have paid handsomely for another form of small technology. In fact, in an alternate time line show in "The Last Avengers Story" we see a universe where Peter has retired and is living a relatively well-off life with wife and child after it is revealed that Hank Pym had talked him into selling the formula for his webbing and the designs for his web-shooters to 3M making Peter rich (David and Olivetti, 2009).

For Peter, the draw of being a hero must make him happy, but he has to forego so many of the other things in life. Fame, albeit masked, is a form of payment, but the sense of a job well done is perhaps payment enough. Still, Peter has to give up careers that would make him happy, and in many cases, he has to forego relationships. Peter faces tragedies in his life. The most famous, is the death of Uncle Ben, but he also loses one love of his life, Gwen Stacey, when the Green Goblin hurls her from a bridge. Spidey is a little too late to save her. Peter marries the other love of his life, Mary Jane (Shooter and Michelinie, 1987). However, despite knowing that Peter is Spider-Man, being the Web-Slinger puts significant strain on their marriage. It is quite possible that an opportunity cost of being Spider-Man is the death of Mary Jane. In *The Amazing Spider-Man* Vol. 2 #13 M.J. is on her way to Paris for a gig as a model when the plane blows up (Byrne and Mackie, 2000). Because Peter was out playing Spider-Man, he was not there to stop her from getting on the plane, or at least to say goodbye.

The people vs. Spider-Man

Peter Parker is the source of many externalities both negative and positive. An externality is when a person does something that has an effect on other persons for better or worse but the original actor receives neither compensation nor penalty for the action. Think of them as unintended side effects. For example, when Spider-Man contributes to stopping the galactic villain Thanos or the Beyonder from destroying all life on earth, or the galaxy or the universe this generates a huge positive externality for all life in the universe. Literally every living thing benefits by way of being saved from death by Spider-Man's contribution to the battle. Often when events are on the cosmic level like Thanos killing all life, the normal population of earth isn't even aware of it. As a result, it not likely Spider-Man will receive any recognition for it, in fact he most likely gets a negative editorial in *The Daily Bugle* instead.

Let's look at a few less cosmic examples. In *Amazing Spider-Man* #172 while giving chase to the Rocket Racer, Spider-Man has to use his webbing to keep the Racer's blast from damaging the nearby buildings. In this case, the owners of the buildings, and the people inside all benefit from Peter Parker's invention of webbing, but Peter is in no way compensated for this by the landlords of the buildings saved. In the same issue while facing the Molten Man, the webbing again is used to put out fires, and keep an entire hospital from burning down, a rather large positive externality to the employees and patients of the hospital.

Another good example of a positive externality is one received both by the citizens of New York City as well as its police department when Spider-Man fights street level crime. This can range from as something simple, like dealing with a mugging, to something more dramatic, such as a full-scale bank robbery or jewel heist. Spider-Man can often respond to a crime faster and more effectively than the police department. Most importantly he can do it non-lethally. This saves police officers from being at risk for injury and death during a crime, as well as innocent bystanders and the perpetrators. Of course, if the subject of the robbery is a bank or jewelry store, the institution benefits as well by avoiding loss. These benefits accrue to others who might offer a thank you, but never actually pay Spider-Man. That's the nature of a positive externality.

This is not to say Spider-Man doesn't create his fair share of negative externalities as well. In *Amazing Spider-Man* #123 while fighting Power-Man[9] (who had been hired by J. Jonah Jamison to bring in Spider-Man), the art work in the comic reveals a lot of damage being done to surrounding buildings as the combatants toss one another around. Damage is also inflicted on the architecture of the city when Spider-Man fights villains, notoriously the Green Goblin. These battles always seem to endanger innocent bystanders and rarely happen in the deserted parts of New York City. Some could argue that Peter Parker is a magnet for such weirdness and this creates some negative externalities. Probably the largest negative externality that Spider-Man imposes on the city of New York is the fact that many of his enemies will attack him anywhere and at any time, with no regard for innocent bystanders, or collateral damage.

Superhero activity entails externalities, which are often at the heart of hero and civilian disputes. People are sometimes killed due to the interactions between the good guys and bad guys. The grieving mother of a child killed during an attempt to apprehend a group of evil doers in Marvel's *Civil War* (Millar and McNevin, 2007) accuses Tony Stark in particular, and heroes in general, of encouraging powered people to work outside the law. In so doing, they bring risks to the general population. But heroes also provide benefits to the population as a whole. The question is whether the good outweighs the bad. As always, answering the question depends on perspective. At the macro level, heroes save the planet on occasion. The collateral damage is lamentable, but given the alternative of destruction for all, the upside outweighs the down. Nevertheless, those who do lose loved ones are harmed.

Externalities are not relegated to superhero stories though. In real life, externalities are relatively common occurrences. If non-heroes were causing the losses, legal remedies for compensation could be followed. That is one way to address, or internalize, the externality. By forcing the party who inflicts the harm to compensate the victim, it raises the cost of engaging in the harmful activity. This raises the intriguing proposition of whether you should be able to sue a hero. If you don't relish the idea of Spider-Man on the witness stand, perhaps regulating hero behavior is a better alternative to internalize the externalities. This is basically what the Superhero Registration Act proposed in *Civil War* is attempting to do. To show his support for the act, Peter Parker reveals to the world at a press conference that he is Spider-Man. In a litigious society though, without indemnification, Peter Parker may be in for a series of lawsuits from people seeking to force the hero to compensate them for damages.

You've come a long way little spider

Let's wrap this chapter up in some webbing and deliver it to the RAFT.[10] Peter Parker has a lot going for him, whether he is in costume as Spider-Man or not. While it seems the world, and to some extent Peter Parker himself, views Spider-Man as his sole contribution to society, it is obvious that even without his powers, Peter Parker would still bring a tremendous amount of human capital to the table. He certainly faces some opportunity costs by not using some of inventions for profit but the utility he derives from being Spider-Man must be greater than those costs because ultimately that is the life he chooses.

His actions also create both positive and negative externalities in the form of what his inventions and powers let him personally accomplish. On the positive side, he fights crime and can save the world in a way a normal police force cannot. On the negative side, you can argue that the battles Spider-Man engages in lead to a lot of destruction and the villains who seek to harm him have no issue putting innocent bystanders at risk.

Peter Parker/Spider-Man's life provides a plethora of examples that illustrate economic principles. He is in many ways a relatable character in that he doesn't start out rich like Iron Man, or as an established scientist like Bruce Banner. He is neither alien nor a god. He gets his start as a normal kid, with all the problems a teen in the real world might have along with some extra problems unique to being a superhero, yet, the hyper-exaggerated situations found in the comics provides a laboratory for studying economic principles. Just watch out for spiders.

Notes

1 The Punisher is example of an Anti-Hero. He is a Vietnam vet who believes that the best way to fight crime is to kill the criminals.

2 Standing for Strategic Hazard Intervention Espionage Logistics Directorate, this is a government organization charged with protecting the earth from threats beyond the scope of other government organizations.
3 A team of superheroes that is funded by a trust from Tony Stark, they provide their members with a weekly $1000 stipend as well medical care.
4 Much later on in the comics he will become a reserve member.
5 Tony Stark is Iron Man and Reed Richards is Mr. Fantastic, of Fantastic Four fame. These two characters are known for not only being superheroes, but also for being incredibly creative inventors and thinkers.
6 Depending when you read this, this company may or may not still be in business, but back in the 1960s thru the late early 1990s this was the place to meet all of your electronic and computer needs.
7 Hank Pym, variously Ant-Man, Giant Man, Goliath, Yellow-Jacket and Wasp, is the inventor of Pym particles which allowed him to shrink to the size of an ant, or grow the great heights. Pym was a genius, but when he found out about the spider tracers, he wondered if Peter might not be even smarter.
8 And Marvel did make him a tech tycoon after the last "Secret Wars" mini-series.
9 Power-Man is a hero who along with his partner Iron Fist hires out his services to others (sort of like a private detective)
10 A prison for super-villains located on Ryker's island.

References

Becker, G. S. (1964). *Human Capital: A Theoretical and Empirical Analysis, with Special Reference to Education.* Chicago: University of Chicago Press.

Byrne, J. and H. Mackie. (2000). *The Amazing Spider-Man*, #13. Marvel Comics.

David, P. and A. Olivetti. (2009). *Avengers: First to Last.* Marvel Comics.

Guggenheim, M. and S. Larroca. (2011). *The Amazing Spider-Man*, #551. Marvel Comics.

Gruenwald, M. and R. Frenz. (1986). *The Official Handbook of the Marvel Universe*, #12. Marvel Comics.

Hudlin, R., B. Tan and M. Buckingham. (2005). *Marvel Knights: Spider Man*, #15. Marvel Comics.

Layman, C. S. (2008). "Why be a superhero? Why be moral?" In T. Morris and M. Morris (Eds.), *Super-heroes and Philosophy: Truth, Justice, and the Socratic Way.* Chicago, Illinois: Open Court.

Lee, S. and S. Ditko. (1962). *Amazing Fantasy*, #15. Marvel Comics.

Lee, S. and S. Ditko. (1963a). *Amazing Spider-Man*, #1. Marvel Comics.

Lee, S. and S. Ditko. (1963b). *Amazing Spider-Man*, #2. Marvel Comics.

Lee, S. and S. Ditko. (1964). *Amazing Spider-Man*, #18. Marvel Comics.

Lee, S. and S. Ditko. (2014). *Amazing Spider-Man Epic Collection: Great Power.* Marvel Comics.

Lee, S. and S. Ditko. (2017). *Amazing Spider-Man Epic Collection: Great Responsibility.* Marvel Comics.

Mankiw, N. G. (2015). *Principles of Microeconomics.* Stamford, CT: Cengage Learning.

Millar, M. and S. McNevin. (2007). *Civil War.* Marvel Comics.

North, R. and J. Chabot. (2016). *The Unbeatable Squirrel Girl*, #11. Marvel Comics.

Shooter, J. and D. Michelinie. (1987). *The Amazing Spider-Man, Annual 21.* Marvel Comics.

PART II
Macroeconomics

5

FROM WEAKLING TO SUPERHERO

The economics of Captain America

John Robinson and William C. Wood

The *Captain America* franchise has wide appeal. From his 1941 comic book debut through multiple feature films in the Marvel Cinematic Universe, Captain America has thrilled and charmed audiences with his toughness, patriotism, and character. Like any person in fact or fiction, he has faced scarcity and choices – but this character is especially suitable as a means of examining fundamental propositions about economic behavior and institutions. Captain America's storyline lends itself particularly to questions of long-term economic growth, whether at the personal or national level, and the recent Captain America movies provide an exceptional setting in which to examine economic approaches to understanding social and political choices.

Captain America took a major leap in modern public recognition with the release of the feature film *Captain America: The First Avenger* (Johnston, 2011). The big screen story is fairly consistent with the comic books. Steve Rogers was an aspiring military recruit at the outset of World War II, but his "4F" classification (physically unfit to serve) prevented him from enlisting. As Steve Rogers, he was severely limited by his weak, skinny frame – but all of that changed when he qualified to be given a super serum by Dr. Abraham Erskine. He was chosen not for being big or strong or fast; the super serum would take care of all that. On the contrary, he was chosen for his strength of character.

Captain America was intended to be only the first of an elite unit made up of multiple super soldiers, but the assassination of Dr. Erskine thwarted that plan. As Captain America, Rogers went on a tour promoting bonds to finance the war effort. His tour was highly successful with domestic audiences, but when his tour went overseas to entertain active duty troops, he was mocked by the soldiers. Determined to prove his worth as a fighting man, he led a dangerous mission behind enemy lines to rescue his longtime friend Bucky Barnes and others held by the Nazi unit Hydra. In true superhero fashion, Captain America succeeded, and marched back into camp with the rescued prisoners. Other successful actions against the enemy followed, and Captain America soon became a beacon of inspiration for the troops as well. Finally possessing the physical strength to match his fearless spirit, Captain America became an archetypal hero. Captain America's military exploits culminated in a daring mission against Hydra that saw him struggling with uber villain Johann Schmidt aboard a heavily armed Hydra aircraft high above the Atlantic. Schmidt was killed by Hydra technology in the struggle, leaving Captain America alone to crash the aircraft in the Arctic to avoid setting off the weapons in a populated area.

Presumed dead for almost 70 years, Captain America was discovered in a state of hibernation underneath Arctic ice in the opening scenes of *Captain America: The First Avenger* (Johnston, 2011). He was revived and was recruited by the supreme counter-terrorist director, Nick Fury, to fight Hydra's modern-day successors. This ongoing fight formed the background for the feature films *Captain America: The Winter Soldier* (Russo & Russo, 2014) and *Captain America: Civil War* (Russo & Russo, 2016). In these films, Captain America continued to achieve superhuman military exploits in fighting evil. At the same time, he became increasingly troubled by S.H.I.E.L.D.'s, the shadowy operation directed by Fury, use of force. The divergence between his own firm moral compass and the actions of his leaders became an increasingly prominent theme throughout the movies. In addition to his title role in these three films, Captain America continued to play a leading part in the *Avengers* series of films. In these films, Captain America is a founding member of the association of superheroes known as The Avengers. In many ways, he becomes the tactical and moral leader of the group. During the events described in *Captain America: Civil War*, he and Tony Stark (Iron Man) take opposing sides over the question of signing the Sokovia Accords, which would turn decision-making authority for the group over to the United Nations.[1]

Key elements of Captain America's personal story, as well as those that arise in his interactions with The Avengers, are surprisingly illustrative of economic themes. His personal history, which spans almost 100 years of American history, highlights what we gain and what we lose as economic growth changes the world around us. His disagreement with Tony Stark about the proper way to govern a group of superheroes demonstrates a conundrum at the heart of public choice economics, which studies the behavior of individuals in the public, or governance, sphere. The important economic principles in Captain America's story are diverse and wide-ranging, including compound return on assets, economic growth and change, inflation, and the provision of public goods.

Did Rogers become rich under the ice?

Steve Rogers spent almost 70 years trapped beneath Arctic ice. Over that time, the economy grew tremendously, changing the world, and changing the fate of individual investors. Few investors can experience 70 years of growth without immediately facing retirement, but Steve Rogers did. His peculiar situation also isolates the growth of a one-time deposit over time from the more typical situation in which a retirement fund grows both from new deposits and from returns on the extant investment.

People tend to underestimate the power of compound returns, but Steve Rogers's situation provides a useful corrective. He might have become wealthy, depending on how much money he had invested and where it had been invested. In *The First Avenger*, Rogers's first continuing task in the Army is to promote the sale of Series E Savings Bonds – alternatively referred to as Defense or War Bonds – which were originally marketed to fund World War II and were sold from 1941 to 1980. We can imagine Rogers purchased some of the very War Bonds he was selling, and their return would have been significant. For every $1000 he invested in these Series E War Bonds, there would be $4,099 in his account when he came out of the ice in 2011. This assumes the minimum guaranteed interest rate on the bonds of 4 percent, and the return would have been even higher, but for the fact that War Bonds only paid interest for 40 years (Rosen, 2001). Without adding a penny to his investment during his 68 years under the ice, he would have found his savings had increased by more than four times.

Though War Bonds would be the obvious investment choice for the ever-patriotic Captain America, we can imagine his more business savvy associate, Howard Stark,[2] guiding Rogers toward a more lucrative investment. If Rogers had been fortunate enough to invest in common stocks in 1943, the growth of his personal assets would have been astounding. The average return would have taken every $1,000 and made it into about $100,000, assuming Rogers's investment matched the average growth rate of the stock market of approximately 7 percent and his dividends were reinvested (DQYDJ, 2017). The enormous difference in these two outcomes is partly due to the higher return earned in the stock market. However, the role of time is critical, as earnings grow and multiply. The widely quoted "Rule of 70" (Investopedia, 2017) shows that an investment growing at 7 percent doubles in 10 years. The doubling of $1000 to $2000 looks unimpressive – and yet if the process can continue for 70 years, that original $1000 becomes $128,000. With Rogers spending about 68 years under the ice, his fortune would have hit $99,563. If Rogers's stocks had been cashed out in 1983 – the same year the War Bonds would have stopped paying interest – his investment would have only been worth about $12,000. Certainly, this is a nice sum compared to the $4,099 from the bonds, but unimpressive next to $100,000.

Other investment possibilities include Rogers finding his way to a mutual fund, as the first of these was created in 1924 (McWhinney, 2017) – but their popularity was not nearly as great in the 1940s as they were when Rogers emerged from the ice decades later. Perhaps it is more likely that Rogers was too busy with his Army job, or simply was not so concerned about his retirement, and so neglected to invest at all. If Rogers had simply kept his money in a typical savings account, bearing an interest rate of 2 percent, his return would have been significantly less. And worse, if he simply hid his $1000 in a safe deposit box, he would have found merely that same $1000 waiting for him in 2011.

Thus far, our calculations have only considered the face value of his investment. These are the sorts of returns achievable if one could go to bed and wake up the next morning with 70 years' worth of compound interest accruing overnight. But a second economic force – inflation – pushes the value of Rogers's investment in the other direction. A textbook might define inflation as the rising price levels in an economy over time, but the equivalent of rising prices is a decline in the value of money. The same $1000 from 1943 would be worth approximately $78 in 2011, after adjusting for inflation (U.S. Department of Labor, 2017a).[3] Economists adjust for inflation to provide a more accurate description of the goods a certain dollar amount can purchase in different years. Just as compounding causes large changes over long periods of time, inflation also has enormous effects on the value of money over many decades.

No matter where Rogers put his money, his wealth upon emerging from the ice would be largely determined by these two forces: interest and inflation. Unfortunately for Rogers, a dollar in 2011 was only worth about 8 percent of what it was in 1943. With all these possible variables, we cannot conclude that Steve Rogers was wealthy in 2011, but we can provide a useful demonstration of the power of compounding. Table 5.1 summarizes the discussion and illustrates how slight differences in interest rates would have made an enormous difference in Rogers's wealth after 68 years in the ice.

To put these numbers into context: Rogers could have purchased a new car in 1943 with his $1,000 (1940s Collector Cars Including Prices, 2017). The same $1,000 would not come close to buying a car in 2011, not a new car anyway. The average annual inflation from 1943 to 2011 was just under 4 percent. Although car prices are influenced by changes in technology – a new car in 2011 is quite different from a new car in 1943 – Rogers probably could have found a car for about $14,000 in 2011, about how much he would have if his investment grew at the same rate as inflation.

Inflation and the illusion of price increases

Many people have heard grandparents say something like, "When I was your age it only cost 25 cents to get into the movies." Today's admission price seems

TABLE 5.1 Value of Rogers's 1943 investment of $1000

Rate of return	*2011* value*	*Inflation-adjusted 2011 value*	*Nature of investment*
0%	$1,000	$78	Burying money in the ground
2%	$3,844	$298	Typical savings account at a commercial bank
4%	$14,397	$1,116	U.S. Treasury Securities (assuming the bond continues to pay interest for the entire 68 years)
7%	$100,000	$7,800	Generalized investment in stocks

* 2011 is the year Captain America came out of the ice.

outrageous by comparison, and seems to represent a high real expenditure of resources. For instance, in 1943, the average movie admission price was $0.29 (Box Office Mojo, 2017). By 2011, it had grown to $7.93. This seemingly large increase is brought down to size when inflation is considered. In real terms, a 29-cent movie admission from 1943 would be $8.84 today (Box Office Mojo, 2017). A minimum wage worker in 1941 would have to work 0.97 hours to earn a movie admission, while in 2011, the $7.25 hourly minimum wage would permit the purchase of a movie ticket after 1.09 hours of work (U.S. Department of Labor, 2017b).

Quality adjustment makes the contrast even more striking. The 1941 movie would have been in black and white or relatively grainy color with a single low-fidelity sound channel. The 2011 movie would have been in full color, much more finely resolved, with enveloping sound effects in the theater. Beyond that, a high-quality cinematic experience could be enjoyed in the home for 17 minutes of minimum wage work ($2 at $7.25 per hour) plus the complementary home theater equipment. Motion pictures were a theater-only experience in 1941.

It is possible that Steve Rogers became a wealthy man during that time in the ice. Perhaps even more interesting than the changes in Captain America's personal wealth, however, were the changes in technology and material wealth for the U.S. as a whole during those 68 years. Rogers woke up to a country that was radically more productive than the one he left. Yet the story is not simply one of unmixed gain and improvement. Rogers experienced profound loss by being buried in the ice for all that time, and the American economy contained many stories of failure alongside all the progress. Also, it is not clear that either Rogers or his fellow Americans were dramatically happier than in 1943. Rogers seems ambivalent at times at his new situation, despite the new and impressive resources at his disposal. These observations provide an opportunity to examine the relationship between growth and loss, and between wealth and happiness.

A dynamic economy: wins and losses

In the previous section, we saw that Rogers might have had some investment success during his time under the ice. However, it is also possible that Rogers invested in a company that went bankrupt in the years between 1943 and 2011, and Rogers could have woken up penniless. In fact, in a dynamic economy, this is a very real possibility. The Fortune 500 did not exist in 1943, but even since the Fortune 500 list began in 1955, there has been significant attrition. Of the 500 companies present when the listing began, only 60 exist today.

The story of Captain America illustrates the two sides of dynamic growth: impressive gains and inevitable losses. Rogers's journey through the ice and into the future gives us the opportunity to compare stark differences in a growing and fluid economy. In this section, we examine the connections between growth and change. Furthermore, we explore the tenuous connections between growth and happiness, examining why individuals and nations might pursue material wealth despite evidence from a variety of fields that wealth cannot buy happiness.

The dynamism of the U.S. economy is evident in the turnover of corporations. At the opening of *The First Avenger*, we see a scene of the Stark Expo in 1943, which demonstrates both the promise and the uncertainty of technological change. The fictitious Stark Expo was modeled after the regular World's Fairs ubiquitous in the 19th and early 20th centuries, which first introduced the world to things like the telephone and the X-ray machine. At the Expo, Howard Stark demonstrates a flying car – a favorite fantasy of the time, lamentably unfulfilled today. At the same time, that exposition vastly underestimates the importance of information technology. Rogers is uniquely positioned to see the long-term effects of these changes, as someone thrust 68 years into the future.

U.S. economic history contains a multitude of examples of once prominent companies that no longer exist. Rogers may have been familiar with Woolworth's (general goods), TWA (airline), Radio Shack (electronics), or a number of other once-famous American companies that failed in the decades before he came out of the ice. These companies had been an integral part of Americans' daily lives, and it is plausible that Steve Rogers would count their disappearance as a real loss. We can imagine how jarring it would be today for someone to wake up and find that Google, Starbucks, or Walmart had disappeared, and how much more disconcerting it could be to discover that cars had entirely disappeared from our landscape.

Certainly, the disappearance of once-familiar companies has taken a toll on individual consumers and households. Economist Joseph Schumpeter coined the term "creative destruction" (Schumpeter, 1943) to describe the phenomenon of messy and sometimes destructive growth. Schumpeter famously called creative destruction "the essential fact of capitalism." In a growing and dynamic economy, individuals and firms may find themselves worse off in the short term, even as the society seems to be constantly progressing as a whole. Although Captain America could have become rich by investing in the overall U.S. economy, unlucky investments in particular businesses would have become worthless. The phenomenon of creative destruction continues to be the inevitable flip side of innovation to this day.

Creative destruction can be difficult to appreciate in its full depth, but its basics are easy to understand in a story that spans decades. When Rogers went into the ice in 1943, television was not yet a common, in-home entertainment option. By 2011, when Rogers came out of the ice, more than half of U.S. households possessed three or more televisions (The Nielsen Company, 2010)! The television industry grew enormously while Captain America slept. Americans love television and it is at least plausible to say that in-home entertainment, and therefore American lives, have improved as well by the growth of this industry.

The development of the television industry, however, was not without its destructive side effects, at least for some participants in the U.S. economy. In providing a new form of entertainment and a new pathway for information dissemination, the television made old forms in these industries less valuable.

Television threatened both the market for radio programming and for general-purpose magazines. Rogers went under the ice in a time saturated with these forms of entertainment, but woke up to a world in which these industries had greatly diminished and were under new assault from the Internet.

Rogers experienced cultural change in addition to technological and economic change. Rogers started his hibernation when society intimately knew and loved baseball. He knew baseball so well that he detected a flaw in a simulated play-by-play radio track that had been intended to make him think he was still living in the 1940s after his 2011 rescue. He woke up in a time when baseball had become just one of many competing attractions for consumers' attention and money, with few interested in baseball to the degree that was common in the 1940s.

When a new technology arrives, it inevitably displaces some older technology. The replacement of horse-drawn carriages by cars surely increased our productivity, and yet the invention of automobiles was not an unqualified good for everyone. Those who had spent their lives developing the skills necessary to support the horse-drawn carriage industry soon found their labor significantly less valuable in the economy.

Change unavoidably means some things are lost while other things are gained. Captain America was talking about cultural changes when he noted painfully to Nick Fury, "They didn't say what we lost," but his sentiment captures a feeling shared by many when economists talk about the enormous material gains due to economic growth in the 20th century.[4] On the whole, economists tend to think economic growth is worthwhile, even when it sometimes leaves particular individuals or industries worse off. In principle, a growing economy creates gains greater in magnitude than any losses incurred, and so material progress could be distributed in such a way that even those who lose the most are eventually made better off by continued growth.

In this vein, while Rogers recognizes all that has been lost while he was under the ice, he acknowledges the increasing material prosperity in the world around him. Material well-being increased markedly, driven by technological innovation that brought us personal computers, the Internet, mobile phones, better medicine, and better transportation. In *The Winter Soldier,* Rogers explains, "The food is a lot better, we used to boil everything. No polio is good. [The] Internet, so helpful" (Russo & Russo, 2014). These improvements in the quality of life for the average American are no small thing. We might be inclined to think that waking up to a world so rich in technology and comfort-enhancing goods would leave Rogers in a constant state of amazement and gratitude. Surely, it is hard for most of us to imagine voluntarily returning to a world without the convenience of computing.

Once again, however, the obvious material improvements tell only a part of the story. Here, another insight from a different branch of economic research – behavioral economics – helps us to make sense of Rogers's situation. First, we observe that doubling the productivity of the economy does not double our happiness, and 70 years of economic growth and technological innovation does not leave Steve Rogers in a hedonistic paradise. In *The Winter Soldier,* Rogers finds that the America he loved exists no longer, and he has outlived most of his friends and loved ones. But more than nostalgia prevents Rogers from attaining true satisfaction. Behavioral economics – which is a sub-field of economics that incorporates insights from psychology into the study of economic choice – gives us the tools to explain why Rogers is not overwhelmed by happiness, even if he truly enjoys modern conveniences.

Economics students are exposed to simple utility models in which individuals always prefer to consume more material goods, and so ought to be happier with more material wealth. Steve Rogers's case provides a useful illustration of the narrowness of this model. While the central thesis of the utility model may hold, we know that expectations and social norms, as well as intuitions about what is right and wrong, all play a role alongside the satisfaction of our material desires in determining how we perceive the world.

While Rogers in 2011 could consume bundles of goods unthinkable in 1943, he is something of a tragic figure, not fully able to resolve his conception of the good with the morally ambiguous choices that superheroes must face during the early 21st century. Captain America began his fight in a time when he felt comfortable with the clear distinction between the good side and the bad. He found it simple to determine the right course of action: to do everything in his power to fight the Nazis and Hydra. His discomfort with Nick Fury's ruthlessness and willingness to play with superhuman technology to achieve his ends made Captain America uneasy, and stripped him of the moral certainty he enjoyed in his previous life. Through this disconnection, we see clearly that material wealth is merely one input into Rogers's (and perhaps our own) happiness, and perhaps not even a dominant one.

Building on the work of psychologists, economists have documented how increases in wealth over the course of a lifetime seem to do little to improve an individual's self-reported levels of happiness (Easterlin, 2003). Curiously, economists studying happiness identify two areas where non-pecuniary life changes have a lasting effect on happiness, both of which might apply to Steve Rogers. The first is health. A deterioration in health reduces the marginal utility of consumption across the board, meaning everything, material or non-material, yields less pleasure (Finkelstein, Luttmer, & Notowidigdo, 2012). Rogers's super-serum gave him the reverse: it turned him from a sickly individual to a paragon of human health.

The other area is relationships. *The First Avenger* illustrates the heartache Rogers experiences in locating his girlfriend from 1943, Peggy Carter. Carter was on the radio with Rogers just before the apparently fatal crash, distracting him with the promise of a future dance in what seemed his final moments of life. Carter went on to marry a soldier saved by Captain America and was elderly when Rogers was revived. Although we are speculating about the degree of unhappiness of a fictional character, we do know that the dissolution of a marriage has a large and variable negative effect on happiness (Amato, 2000). Rogers's unhappiness may have been similar.

Behavioral economics places a high degree of emphasis on the context in which we find ourselves, in how we make decisions, and how we respond to opportunities (Kahneman & Tversky, 1979). The actual pleasure we receive from consumption depends partly on our perceived range of consumption possibilities. Although Rogers was in a continual state of amazement at the society where he woke up from his hibernation, in time he underwent hedonic adaptation – a return to a baseline level of happiness despite significant positive or negative life changes.

One way to explain the seemingly counterintuitive phenomenon is through the concepts of habituation and rivalry (Layard, 2003). Habituation describes that experience of becoming accustomed to a certain good or situation in such a way that turns it from a source of pleasure to a baseline expectation. Air conditioning would have been experienced as a luxury when it was first invented, but for many now it is not so much a source of pleasure as a requisite part our existence. Rivalry, on the other hand, describes the phenomenon that much of our sense of satisfaction comes from our comparison of the things we can consume with the things those around us consume. For instance, Rogers might have been perfectly happy with boiled food when that was what everyone he knew ate, but might have found little enjoyment in it if he saw everyone around him dining on more artfully prepared fare. The importance of consumption's context is not a new point either. Adam Smith noted it in the *Theory of Moral Sentiments*, where he writes that "wealth and greatness are mere trinkets of frivolous utility" (Smith, 1759). Smith recommends against the single-minded pursuit of greater material wealth, suggesting that even if we attain it, we will find that it does not bring with it the expected happiness. On the other hand, Smith also remarks on the wonders of material advancement, commenting in Book 1 of *The Wealth of Nations* (Smith, 1776) that the lowliest worker in his day benefitted from material resources unthinkable even for the rulers of entire nations centuries before. The same continues to be true today when we think of the vast numbers of people and products from around the globe that go into making a simple mobile phone that even the poorest among us are often able to afford.

In summary, despite the consumption opportunities and material means at his disposal in 2011, Steve Rogers's fundamental choices have not changed much. His true happiness is much more dependent on resolving the moral problems he faces – and the problem of confronting evil in a vulnerable world is still very much present. As Captain America's storyline progresses in the movies, the problem of confronting evil becomes increasingly complex, and becomes especially difficult as it becomes apparent that the fight has begun to impose drastic costs on innocent populations around the world. In 1943, Captain America dealt with conventional villains on a battlefield. In 2011 and beyond, both his human and superhuman foes have brought the battle to the civilian landscape, forcing Captain America to confront the tough reality that his actions to protect humanity necessarily involve sacrifices of a dangerous kind. Captain America is not willing to give up the fight altogether and so finds himself grappling with the morality of continuing the fight in spite of these costs, providing an opportunity to look at the economic concepts of public goods and externalities.

Who can provide global defense?

Shortly after rescuing Steve Rogers from his icy sleep in *The Avengers* (Weeden, 2012), Nick Fury recruits Rogers to join the team of superheroes who become the Avengers. In the Marvel Cinematic Universe, the Avengers first operate on behalf of Fury's organization S.H.I.E.L.D., but in *Avengers: Age of Ultron* (Weeden, 2015) they eventually become an essentially private organization, funded by Tony Stark and led by Steve Rogers. Embracing their public personas as superheroes, they find themselves in combat with all manner of terrestrial and extraterrestrial threats to humanity across the globe. While their activities are celebrated by many, they are not without critics, as their fighting inevitably imposes costs on innocent bystanders. These costs come in the form of the destruction of property and even loss of civilian lives, as the Avengers fight across the globe against their various foes. The tension between their heroic deeds and their responsibility for the costs of their actions builds throughout the movie series, and comes to a head in *Captain America: Civil War*. As the world tries to determine how to govern a group of super-powered individuals, economic insights about externalities and governmental provision of services help to explain why the issue is so complicated.

In *Captain America: Civil War*, the Avengers must decide how to react to the increasing costs their activities are imposing on the global population. In the movie, a battle between the Avengers and a group of mercenaries ends in the death of dozens of civilians, and prompts the United Nations to draft the Sokovia Accords.[5] The Accords would regulate the activities of super-powered individuals, effectively placing the Avengers under the governance of the U.N. and criminalizing any unapproved superhero activity. While some of the Avengers, led by Stark, think that the regulation is necessary, others, led by Rogers, resist the idea that their activity should be regulated by bureaucrats.

In economic terms, the Avengers are essentially a private organization providing a public good for the world. Economists define public goods as goods that are non-excludable and non-rivalrous, meaning that once a public good has been provided, individuals cannot be prevented from enjoying its benefits, and the use by one individual does not reduce the availability of the good for others. National defense is a classic example, in that it would be nearly impossible to simultaneously protect some citizens from an external threat while leaving their neighbors vulnerable. Captain America and the Avengers are in the business of global defense by fighting evil that appears in diverse forms, including Hydra and rogue elements of S.H.I.E.L.D.[6] – and, beyond that, extraterrestrial and interdimensional threats. If all their missions succeeded, this would be a perfect example of the private provision of a public good (Bergstrom, Blume, & Varian, 1986).

Public goods present an interesting challenge to market economies. In a market, we generally see sellers receive benefits commensurate with the service they provide and buyers receiving benefits corresponding to the amount they pay. This logic is complicated by the presence of what economists call externalities, which are consequences of economic activity that accrue to unrelated third parties. These externalities can be positive or negative, and will often lead to the under- or over-provision of certain goods. Positive externalities are associated with under-provision because the benefits of the good or service are experienced by more than just those who pay for the good. The people who benefit from the good without paying for it are called free-riders. We can imagine how defeating an enemy out to destroy the earth and all its inhabitants will benefit all of humanity. In theory, every person on the earth should be willing to pay some amount to prevent their own demise. Coordinating the activity of everyone, however, is impossibly costly, and so even though humanity might be theoretically willing to pay a large collective sum to any champion who can defeat the threat, we have no practical hope of doing so. Anyone who can fight against the threat is therefore underpaid, relative to the maximum amount all those who benefit from the heroic activity would otherwise pay.

Thus, evil-fighting will ordinarily be under-produced because of the inability of any one actor – individual or state – to appropriate the benefits. Things change when Captain America and the Avengers enter the picture. Captain America has such a strong personal conviction to fight evil that he is willing to do it, even in the presence of free-riding. Even though he bears much of the cost of his activities and only a small proportion of its benefits, he soldiers on.

There is, however, a similar calculation to be made on the part of negative externalities. The private provision of a public good is innocuous when it is, as an example, a freely provided public park concert by an acapella trio. It is difficult to imagine much of a downside to such a performance. The Avengers' mission is different. The difference lies in lethal negative externalities. These costs are especially prominent in *Captain America: Civil War* when innocent Wakandan aid workers lose their lives.[7]

In the case of positive externalities, we worry about under-provision. Conversely, negative externalities cause economists to worry about over-provision of a good. In this case, we might think that because the Avengers do not bear all the costs of their fighting, they will use excessive force in pursuing their eradication of evil. This incident prompts a perceived need for governmental supervision, and given the international nature of the threat, the United Nations is the obvious governing agency. As a result, the U.N. proposes the Sokovia Accords, setting up a governance structure for individuals with superpowers.

In economic terms, the Sokovia Accords are one attempt to "internalize the externality" by aligning the social costs of superhero activity with the private costs. The Avengers already bear some of the cost of their activities, as their fighting takes a physical and emotional toll on each member. However, they do not bear the full cost of the deaths of the innocent bystanders or the destruction of property that occurs in battles with extraterrestrial threats. The Sokovia Accords could address this issue in a couple of different ways. First, with the requirement that all superheroes identify themselves and wear tracking bracelets at all times, the Avengers can presumably be held financially and even criminally responsible for unauthorized activity that causes harm to third parties. Second, requiring that the Avengers have approval for each mission causes the costs and benefits of their activity to be shared with the U.N. The members of the U.N. council, as representatives of the global population, would take up some share of the responsibility for the successes and failures of the Avengers' missions. Inasmuch as the U.N. represents the innocent bystanders, the international body would consider the potential harm to third parties when deciding whether the Avengers could be called into action.

Members of the Avengers evaluate this logic in different ways. Stark and his followers focus primarily on the problem of the negative externalities of their activity. Stark feels tremendous guilt over the loss of innocent lives resulting from fights between the Avengers and their many foes. As a result, he is eager to support the Sokovia Accords, in the hope that the threat of punishment will effectively constrain the Avengers and cause them to pay greater attention to the harmful side effects of their heroic activity. On the other hand, Rogers focuses on the potential problems with relying on bureaucrats in the U.N. as an effective mechanism for internalizing the externalities.[8] In doing so, Rogers recognizes that the bureaucrats have their own set of interests and are perhaps no more likely than the Avengers to properly balance the social costs and social benefits of superhero activity.

Rogers voices his concern that the United Nations' control will limit the ability of the Avengers to do good when the world needs it. He asks, "What if they want to send us somewhere we don't want to go? What if they won't send us somewhere we're needed?" (Russo & Russo, 2016). Placing the authority in another group's hands does not change the fact that global defense is a public good, and the U.N. likewise will neither receive all the benefit nor bear all the cost for their decisions. He worries that the incentives faced by a bureaucrat might diverge from the interests of the Avengers, and even the world. As he says, the U.N. is "run by people with agendas," which may include goals other than global defense. A bureaucrat supervising the Avengers would incur harsh penalties for future civilian casualties but might not be held to account for the damage of a seemingly unstoppable evil force. The imbalance of incentives would cause a bureaucrat to be overcautious. Whereas the Avengers might overprovide their services because they do not bear all the costs of their action, the bureaucrats might bear costs disproportionately and so underprovide protective services. Rogers had the intuition he was uniquely qualified to make these tradeoffs in fighting evil, and felt that cautious bureaucrats would hamstring the Avengers' effectiveness. Weighing the positive and negative externalities of their actions, Captain America judges that the positive outweighs the negative. In the end, the debate between Stark and Rogers illustrates the complexity of internalizing externalities, and the breadth of potential issues that arise when attempting to coordinate broad social goals – like global defense – with the private interests of any individual or smaller organization.

Conclusion

The story of Captain America is rich with economic insight. Facing the opportunity to consume in an economy vastly wealthier than the one he left decades ago, Steve Rogers experiences material wealth and profound emotional loss. His story provides ready illustrations about the nature of economic growth, economic dynamism and inflation. With his fellow superheroes, he shows how difficult the governance of extraordinary abilities can be. Even though Captain America and his cinematic universe are a fantasy, their example provides useful and novel ways of confronting similar issues that face our society today.

Notes

1 In the comic book version of the story, the legislation is the Superhero Registration Act, proposed by the U.S. government.
2 Howard Stark is the scientist and business mogul who created the Super Serum that turned Steve Rogers into Captain America. He is also the father of Tony Stark, also known as Iron Man.
3 Adjustments for inflation are computed using the U.S. Department of Labor's Consumer Price Index (CPI). This is the standard tool for making such calculations.
4 In fact, Captain America was accusing Nick Fury, a spy and leader of the organization that pulled Rogers out of the ice and helped to put The Avengers together, of compromising on values that Captain America holds dear: respect for liberty and privacy among these. Fury admits to some mistakes but claims the cause is worth the sacrifice.
5 In the *Civil War* comics, the story begins with a disastrous accident caused by a minor group of superheroes and results in regulation from the U.S. government, rather than the U.N. However, the debate follows similar lines and raises many of the same concerns.
6 These rogue elements of S.H.I.E.L.D. – the law enforcement and intelligence agency run by Nick Fury – feature prominently in *Captain America: The Winter Soldier* where they essentially dismantle the organization from within and attempt to use its potent technology to commit mass genocide.
7 Again, the movie differs from the comic somewhat. In the comic, the victims are school children.
8 In the Civil War comic, Captain America leads a violent resistance against the Superhero Registration Act. He eventually realizes how much harm the fight between superheroes causes to their surroundings and relents, allowing himself to be arrested.

References

1940s Collector Cars Including Prices. (2017). Retrieved from The People History: www.thepeoplehistory.com/40scars.html.

Amato, P. (2000). The Consequences of Divorce for Adults and Children. *Journal of Marriage and Family*, 62, 1269–1287.

Bergstrom, T., Blume, L., & Varian, H. (1986). On the Private Provision of Public Goods. *Journal of Public Economics*, 25–49. doi:10.1016/0047-2727(86)90024-1

Box Office Mojo. (2017). Adjusting for Ticket Price Inflation. Retrieved from Box Office Mojo: www.boxofficemojo.com/about/adjuster.htm.

DQYDJ. (2017, July 12). S&P 500 Return Calculator. Retrieved from DQYDJ: https://dqydj.com/sp-500-return-calculator/.

Easterlin, R. A. (2003). Explaining Happiness. *Proc Natl Acad Sci U S A*, 11176–11183). doi:10.1073/pnas.1633144100.

Finkelstein, A., Luttmer, E. F., & Notowidigdo, M. J. 2012. What Good Is Wealth Without Health? The Effect of Health on the Marginal Utility of Consumption. *Journal of the European Economic Association, 11*(1), 221–258.

Investopedia. (2017). Investopedia Terms. Retrieved from Investopedia: www.investopedia.com/terms/r/rule-of-70.asp

Johnston, J. (Director). (2011). *Captain America: The First Avenger* [Motion Picture].

Kahneman, D., & Tversky, A. (1979). Prospect Theory: An Analysis of Decision Under Risk. *Econometrica*, 47(2), 263–291.

Layard, R. (2003). Has Social Science a Clue?: Income and Happiness: Rethinking Economic Policy. Lionel Robbins memorial lecture series. London.

McWhinney, J. E. (2017, July 17). A Brief History of The Mutual Fund. Retrieved from Investopedia: www.investopedia.com/articles/mutualfund/05/mfhistory.asp.

Rosen, D. (2001, January 22). Old War Bonds Are Worth Big Bucks. Retrieved from Bank Rate Monitor: www.bankrate.com/banking/savings/old-war-bonds-are-worth-big-bucks/.

Russo, J., & Russo, A. (Directors). (2014). *Captain America: The Winter Soldier* [Motion Picture].

Russo, J., & Russo, A. (Directors). (2016). *Captain America: Civil War* [Motion Picture].

Schumpeter, J. A. (1943). *Capitalism, Socialism, and Democracy*. Taylor & Francis e-Library.

Smith, A. (1759). *The Theory of Moral Sentiments*. London: A. Millar.

Smith, A. (1776). *An Inquiry into the Nature and Causes of the Wealth of Nations*. London: Methuen & Co., Ltd. 1904 edition.

The Nielsen Company. (2010, April 28). U.S. Homes Add Even More T.V. Sets in 2010. Retrieved from www.nielsen.com/us/en/insights/news/2010/u-s-homes-add-even-more-tv-sets-in-2010.html.

U.S. Department of Labor. (2017a). *CPI Inflation Calculator*. Retrieved from Bureau of Labor Statistics: www.bls.gov/data/inflation_calculator.htm.

U.S. Department of Labor. (2017b). History of Federal Minimum Wage Rates Under the Fair Labor Standards Act, 1938–2009. Retrieved from Wage and Hour Division: www.dol.gov/whd/minwage/chart.htm.

U.S. Department of the Treasury, Bureau of the Fiscal Service. (2017, July 17). *Research Center*. Retrieved from TreasuryDirect: www.treasurydirect.gov/indiv/research/indepth/other/res_othersecurities.htm.

Weeden, J. (Director). (2012). *The Avengers* [Motion Picture].

Weeden, J. (Director). (2015). *Avengers: Age of Ultron* [Motion Picture].

6

THE POLITICAL ECONOMY OF BLACK PANTHER'S WAKANDA

J. Robert Subrick

When the Black Panther attacked Bucky Barnes, the Winter Soldier, in *Captain America: Civil War*, he introduced himself to a much wider audience both within and outside the Marvel Cinematic Universe. Numerous moviegoers witnessed the impressive skills of the Black Panther and the film ended with hints of the wonder and beauty of his country, Wakanda. Even though the Black Panther first appeared in 1966 in *Fantastic Four* #52 (Lee and Kirby, 1966a), he is not as well known outside of comics fandom compared to many of the other Avengers such as Captain America, the Incredible Hulk, Iron Man, or Thor. This changed with the premier of the Black Panther feature length film in 2018. The movie will no doubt increase popular awareness of both the character and his country's history, as well as their role in the Marvel universe.

Despite outward appearances of tranquility, Wakanda is roiling. This chapter explores the tensions that exist within Wakandan society and offers an economic interpretation of what propagates them. After introducing Black Panther, I examine the role of geography in Wakanda's political and economic development. Geography affects the extent of economic integration between Wakanda and the rest of the world. Next I explain why natural resources often undermine economic and political development and how the Black Panther's decisions avoided this natural resource curse. I will briefly compare Wakanda's avoidance of the curse with Botswana's economic history, a country with comparable geography, similarly graced with natural resources and governed by a traditional leader. Then I turn to the interesting question of why Wakanda has invested so heavily in technological development as opposed to the arts or philosophy. Finally, I address some recent developments in Wakanda suggesting its transition to a democracy.

Who is the Black Panther?

An introduction to the Black Panther must begin with the motivations of the character's creators. Stan Lee and Jack Kirby conceived the first significant African superhero in comics during the civil rights movement in the United States, and the evolution of African nations moving out of the shadow of colonialism. Kirby's son Neal explained that the creation of Black Panther was probably an exercise in protest. He believes his father created Black Panther

> because it was the right thing to do at the time. It broke all the stereotypes – a black super hero with a scientific brain … I think he saw this as his personal way of making a statement and "joining" the civil rights movement.
>
> *(Beard, 2016)*

Lee and Kirby relied upon prevalent stereotypes to launch their new hero. The overtly racial tones adopted by the Fantastic Four to describe the mysterious Wakandans include, as noted below, the incredulity that a black person could be technologically advanced, intelligent, and a competent leader (Lee and Kirby, 1966a). Not only was this used to set up false expectations for the readers, but these sentiments were also drawn from the headlines. By running counter to the persistent view that blacks could not be the equal of whites, "two middle-aged Jewish men working in 1966 New York City" who might have been driven by "a mix of white guilt, black empowerment fantasy and market opportunism" began, in a small way, to break the mold (Narcisse, 2016).

In this spirit, Lee and Kirby came up with The Black Panther, the leader of the small, insulated, landlocked African country of Wakanda. Thousands of years ago, a meteor containing a rare and virtually indestructible metal, called vibranium, crashed into Wakanda. An unfortunate side effect of vibranium is its radioactivity which mutates humans, sometimes permanently. The vibranium affected the initial discoverers, mutating them into "demon spirits." Bashenga, the mightiest warrior at the time, prayed to the Panther God to give him the strength to defeat these demons. He vanquished them and as a result became the first "Black Panther." Under his leadership, the various tribes in the area were united to form the nation of Wakanda (Kirby, 1978).

Bashenga recognized the threat and promise of vibranium and established the precedent of hiding the metal from the outside world. Through the generations, the subsequent Black Panthers, who inherited the title, have protected the citizens of Wakanda from the harmful effects of vibranium, and defended the precious resource from the exploitation of outsiders. Vibranium absorbs sound waves and kinetic energy. If a piece of vibranium that had stored up energy were smashed, it would release an explosive force of great magnitude. It is also nearly indestructible making it a perfect material for building weapons. As a result, a small amount of vibranium in the wrong hands might lead to a war (Hannigan and Perlin, 1980).

Unfortunately, obtaining vibranium is fraught with risks. Vibranium is highly radioactive and has altered some of the Wakandan plant life, creating unusual flora like the Heart-Shaped Herb, the secret to the Black Panther's superhuman powers. Consuming this herb enhances agility, endurance, speed, senses, and strength. It confers the ability to "see in total darkness, track any scent, and hear an enemy's heartbeat" (Heart-Shaped Herb, n.d.). In other words, it gives Black Panther abilities comparable to a super-soldier like Captain America. This mystique allows him to govern relatively unchallenged. Who would challenge him unless they too possessed super-human abilities? Even an exceptional human is no match for the Black Panther.

The Black Panther introduced in the 1960s, and typically the version of the character who appears in the comics and movies, is named T'Challa. During his customary rite of passage, as a young man, he wandered the land (Claremont and Byrne, 1980). After roaming the African landscape, T'Challa went to the United States and England to study, as did many of the early post-colonial African leaders. He announced his presence to the world when he invited the Fantastic Four to Wakanda. His displays of Wakandan technology impressed Reed Richards, aka Mr. Fantastic, who accepted an invitation to visit the African nation. Little did they know T'Challa had an ulterior motive. When the group arrived in Wakanda, the Black Panther attacked them, and nearly succeeded in capturing them. In the end, the Fantastic Four turned the tables on him. He explained that his motive was to test himself against the superhero team. If he could fight them successfully, he would be ready to face his nemesis: Klaw (Lee and Kirby, 1966b). Since then, the Black Panther has periodically joined the Avengers, worked with Daredevil, fought the Ku Klux Klan, and protected his country from Doctor Doom's attempt to expropriate its rare metal. Until recently, T'Challa was the wealthiest person in the world. His estimated worth was about $90 trillion, more than world GDP in 2014.[1] His downfall occurred as Wakanda experienced a civil war where two insurgent groups challenged the legitimacy of the Black Panther's rule. The latest insurrection has put Wakanda on the road to constitutional democracy after centuries of monarchy.

The Wakandan puzzle

The story of the Black Panther and the fictional land of Wakanda presents a puzzle to economists familiar with patterns of development as they've played out in the real world. For much of its history, the location of Wakanda was shrouded in mystery and the country had very little contact with the outside world. Its legendary existence encouraged numerous villains to attempt to discover its specific whereabouts in order to exploit its resources. The threat of expropriation led the country to evolve independently from the rest of the world, untouched by historical events. Unlike almost all of Africa, Wakanda has no colonial history nor did the slave trade adversely affect it. Its history offers a hypothetical instance of an African nation developing organically with minimal interference from the rest of the world.

One of the most intriguing aspects of Wakanda is its technological advancement. There has been no Western influence on its scientific progress, yet Wakanda has developed technologies well beyond the rest of the world's capabilities. For example, when Black Panther is introduced, the reader sees the Fantastic Four zooming around New York in a space age, flying car. Ben Grimm, aka the Thing, is awed by the technology but incredulous that its source is "some refugee from a Tarzan movie" (Lee and Kirby, 1966a). Not only is Mr. Fantastic similarly astonished by the vehicle, he is also impressed by the communication devices utilized by the Wakandan emissary. Unbeknownst to Mr. Fantastic, Wakandan inventions are not limited to transportation and communiqués. Wakandan scientists discovered a cure for cancer and its citizenry has the longest life expectancy in the world (Maberry and Eaton, 2010). The extraordinary focus of the Black Panther on Wakandan science and security has allowed the secluded nation to attain unprecedented levels of technological know-how, and economic well-being. But as we will see, this comes at a cost.

This brings us to the first part of the Wakandan puzzle. In general, countries that are open to international trade tend to have high levels of income, productivity, and superior technology. The exchange of goods, services, and ideas promotes specialization that, in turn, increases productivity. In contrast, countries that have established trade barriers forego the benefits of specialization and remain relatively poor. Wakanda has followed the path of isolationism yet experienced some of the expected benefits associated with integration. How could the country attain such high levels of technological advancement without engaging and learning from the collective stock of scientific knowledge?

Wakanda's scientific achievements stem from the use of the revenue obtained from the sales of vibranium. Sales to the world provide the financial support for scientific research and development (Lee and Kirby, 1966b). In a sense, the money has been used wisely to develop advanced technologies. But this simply pushes the puzzle of Wakanda back another level of analysis. Most countries dependent upon the sale of natural resources for income fall under what economists call a natural resource curse. This curse appears when, as is often the case, nascent governments use revenues from natural resources for self-aggrandizement. In many post-colonial African countries, money from the sale of natural resources turned into Rolls Royces, additional homes in foreign countries, and immense personal savings accounts for members of the government. It did not finance education, health care, or infrastructure. The question of why Wakanda was able to avoid the natural resource curse, a plague for many real, post-colonial African governments, is answered through the Black Panther's leadership. He chose to the use the money for the betterment of the country.

This answer leaves us with yet another question. Using the vibranium revenues to help the citizenry makes sense in a democratic regime but Wakanda is not a democratic regime. In democracies, elected officials are more likely to use natural resources for the public's benefit than autocrats since elected officials depend on greater levels of public support to maintain their power. In a country where leaders are elected, using revenues for personal gain, if exposed, will almost always reduce the chances of winning the next poll. So why does the benevolent dictator not turn bad? Before proposing an answer to this question, let's examine some of the challenges for Wakanda, beginning with geography.

The geography of Wakanda – good fences make good neighbors

The exact location of Wakanda has varied throughout the assorted versions of the Black Panther story. In general, it is located in north-eastern Africa. In the movie, *Captain America: Civil War* (Russo and Russo, 2016), Wakanda was shown on a map at the northern end of Lake Turkhana, the world's fourth largest saltwater lake. Such a location would have Wakanda bordering Ethiopia, Sudan, Uganda, and Kenya, bringing with it a number of difficulties for Wakandan economic, political, and technological development. First, it faces significant barriers to trade since it has no direct access to the Indian Ocean. Second, even if trade costs were low, its neighbors hardly represent bastions of economic and political development. The likelihood of Wakandan goods reaching ports fully intact is small. Neighboring governments would probably extract some of the goods and services for themselves. Transparency International (2017), who measures corruption, ranked Ethiopia 108th, Kenya 145th, Uganda 151st and the Sudan 170th. The Heritage Foundation (Miller and Kim, 2017), which measures trade policy, ranked Uganda 93rd, Kenya 146th, Ethiopia 153rd, and the Sudan 181st in their 2017 report. Wakanda is a landlocked country with "bad" neighbors. Corruption and inward looking trade policies both generally contribute to relative economic underdevelopment and technological backwardness (Collier, 2007).

Similarly, landlocked countries tend to be poor. More directly, lack of access to the sea or navigable waterways raises the costs of economic integration, while navigable rivers reduce the costs of trading. Floating goods down rivers is less expensive compared to the costs of transport over land. As a result, a dearth of deep and wide waterways limits the extent of trade. As far back as the late 1700s, Adam Smith (1776/1994) recognized the problems facing sub-Saharan Africa's economic underdevelopment resulting from their lack of access to the sea. He wrote

> All the inland parts of Africa … seem in all ages of the world to have been in the same barbarous and uncivilized state in which we find them at present … here are in Africa none of those great inlets … to carry maritime commerce into the interior parts of that great continent: and the great rivers of Africa are at too great a distance from one another to give occasion to any considerable inland navigation.[2]

What was true in Smith's time remains true today. If a region has access to the sea, it is probably one of the richest parts of a country. The coastal regions of the US tend to have higher incomes than the landlocked regions. Boston has significantly more wealth than Morgantown, West Virginia for example. The few exceptions such as Chicago have access to waterways that allow it to overcome its distance from the ocean. In Europe, Switzerland is another obvious exception. It is a mountainous country with no direct access to the Mediterranean Sea or the Atlantic Ocean. The Swiss experience illustrates that being landlocked and rugged alone is not a guarantee of poverty. It also shows the importance of one's neighbors.

Good neighbors create substantial spill-over benefits. For one, they reduce transportation costs. Well-governed neighbors usually have a well-maintained infrastructure to move goods and services efficiently. They also tend to have relatively few problems with corruption. In contrast, poorly governed countries lack infrastructure and petty corruption acts as a plague on transactions. For example, in early 2000s, about 12% of the roads were paved in Ethiopia and Kenya, 23% in Kenya, and about 36% in the Sudan (International Road Federation, n.d.). Paved roads make for more effective transportation of goods, and without them, trade is more costly. Additionally, as goods move from the landlocked regions to the coastal areas, the likelihood of the good disappearing or the transporters paying "fees" to roadside "tax-collectors" increase (Collier, 2007). The goods sent to the ports may never reach their destination. They may be confiscated by rogue groups or by agents of the government. In any case, the presence of bad neighbors curtails the extent of likely economic integration into the global division of labor where the gains from trade extend well beyond national borders and present nearly boundless opportunities to increase productivity and prosperity.

Wakanda's neighbors do not represent the poster children for well-governed and non-corrupt political regimes. They have long histories of extensive poverty, widespread corruption, and poor governance. None of the neighboring countries have experienced prolonged periods of either economic progress or democratic political stability. Even if political stability existed, trade would be minimal because Wakanda's neighbors are also poor, each having incomes outside the top 150 countries in the world. According to the Central Intelligence Agency's (2017) *World Fact Book*, the GDP per capita in the Sudan is $4,500 (172nd in the world), Kenya $3,400 (187th), Uganda $2,100 (203rd), and Ethiopia $1,900 (208th). Poverty and corruption surround Wakanda. Bad neighbors indeed!

Vibranium: blessing or curse?

The geographic endowments of Wakanda suggest it too should be a poor country. Lack of access to the sea along with poor, corrupt neighbors greatly increases the cost of trade. On the other hand, it seems obvious that countries with large amounts of natural resources would attain high levels of income. Natural resources are practically "free" goods available to trade. Oil reserves, diamonds, and gold exist even though no human made them. They provide revenue to firms and governments so long as they remain cost-effective to extract, which, in theory, can be used for public investments in infrastructure, or improve public education or health care, but the history of natural resource rich countries indicates that natural resources alone do not guarantee prosperity. Frequently they become a curse.

Often when people consider the relationship between natural resources and prosperity, they think about the economic history of Australia, Canada, or the United States. Australia attained the highest level of income per person in 1870 with the discovery of massive gold deposits and it has remained a wealthy nation since. Both Canada and the United States exported large amounts of natural resources such as timber during the 18th century. This was also the time-period when both moved closer to the top of the world's income distribution. By the end of the 19th century it seemed as if economic prosperity depended in part on access to the world's natural resources. If you had them, you could trade for finished products and increase societal well-being. National wealth creation became possible as revenues from the sale of these resources were used to fund private and public investments. This, in turn, improved the prospects for economic growth. The money could be used to fund primary education and increase literacy rates. It could be used to subsidize health care costs. It could be allocated to infrastructure projects such as paved roads, highway systems, or port development. It could be utilized for police and defense purposes so as to discourage crime and better protect the property rights of the citizenry. It allowed governments to pay salaries that discouraged the acceptance of bribes. Potentially, natural resources provided the basis for economic development. Natural resources were like manna from heaven. If you lived in a natural resource rich area, the keys to prosperity were readily available (Stiglitz, 2005). If you didn't have resources, you might go to war to get them.[3]

Yet as Sachs and Warner (2001) show, the evidence does not support this rosy picture. Throughout sub-Saharan African and the Middle East, the natural resource curse has spread. Some government regimes used revenues generated through the sale of natural resources such as oil or diamonds to consolidate power. They devoted resources to police protection for themselves rather than for the citizenry. They spent money on multiple residences rather than public good provision. They had access to the finest health care in the world while the average person languished in underfunded hospitals that lacked competent staff and basic medical products. They used the money to buy off supporters and punish dissidents. In general, the political elite used the sale of the country's natural resources to enrich themselves and impoverish the rest of society (Mehlum, Moene, and Torvik, 2006).

In extreme cases, the revenue became the reason for confrontations. Blood diamonds in Liberia financed the government's brutal wars from 1989 to 2003. During apartheid in South Africa, revenue from gold sales provided financial support to the government, which allowed them to enforce the labor market discrimination that characterized the regime. The former dictator of Zaire (Democratic Republic of the Congo) Mobutu Sese Seko accumulated enormous wealth by selling off the country's resources. By the time he fled the country in 1997, the average Congolese citizen's income had fallen by approximately 77% from its peak to an annual income of approximately $139.[4] He sold the minerals extracted through harsh labor conditions and kept the money for himself and his close supporters. During the Arab Spring, the Saudi government used oil revenues to pay its citizens to not protest. The king spent $10.7 billion on programs to appease unemployed labor and provided pay raises for government employees. The king's policies did not address the underlying political problems; there were no political reforms. Instead the oil revenue provided a means to stay in power without addressing long-run issues pertaining to economic, political, and technological development (Ross, 2012).

Botswana: the real world Wakanda?

Fortunately, geographic endowments need not determine a country's destiny. Within sub-Saharan Africa, another landlocked country with bad neighbors has performed exceptionally well since the Second World War, even though its primary export was a natural resource. Like Wakanda, Botswana has "bad" neighbors: South Africa to the south, Namibia to the north and west, and Zimbabwe to the east. All of Botswana's neighbors had apartheid or apartheid-like governments in the second half of the 20th century. Well-governed, they were not. Yet Botswana prospered.

Botswana became an independent country in 1966 after a period as a protectorate of the United Kingdom. From independence until 2016, its GDP per capita increased from \$77 to \$6877. Its growth has been driven by its primary export, diamonds. Traditionally, a chief led the Bamangwato, the largest tribe in Botswana. Not surprisingly the traditional chief of the Bamangwato, Seretse Khama, led the independence movement and became its first president. Khama's personal life greatly increased the costs of having "bad" neighbors. In 1947 while living in London, he married Ruth Williams, a white woman. This led to enormous pressure from the South African government on the British government to prevent his return to his home country. Eventually he and Mrs. Khama did return but the neighboring countries boycotted trade with Botswana. Once he returned, Khama led Botswana through its formative years and established a precedent of fiscal prudence, monetary stability, and increased openness to international trade. As the theory suggests, he devoted diamond revenues for the provision of public education, health care, and infrastructure. Systemic public corruption did not emerge. In other words, he provided sound leadership for the development of a well-governed country (Beaulier and Subrick, 2006).

In many ways, the story of Wakandan exceptionalism parallels the economic miracle in Botswana. Against the geographic odds both countries attained levels of development well-beyond their bordering countries. They overcame the curse of geography and dysfunctional neighbors. Traditional leaders who governed wisely led both countries. They both adopted policies that allowed them to avoid the natural resource curse. The most glaring difference is that Botswana transitioned to a multi-party democracy. As a result, the possibility of losing an election disciplined the governing party to spend wisely. Frequent and fair elections now characterize the Botswanan political system. The diamond revenues were used for public good provision rather than self-enrichment. When droughts came, the ruling party used the diamond revenue to assist both those who supported the government and those who were opposed (Holm and Morgan, 1985). Unlike Botswana however, no democratic transition has occurred in Wakanda.

The economics of non-democratic societies

Democracies provide a framework for sustained economic development and peaceful social cooperation. They tend to have institutions that secure contract and property rights from theft, and they protect individual rights better than autocratic regimes (Easterly, 2013). When elected officials adopt policies that unjustly violate a citizen's property or civil rights, people protest and vote for someone else to govern. The threat of these actions encourage public officials to adopt public policies that satisfy the citizenry. According to Acemoglu and Robinson (2009), these actions lead to the emergence of democracies.

Once in place, elections provide a mechanism by which political competition becomes peaceful. Rather than threaten violence after losing an election, a political party can regroup and try again next time. This reduces social instability and allows citizens to go about their lives. By providing a framework for peaceful conflict resolution and peaceful transition of political power, democracies provide the incentives for economic development and good governance.

Wakanda has yet to develop into a democracy where the Black Panther earns his title by winning elections. One does not become the Black Panther after months of campaigning across the countryside, kissing babies, and developing policy positions. The title is largely hereditary, but one seeking to become the Black Panther must defeat the current Black Panther and then fight six of Wakanda's greatest warriors all at once. If successful in these two trials (along with a few more), you become the Black Panther (Thomas and Buscema, 1971).

The job description

In Wakanda, the Black Panther is the head of state, making most of the governmental decisions. Although the Black Panther has an advisory council, the Black Panther largely rules on his own. As a result of living under a hereditary, tribal leader, Wakanda has no democratic tradition. Although the Black Panther has retained political legitimacy throughout the centuries, in the new millennium Wakandans have begun to question the validity of their government. The Black Panther's support depends on his ability to provide the most basic of public goods – security from outside invasion and domestic turmoil. In the story arc "A Nation Under Our Feet" Ta-Nehisi Coates and Brian Stelfreeze describe a Wakanda on the verge of civil war. The combination of the never-ending attempts by outsiders to steal vibranium, recent internal challenges to his rule, and political intrigue, not to mention a terrorist organization poisoning the minds of the people, have raised the question of whether a monarchy and freedom are compatible. Government by a monarch in the age of democracy creates tensions within society. Furthermore, high levels of income inequality exacerbate these societal pressures. In Wakanda, traditional ways of life exist in the presence of the world's most sophisticated technologies. Citizens live in huts that are located next to the factories. A disenfranchised and relative poor citizenry are beginning to demand massive social change.

There is a Wakandan proverb that says, "Power lies not in what a king does but in what his subjects believe he might do" (Coates and Stelfreeze, 2016a). Perceptions matter at least as much as actions. If the citizens think the Black Panther will severely punish those who challenge his reign, they will refrain from doing so. The proverb echoes the opening sentences of David Hume's (1742/1987) essay, "Of the First Principles of Government" where he wrote:

> Nothing appears more surprising to those, who consider human affairs with a philosophical eye, than the easiness with which the many are governed by the few; and the implicit submission, with which men resign their own sentiments and passions to those of their rulers. When we enquire by what means this wonder is effected, we shall find, that, as force is always on the side of the governed, the governors have nothing to support them but opinion. It is therefore, on opinion only that government is founded; and this maxim extends to the most despotic and most military governments, as well as to the most free and most popular.

Opinion forms the basis of government. The political elite always lacks the numerical numbers to impose their rule. Because there are too few of them to govern by force, they must persuade the citizenry to accept their decisions. This is as true for democracies as it is for African governments led by traditional leaders.

Don't question the dictator: study STEM instead

Whether their rule is benevolent or not, a dictator's biggest threat is change. When people living under the dictator's rule begin to view their lot as oppressed, and particularly when they begin to compare themselves to other political and economic systems, the legitimacy of the dictator is at risk. Not surprisingly dictators, including the Black Panther, have enacted policies to limit this threat. One method to protect the dictator relies on education, but not necessarily indoctrination. Bruce Bueno de Mesquita and Alistair Smith (2011), in *The Dictator's Handbook*, provide a framework to understand this aspect of the Black Panther's political decision-making. They argue that dictatorships do not invest many public resources in fields such as sociology, political science, or philosophy. Such disciplines promote independent thinking and inspire people to consider the foundations of government. Additionally, these fields encourage people to think about the legitimate use of coercion. They foster critical thinking skills and the questioning of long established traditions. Instead dictatorships promote the study of the STEM fields (science, technology, engineering, and mathematics). These fields rely less on questioning and searching for answers to fundamental social questions. Instead, they concentrate attention on command and control type problems that often have unambiguous answers. It is the mechanical application of rules rather than development of ideas that a dictator prefers. Such thinking reduces the likelihood of social movements emerging that challenge the legitimacy of the political system.

True to form, the Black Panther has primarily allocated education resources to the STEM fields. He has not used the money to create the world's leading departments of political science, philosophy, or sociology; rather Wakanda has used its revenues to develop the world's most-sophisticated technologies that protect citizens from outside threats and help them live long, healthy lives. However, these educational investments did not protect the Black Panther when troubles arose that led to the questioning of his mystique.

In the series "A Nation Under Our Feet," a group of insurgents led by Tetu, a shaman, convinced many people to consider new ways of governance. The university teacher Changamire provided inspiration for this movement. Changamire expounded on Enlightenment ideas and taught the political legitimacy doctrines of John Locke, including ideas about the origins of rights, the importance of pre-political civil society, and the social contract as the basis of government (Coates and Stelfreeze, 2016b). These ideas motivate and possibly justify political change. These ideas resonated first with university students, then spread to the general population, as periods of crisis developed in Wakanda. The citizenry increasingly demanded change as the Black Panther failed to provide the most basic of public goods, security. For example, the super-villain Thanos invaded Wakanda only to be thwarted by Black Panther and the Avengers (Hickman and Deodato, 2013). That attack was followed by an attempted invasion from the supervillain Doctor Doom which threatened the viability of the Wakandan nation-state (Maberry and Eaton, 2010). A civil war erupted. A pro-democracy movement emerged with the motto, "No One Man." The movement's members believed the Black Panther had gained too much political power. They insisted that political power should be spread among the people and that decentralized decision-making should replace the centralized power of the Black Panther.

The foundation for the Wakandan revolution, was based on the same ideas underpinning the upheaval of English society in the 17th century. In his post-mortem, Locke sought to develop an argument against monarchism and in favor of the consent of the governed. Changamire quoted from Locke's second treatise to a class full of students:

> The injury and the crime is equal, whether committed by the wearer of a crown, or some petty villain. The title of the offender, and the number of his followers, make no difference in the offence, unless it be to aggravate it. The only difference is, great robbers punish little ones, to keep them in their obedience; but the great ones are rewarded with laurels and triumphs, because they are too big for the weak hands of justice in this world, and have the power in their own possession, which should punish offenders. What is my remedy against a robber, that so broke into my house?
>
> *(Locke, 1689/2003, p. 179)*

The class ends on Locke's question. Changamire wants the students to reconsider the Black Panther's legitimacy. He is a "great robber" who lives above the people and beyond the scales of justice. How would things differ under in a democratic society, one where one man does not have near absolute authority? He wants a society governed by the rule of law where no one, including the Black Panther, receives special treatment before the law. He wants the Wakandans to govern themselves. He wants a political revolution.

Later when meeting with T'Challa, Changamire discussed Edmund Morgan's *American Slavery, American Freedom* (Coates and Sprouse, 2017). Morgan's book explores the paradoxical relationship between the emergence of political freedom in Virginia in the early 18th century and its relation to the expansion of slave labor within the colony. How could democracy emerge in a society where simultaneously more and more people had no rights at all? This perplexes T'Challa and he appears unsure how it related to the crisis in Wakanda. As the conversation continues, the question arose about the proper type of education the state should provide.

CHANGAMIRE: Your father did a lot for Wakanda's educational system. But he did not have much use for the humanities.
T'CHALLA: We are a country of crafters and warriors.
CHANGAMIRE: But not of thinkers?

(Coates and Sprouse, 2017)

Changamire's response indicated he believed that the Black Panther had followed the path of dictators. Citizens with degrees do not necessarily become educated. Yes, they know how to build things. Yes, they solve problems in science, engineering, and mathematics, but they lack the information and knowledge to create and sustain a self-governing society when "no one man" decides. Rather they debate technical questions about how to best produce technologies. They do not debate the relative merits of parliamentary and presidential systems nor do they consider the proper scale and scope of governmental activities.

As the conversation returned to Morgan's book. T'Challa wants to know what he should do. How should the Black Panther respond to the insurgents? He does not wish to harm fellow citizens, too much blood has been split already, but he must protect the country and provide stability for his people. Changamire does not respond directly but points back to the lessons of Morgan's book: "[t]hat book chronicles the attempt to raise an entire race of kings. And every year thousands of them were born and charged with keeping thousands underfoot" (Coates and Sprouse, 2017). The process leads to an unstable situation. A political elite emerged who had to enslave others to remain in power. A similar situation was occurring in Wakanda. The elite control the resources such as vibranium and the public decision-making rights while the vast majority of citizens have control over neither. They are not equals economically or politically to the Black Panther and his close friends and advisors. In Wakanda, the future remains uncertain although political change seems inevitable, but will the change take the form of a revolution that culminates in regicide or will a relatively peaceful transition take place?

Kiser and Barzel (1991) claim that the transition from a monarchy to democracy can occur without a bloody revolution. Kings and queens and Black Panthers want to maintain power at minimal cost. They do not want to incite protests, revolutions, or regicide. They would like an extra palace or two for vacations but they recognize that expropriating too much from the citizenry may encourage discontent. The king does not want valuable assets destroyed in the struggle for power. Thus, an opportunity arises for a mutually beneficial exchange that makes both parties better off. What can the king offer to appease the potential revolutionaries? One possibility is decision-making rights. That is, the opportunity to affect public decision-making. Then the people can decide for themselves how they wish to be governed. What can the people offer? A commitment to avoid future revolutions, and instead to solve social problems peacefully. With such a bargain, the king remains in power and, more importantly, breathing. By giving up some decision-making rights for some social stability, everyone wins. Furthermore, the society moves down the road to democracy without rivers of blood flowing next to it.

After successfully thwarting the revolution, T'Challa decides to move towards democracy. The logic of political survival propels him in that direction. Wakanda will adopt a new constitution. T'Challa will remain as the head of state but he will no longer rule as "one man." Democracy will emerge. If the Wakandans can maintain it, only time will tell.

The future of Wakanda

The history of the Black Panther illustrates a number of economic principles. It highlights the role of geography in economic development and draws attention to the importance of one's neighbors in participating in the global division of labor which allows people to realize the gains from specialization. Additionally, it portrays the importance of political leadership in the management of natural resource revenue. Furthermore, it exposes the tensions that exist in a society that devotes its public resources to science and ignores the role of other disciplines in the social sciences and the humanities. Finally, it elucidates how a traditional monarchy evolves into a democracy under the threat of revolution.

Wakanda is supposed to be an exceptional country. It has attained high levels of literacy and life expectancy while developing the most sophisticated technology in the world, yet at the same time avoiding colonization throughout its existence. Nevertheless, as Changamire, the philosopher who inspired the revolutionaries, said, "Wakanda has all the intelligence any advanced society would want, and none of the wisdom that any free society needs" (Coates and Sprouse, 2017). Materially Wakanda has done reasonably well, but it lacks both economic and political freedom. The citizens have neither the right to trade with foreigners, nor the right to choose their leaders. At the end of *Captain America: Civil War*, T'Challa agrees to let Bucky Barnes stay in Wakanda until his brainwashing is cured. Barnes had been falsely identified as the killer of T'Challa's father. Once the Black Panther learned the truth, he decided to help Barnes. Captain America tells T'Challa the Avengers will come looking for them since Barnes is a wanted man. T'Challa responds, "Let them try." Try they will but it remains to be seen when they leave whether Wakanda will still be ruled by the Black Panther or will a democratic transition begin.

Notes

1 According to the comics, the material costs $10,000 per gram, and Wakanda's Vibranium vaults have 10,000 tons of the stuff (Black Panther: Doomwar #1). http://time.com/money/3950362/richest-superheroes-comic-con/. Accessed on 8 August 2017
2 This material is found in Book 1, Chapter 3.
3 As just one of many possible examples, much of the conflict between Japan and China during the late 1800s centered around access to resources. Japan was resource poor and required more inputs to expand their empire.
4 This calculation is based on data from the World Bank's "World Development Indicators" (http://databank.worldbank.org/data/reports.aspx?Code=NY.GDP.PCAP.CD&id=1ff4a498&report_name=Popular-Indicators&populartype=series&ispopular=y).

References

Acemoglu, D. and J. Robinson. (2009). *The Economic Origins of Dictatorship and Democracies.* Cambridge: Cambridge University Press.

Beard, J. (2016, August 25). "Jack Kirby Week: The Black Panther." *Marvel.* Retrieved from https://news.marvel.com/comics/26638/jack_kirby_week_the_black_panther/.

Beaulier, S. and J. R. Subrick. (2006). "The Political Foundations of Development: The Case of Botswana." *Constitutional Political Economy* 17(2), 103–115.

Central Intelligence Agency. (2017). *World Factbook 2017.* Retrieved from www.cia.gov/library/publications/the-world-factbook/index.html.

Claremont, C. and J. Byrne. (1980). *Marvel Team Up*, #100. Marvel Comics.

Coates, T. and B. Stelfreeze. (2016a). *Black Panther*, #1. Marvel Comics.

Coates, T. and B. Stelfreeze. (2016b). *Black Panther*, #2. Marvel Comics.

Coates, T. and C. Sprouse. (2017). *Black Panther*, #10. Marvel Comics.

Collier, P. (2007). *The Bottom Billion: Why the Poorest Countries are Failing and What Can Be Done About It.* Oxford: Oxford University Press.

De Mesquita, B. and A. Smith. (2011). *The Dictator's Handbook: Why Bad Behavior Is Almost Always Good Politics.* New York: Public Affairs.

Easterly, W. (2013). *The Tyranny of Experts: Economists, Dictators, and the Forgotten Rights of the Poor.* New York: Basic Books.

Hannigan, E. and D. Perlin. (1980). *The Defenders*, #78. Marvel Comics.

Heart Shaped Herb. (n.d.). Retrieved from http://marvel.wikia.com/wiki/Heart-Shaped_Herb.

Hickman, J. and M. Deodato. (2013). *New Avengers*, #9. Marvel Comics.

Holm, J. and R. Morgan. (1985). "Coping with Drought in Botswana: An African Success." *The Journal of Modern African Studies* 23(3), 463–482.

Hume, D. (1987). "Of the First Principles of Government." In E. Miller (Ed.), *Essays, Moral, Political, and Literary.* Indianapolis, Indiana: Liberty Fund, Inc. (original work published in 1742).

International Road Federation World Road Statistics. (n.d.). Retrieved from www.econstats.com/wdi/wdiv_579.htm.

Kirby, J. (1978). *Black Panther*, #7. Marvel Comics.

Kiser, E. and Y. Barzel. (1991). "The Origins of Democracy in England." *Rationality and Society* 3(4), 396–422.

Lee, S. and J. Kirby. (1966a). *Fantastic Four*, #52. Marvel Comics.

Lee, S. and J. Kirby. (1966b). *Fantastic Four*, #53. Marvel Comics.

Locke, J. (2003). "The Second Treatise: An Essay Concerning the True Original, Extent, and End of Civil Government." In I. Shapiro (Ed.), *Two Treatises of Government: And a*

Letter Concerning Toleration. New Haven: Yale University Press (original work published in 1689).

Maberry, J. and S. Eaton. (2010). *Doomwar*, #1–#6. Marvel Comics.

Mehlum, H., K. Moene, and R. Torvik. (2006). "Institution and the Resource Curse." *Economic Journal* 116(508), 1–20.

Miller, T. and A. Kim. (2017). *The Heritage Foundation: 2017 Index of Economic Freedom*. Retrieved from www.heritage.org/index/pdf/2017/book/index_2017.pdf

Narcisse, E. (2016). "The Politics of Marvel's Black Panther." *Kotaku*. Retrieved from https://kotaku.com/the-politics-of-the-black-panther-1766701304

Ross, M. (2012). *The Oil Curse: How Petroleum Wealth Shapes the Development of Nations*. Princeton, New Jersey: Princeton University Press.

Russo, J. and Russo, A. (Directors). (2016). *Captain America: Civil War* [Motion Picture]

Sachs, J. and A. Warner. (2001). "The Curse of Natural Resources." *European Economic Review* 45(4), 827–838.

Smith, A. (1994). *An Inquiry into the Nature and Causes of the Wealth of Nations*. New York: Random House (original work published in 1776).

Stiglitz, J. (2005). "Making Natural Resources into a Blessing rather than a Curse." In S. Tsalik and A. Schiffrin (Eds.), *Covering Oil: A Reporter's Guide to Energy and Development*. New York: Open Society Institute.

Thomas, R. and S. Buscema. (1971). *Avengers*, #87. Marvel Comics.

Transparency International. (2017). *Corruptions Perceptions Index: 2016*. Retrieved from www.transparency.org/news/feature/corruption_perceptions_index_2016

7

TRUTH, JUSTICE AND THE ECONOMIC WAY

Brian O'Roark

The introduction to the man from Krypton from the 1952 television series is familiar to nearly every fan of Superman, and to many who are entirely indifferent to him or comics in general. It is here where we learn of some of the characteristics that make Superman so, well, super. He can redirect rivers, bend steel with his hands, leap tall buildings, outrace trains and, most importantly, he is on our side, fighting for "truth, justice and the American way" (Maxwell and Carr, 1952).

Interestingly, the familiar credo originally claimed that Superman was engaged in "a never-ending battle for truth and justice." The "American way" part appeared in the Superman animated series of the 1940s. This was, of course, a reaction to World War II. The phrase became engrained in the civic consciousness during the run of the 1950s Superman television show and was revived during the 1970s and 1980s Christopher Reeve movie portrayal of Superman (Cronin, 2010). The advent of this phrase during the war was no accident. Comics were a part of the war effort as much as metal drives and victory gardens. The writers of Superman wanted to create a clear connection between Superman and America, and one way to do that was to remind everyone why the war was being fought. There was a way of life to defend not just in Europe, but in America as well.

A common misconception is that the American way is the same as the America dream. That's not the case. There are many interpretations of what constitutes the American dream, and that concept is malleable over time. But that is not what Superman stands for; he stands for the American way, and in the context of truth and justice, it is safe to say that the American way is part of the structural elements that make America, or any society for that matter, work.

But what does this have to do with economics? Quite a bit actually. In economics the American way, along with truth and justice, is part of what we refer to as institutions. Superman is fighting for truth and justice. Right and wrong are clearly defined in the early comics, and those lines are never blurred. The readers are as clear as Superman is on what he should do when confronting a villain. Institutions, or the American way, involve the processes for defending truth and justice. These are the rules and guidelines within which people behave. Economist Douglas North (who won a Nobel Prize in economics which means he is really smart) said that "Institutions are the rules of the game in a society, [...] the humanly devised constraints that shape human interaction. [...] They structure incentives in human exchange, whether political, social or economic" (North, 1990, p. 4). Institutions include all the things that order life, not just the legal issues such as property and contact laws, but also, and often times more importantly, the religious aspects, norms and cultural approbations of society.

Without institutions, social order becomes chaotic. There is a clear consensus in economic research that institutions foster an environment in which economic growth can flourish. The certainty brought about by institutions enables and encourages businesses to expand, and fosters more economic transactions. While not every institution is perfectly transportable to all societies – as a result of other institutions within that country – there is a pretty well-developed set of institutions that are good predictors of economic success. Interestingly, two of those are truth and justice. Because of the importance of institutions, and because of what those institutions are, perhaps it isn't too big of a leap to say that Superman is fighting for truth, justice and the economic way.

Not convinced? Let's take a look at how Superman has changed over time. In three stages, we'll examine the original comic which sets up Superman as a defender of the economic way. We'll start at the beginning, with *Action Comics* #1 (Siegel and Shuster, 1938). We'll then move on to how he maintains the values that protect the economic way. Finally, we'll consider what the world would look like if Superman turned to the dark side and became a dictator. Suffice it to say, the world would be a much different and a much less pleasant place.

The origin of the economic way

Let's begin with Superman as the general public knows him. Born on a dying world, Superman's parents launched him into space moments before the planet, Krypton, exploded. Baby Superman, with the Kryptonian name Kal-El, is the only survivor, the last of the Kryptonians. Fortune smiles on the child as his ship crash lands in Kansas where he is found by the all-American Kent family. Ma and Pa Kent name him Clark and raise the boy as their own, helping him understand his power, and the responsibility that comes with being special. Their well-honed set of values serves Clark Kent well as he heads to the big city of Metropolis. As an intrepid reporter, he uses his powers to keep people safe, clean up the streets, and get the scoop for *The Daily Planet*.

In *Action Comic* #1 (1938), the first Superman comic, after a brief introduction to the character, Superman is seen speeding to the house of the governor (presumably of New York) to present evidence that will save the life of a woman condemned to be electrocuted. He then goes on to save a woman being beaten by her husband. Later he deals with a corrupt politician who has proposed a bill that will embroil the United States in Europe. While showing Superman as a defender of the downtrodden, protector of the weak, and guardian of democracy, creators Jerry Siegel and Joe Shuster not only establish the essence of their character as a champion of the oppressed, but they also, unknowingly, encapsulate the relationship between Superman and the institutions that define America.

Institutions are important because they set the stage for economic activity. Economic researchers have examined how institutions impact economic development and growth and found them to be at least as important as the amount of resources a country has. Think about a poor country in Africa. There are millions of people so labor is plentiful. There may be lots of natural resources, such as oil and mineral deposits. The country might be located on the ocean so if they produce goods they can ship them with relative ease. Nevertheless, this country is poor. To help this country get its economic house in order, and show what great guys they are, a rich, western country steps in and builds a hydroelectric dam. This will provide electricity for the poor country and start it on the path to prosperity. The dam is a magnificent, modern structure, unlike anything seen in the country before. The ribbon cutting ceremony is a great event and when the rich country leaves, patting itself on the back for its generosity, there are high hopes. But in a few years, the country is just as poor as ever. What is the problem?

While the dam provides the electricity, there is no infrastructure upon which to carry the power. There is little interest or expertise on the part of the government in providing upkeep for the capital investment. No private power company exists so there is no profit motive to expand capacity, make sure the customers are served or fix any malfunctions. Add to this, the politically unstable environment of the country. While the ruler in charge when the dam was completed hailed this as a great achievement, no one sees any real difference in their lives. The political system itself is ripe with corruption so the only benefits seem to be to the relatives of the ruler who now have government jobs running the power station, that doesn't actually produce power. So, despite the huge capital investment, the country doesn't change. Poverty still plagues the people in this country.

The gift of the dam was indeed generous, and in a perfect world, it would have led to an increase in the well-being of the population. However, because the institutions – the rules of the game that govern economic interaction – were not changed, the dam falls into disrepair. The dam, or more loosely the capital project, was the way economists used to think of economic growth.

Robert Solow (another really smart guy who also won a Nobel Prize) started modern day economic growth theory with his 1956 paper "A Contribution to the Theory of Economic Growth." Economic students today struggle through Solow's growth model and when they finally think they have it, devious economics professors deal the fatal blow: Solow didn't have it right. Solow's original model targeted capital – tools, machinery, factories and the like – as the prime driver of economic growth. If a country was able to increase its stock of capital, and keep it growing faster than it was being depleted, then that country should experience economic growth. This is why rich countries in the 1960s and 1970s gave poor countries all kinds of stuff. Dams were one thing, but bulldozers, tractors and other machinery was (and still is) given to poor countries as well. However, poverty has not been overcome based on the amount of machinery a country possesses.

Consider North and South Korea, a petri dish of comparing economies if ever there was one. There are lots of people in both countries. Neither has a particular geographic advantage over the other. The cultural background of the two counties is still essentially the same. Obviously though, there is a huge difference in the standard of living of the people. In one place, there is subsistence living, while in the other, the most modern of conveniences. In one, the government spends on military dominance, while in the other government spends on infrastructure and attracting foreign business. In one, there is no freedom while the other is one of the freest countries in the world.

Economists who were trying to understand why the bulldozers they sent to Sudan didn't make the country into an economic dynamo began looking at institutions in earnest in the 1980s. It turns out growth doesn't just come from having resources to produce things. There were inconspicuous factors as well. This led to an explosion of research into the role institutions play in economic growth from examining thing like the financial systems of countries, down to whether they have term limits for their legislators. The results have been stunning. Today, economists realize the importance of not only having capital, but also providing it to people who live in countries where the institutions will provide an environment which fosters the effective use of that capital. For instance, if there are no private property rights ensuring that the farmer gets to keep what he grows and allows him to sell it for a profit, then it doesn't matter if he has the most advanced tractor in the world. When private property rights are diminished, the farmer might continue to farm, but it is just as likely that he chooses to give up on that occupation because, let's face it, farming is hard work.

The necessary institutions – what makes up the economic way

There are lots of different aspects of life that fall under the heading of institutions. Politically, socially and economically, there are myriad choices society must make about the rules of the game that will determine how people interact and get along. On the political side, you have things like the way your government is set up: do you have a congress or a parliament; are there term limits for the legislators; who has the right to vote. Socially there are also many different institutions including things like: do you have freedom of religion; how are minorities treated; is there a public-school system. Of course, the focus here is economics, so let's turn our attention to three of the basic institutions necessary for economic development: impartial courts, protection of property and eliminating corruption. These are not the only institutions a country could adopt, but as far as economic development is concerned they are three of the more important ones.

A fair court is at the heart of a democracy. The role of the court is to enforce the laws correctly and equitably. When a population loses faith in the findings of the courts or when those courts become vehicles of oppression, then democracy suffers. People begin to view the courts as a vehicle through which despots entrench themselves and not a place where truth or justice are found. However, this also harms the economy. Economic activity is based on a number of things, but one of the principle foundations is trust. In his book, *Trust: The Social Virtues and the Creation of Prosperity*, Francis Fukuyama (1995) provides a convincing argument for why economic and social life go hand-in-hand. In societies where trust is absent, economic activity will flounder. The connections needed to build a company that can compete on a global scale are not possible where trust does not exist. Courts are necessary components of authenticating that trust. Upholding and enforcing contracts, along with divining the intent of laws establish the ground rules and the expectations for the actors in an economic transaction. If you do not naturally trust someone you probably will not engage in trade with them (and remember, trade is a good thing). A fair court system encourages trade because even if you do not trust someone there is a way to define what each party to a trade must do to satisfy the other, and a way to enforce an agreement that the parties enter into.

The second institution essential for economies to grow is the protection of property. This institution provides the incentive to create and maintain property. When property is owned, the owner can benefit financially from its use or sale. If property rights are unclear, courts can help provide clarity. One of the great papers in economics, written by Ronald Coase (1960) (yet another really smart guy who won the Nobel Prize in economics), established that when property rights are not clearly defined, economic outcomes are sub-optimal. Defined property rights ensure that transactions that do occur move goods to those who value them the most. As such, the agents who need resources to be productive will get them. This outcome also encourages investment in businesses (Besley, 1995). If it is well established that courts will protect the investments that individuals make in their businesses, then business will begin to expand. This leads to more production, more hiring and eventually greater income.

Protection of property rights also expands the scale of market transactions. Consider the process of buying a car. Whether you buy one new, used, from a dealer or on eBay, one of the important aspects of that transaction is that the seller provides evidence that they own the car and therefore have the legal right to sell it. This is done through producing a title, the piece of paper that the government uses to identify the owner of the car. When the car is traded, the title goes with it. This way there is a paper trail of property ownership. In some parts of the world however, this paper trail simply doesn't exist. Thus, establishing who owns something is a much more difficult process. It is entirely possible that even when you think you have bought a car, you really haven't, even though money has been exchanged and you have possession of the vehicle, because the seller wasn't legally entitled to sell it. The problem is that if that happens enough times, where original ownership is not clearly established, people stop engaging in transactions. If the courts either can't establish who owns what, or if they do so by favoring their friends and the connected people of society, transactions grind to a halt.

Economists are convinced that reducing the number of transactions is a very bad thing. People try to address their wants and needs in a number of different ways. Consider two options: you can buy things you want or steal things you want. We'd like to limit thievery, but sometimes you don't have enough in the bank account to buy what you want. An alternative method, and a very effective way of getting what you want, is to trade for things. Either you trade money or you might trade something the seller wants. Maybe they want your iPhone and you really want a car. You could swap one for the other, or use the phone to reduce the monetary amount you owe. But again, if that phone isn't really yours to trade – maybe it is your sister's – then there is a problem. If your sister tries to get it back, and the court says that she can't because you are paying off the judge, then your sister, and others, may choose not to buy phones in the first place. This slows the cell phone market down and harms the economy. Not only that, but more directly, your sister is worse off. Presumably she bought the phone because it was going to provide some value. If she doesn't buy a new one because it might be taken from her, the value she received from having a phone is no longer created, and that is bad for her and the economy.

The final of our three institutions in focus involves limiting corruption. Corruption is a way for the connected to get what they want at the expense of everyone else. The corruption tends to enrich a small group of people (like the judge you paid off) at the expense of a larger group. Simply, corruption reduces economic growth. This is the main finding of papers by Paolo Mauro (1995) and Arvind Jain (2002). (Sorry guys, no Nobel Prize for you. Those things are actually hard to get.) If the only people who are able to do business are the ones connected to the government, there is no incentive to experiment, innovate or create. No matter what you do, there is some impediment keeping you from moving ahead. Corruption can also cause resources to flow from where they are needed to pet projects of bureaucrats. Think about taking food aid from the poor due to tight budgets. That tight budget might be the result of a sports stadium that was built for a politician's favorite team. Perhaps it is the case that in order to open a shop you need to pay off the local sheriff. This will ensure that no competitors enter the market, that is unless they pay more than you do. While it might be the way business gets done in parts of the world, corruption is not efficient, nor does it encourage business activity. In many cases, it drives activity away.

"All right" you say. These institutions are pretty obvious, but where does Superman fit in? Remember the endeavors of Superman in *Action Comics* #1. He is stopping the miscarriage of justice. An innocent woman is minutes away from being executed and Superman has evidence to exonerate her. Not only is he protecting the innocent, but he is trying to uphold the integrity of the court system.

The woman who is being beaten by her husband is, in essence, having her property taken away from her. She isn't being robbed of a material possession, but her life is at risk. This violation of her property rights is an obvious situation where protection should be afforded. It may not be possible for the police or the courts to act in a timely fashion, but Superman can.

The corrupt politician is, well, corrupt. He is violating the trust of the people he represents. The lobbyist states unequivocally that the politician will be financially taken care of. In issue #2, the readers find out that the bribe is coming from a munitions magnate intent on instigating a war in Europe so he can sell more guns. Superman tracks him down, and forces him to the war front to experience the destruction caused by his weapons.

More recently, we can see that people still expect Superman to uphold the economic way. In *Superman* #713 (Straczynski and Roberson, 2011), Clark Kent quits being Superman. He is writing a piece about whether there should be a Superman and considering just doing good as Clark Kent, when a fan shows up, reads the draft and can't believe that Clark Kent, who has been writing about Superman for so many years, has so little perspective on what Superman means to people. The fan takes Clark Kent around town, conducting impromptu man on the street interviews. One person is asked about whether Superman kills people. He answers that some crimes call for a stricter form of justice than Superman doles out. If the task were his, he continues, he might not be able to restrain himself. Then he pauses and says "But I guess if I was the one accused of a crime, I'd want a court to decide if I was guilty or innocent, and not some guy, super or not. Wouldn't you?" (p. 22). These conversations confirm for Clark Kent that the world wants to see Superman, and that they believe in his modus operandi.

Superman's original story establishes him as the doer of good deeds, but these actions have an ulterior motive. No, Superman's creators did not consider this while writing the story. It is impossible to imagine that two kids, Jerry Siegel and Joe Shuster, were subliminally attempting to equate their creation with economic institutions. There is no economic symbolism hidden in the cartoon they drew. Nevertheless, this character who has world-wide recognition upholds the institutions that make successful economies thrive. That's part of who this character is. While that was true at the beginning, things can certainly go awry. Siegel and Shuster were fired from DC comics in 1946, eventually signing away any claims to their creation. So, did Superman change as a result? Of course, but while his appearance has gone through some alterations, Superman's ethos remained consistent. He could choose to stop defending the economic way, but he doesn't.

Defending the economic way ...

Consider that Superman can improve the lot of humanity but he doesn't. If Superman can change the course of rivers, then he should be able to end drug smuggling. If he battles physically powerful aliens and defeats them, then he should be able to put an end to crime. If he has resources and technology at his fingertips that are light years ahead of their time, then he could prevent nuclear wars. Despite all of this, the reader is forced to accept a reality in which Superman does not do these things. In fact, he is a fragile hero – he has run away from earth, and left the public eye at times, feeling pressured, unwanted or just needing a break (for instance, Bates and Swan, 1967; Waid and Ross, 1996/2008; Straczynski and

Robertson, 2011). Even his Fortress of Solitude provides a great, temporary escape for contemplation and rejuvenation. He could be more involved, could interfere more with the day to day lives of humans, but he hasn't. This behavior is both vexing (see Lois Lane and Lex Luthor below) and liberating. While he could be a benevolent dictator, he chooses not to be.

In *Superman* #234, the Man of Steel is trying to stop a volcano from erupting and killing the inhabitants of an island. Unfortunately, the location of the volcano is the private property of a wicked plantation owner called Boysie Harker. Harker tells Superman that he is not welcome on the island and to vacate the premises or else face the law. Superman knows he can't legally get to the volcano, so he comes up with an alternative plan. He is bound and determined to obey the law even as the volcano threatens hundreds of native residents of the island. Nevertheless, Superman notes that "if worst comes to worst, I'll have to defy Harker – and take the consequences! Because there's a moral law that's above some man-made laws!" (O'Neil and Swan, 1971, p. 9)

Here he is, thirty-three years after his creation, still abiding by the economic way. Private property protections apply not just to individuals, but to the hero as well. He will only intervene if there is no other alternative. It isn't his job to interfere. *Superman* #247 (Maggin and Swan, 1972) expands on this point. Superman is working with the Guardians, an alien species who oversee the universe. While healing him after a successful mission, the Guardians plant an idea in his mind that Superman is creating a cultural-lag on Earth. This leaves Superman confused about how much he should be interfering with events on his adopted home planet. When he returns to Earth he finds a boy being beaten by a field boss. After saving the boy, the oppressed migrants cheer and begin asking Superman to do all manner of things for them from throwing the boss in jail to rebuilding their houses. Superman begins to think that perhaps people are not moving forward because they are too dependent on him to fix their problems.

This point is further illustrated in the graphic novel *Kingdom Come* (Waid and Ross, 2008). Heroes are not supposed to interfere. When they do and people no longer have to fend for themselves, they stop being productive. Pastor Norman McCay is remembering his friend Wesley, who lamented that the aging heroes had given way to a new generation of super humans, a generation that did not fight for right, rather, they just fought. Norman recalls Wesley saying that "human initiative began to erode the day people asked a new breed to face the future for them" (p. 17). The dilemma Superman faces is that there are things a superhero should do, but creating dependency isn't part of the plan. Heroes should work within the system, not replace the system, even if the system is flawed.

This is particularly evident within the context of how Superman does his job. When the relevancy of a hero who does not kill the bad guys is questioned, Superman finds a way to hold to the rules that keep dictators at bay. In *Action Comics* #775 (Kelly, Mahnke and Bernejo, 2001) titled "What's So Funny About Truth, Justice, and the American Way?" a new group of vigilante, super-powered humans appears. They execute wrong-doers with prejudice resulting in a conversation among the people of earth over whether this is the proper way to deal with criminals. This group, called The Elite, asks whether the era of Superman might be over. They fight evil, but they step over the line Superman has set for himself and expects from other heroes. By being willing to kill, The Elite get around the system. There are no due process rights, no right to face accusers, no trial. It violates Superman's ethos, but it is economical as costs are minimized. If there are no trials or incarcerations, or appeals the government is not expending resources, but such vigilantism certainly eliminates justice from the process.

Curiously though, the actions of the Elite also address a peculiarity in comics: when heroes act with restraint they deposit villains in jails that rarely hold them. Escapes are enacted, and more people are harmed. This theme recurs across characters and stories. In graphic novels such as *The Killing Joke* (Moore, Bolland and Higgins, 1988) and *Injustice: Gods Among Us* (Taylor, Raapack and Redondo, 2016), along with Superman, civilians question the tactics used by heroes. Heroes, however, understand the necessity of justice better than the mob. Superman is indignant as he chastises The Elite. "You're murdering people and calling yourself 'heroes!' This is not the way the job gets done!" Manchester Black, the leader of the Elite responds "Good pounding the snot out of evil in bright tights. No questions. No 'grey areas'. … Reality is a mite bloodier than sitcoms or comics. The greys stretch out further."

… Working within the system…

For Superman, there are rarely areas of gray because he believes in the system. He is part of the system. So, what is the system? In economics, we divide macro economies[1] into systems. These systems coordinate how societies decide to allocate resources, goods and services by asking three questions: what will we produce, how will we produce it and for whom will things be produced? In the most elementary way, economic systems can be illustrated along a continuum; at one end is the capitalist system, the other the pure command system. Capitalism is associated with markets, profits and choices, whereas command systems are organized by governments.

Capitalism is typically accompanied by economic and political freedom, higher standards of living and more innovation among other things. The largest drawback for the capitalist system though is income inequality. There is the potential for great wealth to be generated in a capitalist system, but that income need not find its way to the poorest. The rich are free to give away what they make to help the poor, but there is no compulsion to do so. To put it bluntly, capitalism is not fair.

Command systems are characterized by strict government control. All production decisions, resource allocation and goods distribution are determined by a government bureaucracy. The attempt is to create equality across the society. If one group has more than they need, a benevolent dictator will reallocate material goods so that no one has more than anyone else. Fairness is a focal point. Unfortunately, the determination of what is fair is usually made without consulting the people. There is little to no freedom of choice economically or politically. Profit motives that drive innovation are absent, resulting in slow economic growth and very slow changes to the overall living conditions of people.

In reality, neither of these systems actually exists. These two types of systems are the extremes. A society chooses how to organize itself and inevitably mixes components of the two types of systems. A capitalist system is likely to have some restraints on what firms can acceptably do to earn a profit. Slave trading is profitable, but outlawed. There are environmental rules that must be followed, even if polluting the local river would keep costs down. Pharmaceuticals must be tested in the lab before human trials can start even though that will lengthen the time it takes to bring a drug to market. Government still exists and must be paid for so tax collection plans are imposed even though this hurts the bottom line.

Similarly, command systems have some aspects of capitalism. Innovations happen and markets exist, even if they occur in the dark. There are rich people living in command economic systems, they just tend to be the ones making the rules. The rich have found a way to profit from the economic system in which they live, even if it is at the expense of those who are otherwise prohibited from doing the same.

Regardless of which economic system a society chooses, there are institutions that govern those systems. Systems and institutions go together like Superman and Lois Lane. It just so happens that capitalist systems have those growth promoting institutions like a fair court system, protection of property rights and less corruption, that coincide with Superman's mission statement. It isn't that capitalist systems never have problems with their institutions, they are, after all, "man-made," still, the choice of a capitalist economic system and adopting institutions that foster that system (and genuinely trying to implement them) are more likely to lead to economic growth. By defending this system over another, Superman is promoting economic well-being.

... Most of the time?

Superman is thought of by many as a perfect hero: he is good, he stands up for those who can't defend themselves, he is sympathetic. Superman is also a good example of a number of economic ideas that aren't covered in this chapter but were covered in prior chapters: he is unbound by scarcity, he has a comparative advantage in nearly all aspects of his powers – that is why he never adopts a permanent sidekick, his opportunity costs are very low for all of his activities because he can act so quickly, his powers enable him to be incredibly productive. He also gets a lot of satisfaction out of being a good guy. Layman (2008) offers an interesting application of Spider-Man's credo to Superman. He suggests that for Superman, the credo could be "With great power comes great personal satisfaction" (p. 195). Powers certainly could be used to help yourself, your friends and your family, and harm those who get in your way. But heroes don't do that. Why not? A series of essays of which Layman's is a part deals with superheroes and philosophy, where the question of superhero morality is debated. In economics, we have another explanation for why superheroes are good: utility. This is the measure of personal well-being people receive for consuming goods or services. Basically, utility is an attempt to quantify happiness. A higher utility score means a happier person. Heroes could just take what they want, but it isn't just how much you have that makes someone happy. Layman goes on to suggest that one reason to be good is that it brings peace of mind. Helping others is its own reward.

Superman is such a perfect economic agent, and he is so powerful we could ask: What keeps Superman from taking over the planet? He might be happier if he didn't have to fight all the time. He could help others by being proactive to eliminate crime rather than reactive. Some might say that other heroes wouldn't let him take such drastic actions, but economics presents us with a more nuanced view. Superman has chosen to be bound by the rules of the game, partly because he finds utility or satisfaction in doing so. Forcing compliance makes him a dictator, but even Superman has his limits. Right?

Critics of Superman hound him as one who shakes their fist at God – "Why didn't you prevent this?" some shout. Pa Kent tries to tell him that he can't save everyone, but he tries nevertheless, and when he fails, he is left reflecting on his own shortcomings. What explains this behavior? It is vexing to friend and foe alike. Lois Lane considers, with some incredulity, that this man from the sky who can do anything with this power repertoire, decides to "be a hero" in a world where "nobody sticks their neck out for anybody … here's this … this … man sticking his neck out for everyone. Way, way out." (Loeb and Sale, 1998, pp. 66–67).

Unable to imagine that someone could use these powers for good, Lex Luthor, Superman's arch nemesis, after a thorough data analysis which concludes Clark Kent and Superman are the same person goes on a rant. "I know that no man with the power of Superman would ever pretend to be a mere human! Such power is to be constantly exploited. Such power is to be used!" Luthor then fires the data analyst who reached the correct conclusion by saying "I have no place in my organization for people who cannot see the obvious!" (Byrne and Austin, 1987).

The preconceived notion of what it means to be powerful keeps both Lane and Luthor from identifying the obvious: Clark Kent is Superman. Consider it a form of rational ignorance. Becoming fully informed shatters their world-view. Lois reflects on the coincidence that when Clark Kent is not around, neither is Superman. When she connects the dots she almost immediately dismisses the idea, chiding herself "Lois Lane, that's the stupidest idea in the world" (Loeb and Sale, 1998, p. 165).

While it sounds impossible to Lane and Luthor, Clark Kent likes helping people. He derives value from making others safer. Even when he doesn't don the cape there are instances of Kent protecting people from harm. In the *Green Arrow* #28 (Percy and Schmidt, 2017) comic the Green Arrow teams up with Superman to take on a criminal financier. In one panel, we see Clark Kent walking down the street and in the span of about ten seconds he thwarts a robbery, prevents a kid from being clocked by a falling paint can and opens a taxi cab door for a little old lady. Economists say that being a Boy Scout is utility enhancing for Superman.

Everyone else says such acts make him happy. But what if what made Superman happy was something entirely different? What if his sense of doing good is a product of the system in which he was raised?

Dark times for the economic system

For the majority of Superman story arcs, he toes the company line. He is the unassailable fighter for truth, justice and the American way. Superman has continually fought to protect and defend the system, battling all manner of organized crime, insanely smart evildoers and alien invaders. While he may not always agree with the people in charge, it is the system to which Superman adheres. In *The Dark Knight* (Miller, 2016), Superman (Clark Kent) and Batman (Bruce Wayne) have a discussion on their next course of action, after the president of the United States has asked Superman to talk to Batman about the vigilante's excessive use of force. As he reflects on their conversation Superman admits some things to himself. Batman has an agenda, and he will not waver no matter the cost. While the rest of the superheroes have come to terms with some degree of government oversight, Batman does not acquiesce. Superman admits that while there is an unsteady peace between the government and heroes, Batman's obsession might end the truce. "I gave them [the government] my obedience and my invisibility," Superman recalls. "They gave me a license and let us live. No, I don't like it. But I get to save lives – and the media stays quiet. But now the storm is growing again – they'll hunt us down again – because of you [Batman]."

The question of what would happen if Superman followed his own agenda, as Batman does, has led to some intriguing story lines regarding Superman. One of the better known of these alternative realities is *Superman: Red Son* (Millar and Johnson, 2014). In this Elseworlds[2] story line Kal-El lands on a Ukrainian collective farm rather than in Kansas. Instead of fighting for "truth, justice and the American way" he is converted to one "who as the champion of the common worker, fights a never-ending battle for Stalin, socialism and the international expansion of the Warsaw Pact" (p. 5). Underneath the Soviet trappings, Superman is, at least initially, the hero readers expect. He saves America's Metropolis from certain destruction when a satellite falls out of orbit and is heading for what will be a cataclysmic impact. Mid-flight he concedes that he isn't a soldier. He didn't hate the enemy or fight only for his people. He "fought for what was right" (p. 11). Notice the past tense.

He repeatedly turns down political advancement in the Communist party claiming he doesn't want to be the leader. He even notes that his "privileges" should disqualify him as leader of the socialist republic. Making him the leader would be "in complete contradiction to everything we were ever raised to believe in" (p. 33). But that all changed when he sees an old friend and her children in a bread line. Seeing hungry people prompts Superman to act. His friend Lana tells him that he "can't take care of everyone's problems" (p. 46), but in a command economic system he can. "Superman is here to rescue them" (p. 47) and Superman is nothing if not a man who works within the system. Earlier the question of whether Superman should interfere was raised and Superman tried to avoid this whenever possible. It isn't part of being a hero. By the end of *Red Son* though, he has become a dictator, whose subjects are entirely subservient to the Man of Tomorrow. People have given up taking responsibility for themselves, and have so given over control of their lives to Superman that they stop wearing seatbelts or life jackets. The difference between being in a capitalist system and a command system is that in the capitalist system, Superman would be convicted that he was stepping beyond his bounds, moving outside the system. In the command structure, while Superman feels a little guilty at first about taking too much control, he progressively takes over more and more of the society. In fact, as the story continues, he eventually demands this obedience. In his global Soviet Union only the United States resisted, and it was beset by civil war. Everywhere else,

> every adult had a job, every child had a hobby, and the entire human population enjoyed the full eight hours sleep which their bodies required. Crime didn't exist. Accidents never happened. It didn't even rain unless … everyone had an umbrella. Almost six billion citizens and hardly anyone complained. Even in private.
>
> *(Millar and Johnson, 2014, p. 98)*

Dependency on government is part of the command system. And after all, Superman defends the system.

Conclusion

Superman is the personification of any super power you could want. He can fly, has super strength, can run fast, has x-ray vision, heat vision, super hearing, super breath, is impervious to most weapons, has remarkable stamina and over time has utilized a variety of other variously appearing and disappearing powers – such as telekinesis, ventriloquism, an eidetic memory and hypnotism. Yet, despite all of these powers, Superman is a Boy Scout. If at all possible, he avoids killing people. In fact, in story arcs where people die or are hurt, he is consumed with feelings of inadequacy. What could he have done differently that would have prevented the outcome? The one area of his superhero life where things seem to never go wrong is his ever-lasting fight to protect the economic way.

Defending the economic way is a balancing act. When you have super powers, it would be much easier, and much less messy to just take over, subject everyone to your will and eliminate the opposition. But if Superman did this, he would be the personification of the evil being fought in Europe when his credo was codified. This is what Hitler, Mussolini and Hirohito would do and taking such actions wouldn't fit the character of Superman.

From his first appearance to the present, Superman has been a hero who sets the standard for all heroes. He fights for truth and justice. He battles the bad guys where ever they come from and defends anyone and everyone from the forces of evil. Superman also fights to uphold the process by which truth and justice themselves are protected. He protects the institutions that govern society so that he doesn't have to be the judge. He lets the system play out, and subjects himself to the rules that he works so diligently to uphold, even though he doesn't have to. When we see what the alternative could be, we shudder, and realize, it's a good thing Superman landed in Kansas. The American way, and the economic way, are in good hands.

Notes

1 Macroeconomics is one of the primary divisions in the study of economics. Macro looks at the big picture, specifically, at economic activities that occur on the national and international level. This is opposed to microeconomics which focuses on smaller decision making units such as individuals and corporations.

2 Elseworlds is a DC series of alternative reality story lines.

References

Bates, C. and C. Swan. (1967). *Superman*, #201. DC Comics.

Besley, T. (1995). "Property Rights and Investment Incentives: Theory and Evidence from Ghana." *Journal of Political Economy* 103(5), 903–937.

Byrne, J. and T. Austin. (1987). *Superman*, #2. DC Comics.

Coase, R. (1960). "The Problem of Social Cost." *Journal of Law and Economics* 3, 1–44.

Cronin, B. (2010, September 3). *Comic Book Legends Revealed*, #276. Accessed www.cbr.com/comic-book-legends-revealed-276/.

Fukuyama, F. (1995). *Trust: The Social Virtues and the Creation of Prosperity*. New York: Simon and Schuster, Inc.

Jain, A. K. (2002). "Corruption: A Review."*Journal of Economic Surveys* 15(1), 71–121.

Kelly, J., D. Mahnke and L. Bernejo. (2001). *Action Comics*, #775. DC Comics.

Layman, C. S. (2008). "Why Be a Superhero? Why Be Moral?" In T. Morris and M. Morris (Eds.), *Super-heroes and Philosophy: Truth, Justice, and the Socratic Way*. Chicago, Illinois: Open Court.

Loeb, J. and T. Sale. (1998). *Superman for All Seasons*. Burbank, California: DC Comics.

Maggin, E. and C. Swan. (1972). *Superman*, #247. DC Comics.

Mauro, P. (1995). "Corruption and Growth." *Quarterly Journal of Economics* 110(3), 681–712.

Maxwell, R. (Writer) and T. Carr (Director). (1952). "Superman on Earth [Television series episode]. In B. Luber (Executive Producer), *The Adventures of Superman*. Los Angeles, California: Superman Inc.

Millar, M. and D. Johnson. (2014). *Superman: Red Son*. Burbank, California: DC Comics.

Miller, F. (2016). *Batman: The Dark Knight Returns, 30th Anniversary Edition*. DC Comics.

Moore, A., B. Bolland, and J. Higgins. (1988). *The Killing Joke*. Burbank, California: DC Comics.

North, D. (1990). *Institutions, Institutional Change, and Economic Performance*. Cambridge: Cambridge University Press.

O'Neil, D. and C. Swan. (1971). *Superman*, #234. DC Comics.

Percy, B. and O. Schmidt. (2017). *Green Arrow*, #28. DC Comics.

Siegel, J. and J. Shuster. (1938). *Action Comics*, #1. DC Comics.

Solow, R. (1956). "A Contribution to the Theory of Economic Growth." *Quarterly Journal of Economics* 70(1): 65–94.

StraczynskiM. and C. Roberson. (2011). *Superman*, #713. DC Comics.

Taylor, T., J. Raapack and B. Redondo. (2016). *Injustice: Gods Among Us: Year One*. DC Comics.

Waid, M. and A. Ross. (2008). "Kingdom Come." In B. Kahan (Ed.), *Kingdom Come*. Burbank, California: DC Comics. Originals published in 1996.

PART III

Advanced

8

FROM THE COMIC BOOK TO THE REAL WORLD

The principal-agent problem and moral hazards when Iron Man flies over your backyard

Deborah Kozdras and Antoinette Criss

Comic book superheroes inspire the imaginations of readers. However, beyond where would you go, what would you do if you were given great superhero powers? And what would society do if the powers of a superhero like Iron Man were actually within reach? As the technology that underlies Marvel's armored Avenger gets closer to reality, the field of economics can help illuminate the issues we might face.

In comics, superhero powers come from a variety of sources including science experiments going wrong, magical means and innovation. In the latter category is Iron Man, a comic book superhero who derives his powers from his own technological ingenuity – something which places him close enough to our own reality to propel not just popularity, but inspiration. As Dunn (2010) noted, "the enduring appeal of Iron Man owes a great deal to how Tony Stark personifies the spectacular promise of technology to turn our dreams into reality, a promise that has stoked a fire in the bellies of countless men and women" (p. 8).

Though it is unlikely that we'll have to deal with aliens, super-powered mutants, Norse deities or students bitten by radioactive spiders anytime soon, innovations like Iron Man's suit are within the reach of today's technology. For example, the army constructed a new type of wearable armor – Tactical Assault Light Operator Suit (TALOS) – that is based on the Iron Man suit. The serial entrepreneur Elon Musk, who has been compared to Tony Stark, is rumored to be creating his own version of Iron Man's suit (Blumenthal, 2016). That means that the premise of Iron Man – the possibility that an unaccountable individual could wield superhuman powers derived from technology of their own invention – is a real possibility. So what concerns does that raise? What rights do society and government have relative to the individual intellectual property (IP) rights owner in a situation where the IP grants that person extraordinary abilities with broad social ramifications? What happens when an Iron Man prototype flies over your backyard?

The unintended consequences of technological innovation are a topic of interest to social scientists from various disciplines. Because Iron Man has been exploring these issues in comics and movies for more than 50 years, the stories provide a good template for understanding the issues and playing through different scenarios.

This chapter will explore Tony Stark, risk-taking inventor, as his character has evolved from comics to the big screen, paying particular attention to the nature of his inventions. We begin with the Iron Man origin story and particular aspects of the decision-making process, such as trade-offs, utility and rationality, that Tony Stark faced while creating his suit. Then we expand the lens to include the overall theme of information asymmetry, the principal-agent problem and moral hazards associated with superheroes in both the comics and the films. We follow this by asking at what point might it be appropriate for the government to step in to limit the actions of heroes. Finally, we will explore these issues as prototypes of the Iron Man suit are making appearances in the real world.

The origins of Iron Man

Iron Man debuted in 1963 in *Tales of Suspense* #39 (Lee & Lieber, 1963), part of the pantheon of Marvel superheroes co-created by Stan Lee and Jack Kirby. As Genter (2007) and Fellman (2010) have noted, the character was the product of Cold War-era anxieties, and drew many of its themes, characters and scenarios from the global competition between the United States, the Soviet Union, China and the war in Vietnam. Like many Marvel comics from this era, Iron Man appealed to young adults and college students, not just the traditional comics audience of young children.

Iron Man was an unusual archetype for a superhero. Tony Stark was a rich industrialist, who manufactured weapons for the military. In a biography, writer Stan Lee stated that he assumed his readership would initially hate the character: "You know what would be fun? Let's create a character who wouldn't have a chance to be a success right now and let's find a way to make him popular" (Lee & Mair, 2002, p. 160).

Like many Marvel characters, Iron Man's origin includes a tragic element that adds a human dimension to the fantasy story. The carefree industrialist Tony Stark is injured and kidnapped while deploying some of his weaponry in a war zone (Vietnam in the comics; Afghanistan in the movie). The enemy, a local warlord, forces him to develop a super-weapon for his army, in collaboration with another scientist who is also held hostage. Stark's heart was left vulnerable to a piece of shrapnel, embedded in his body during the attack. To prevent the shard from puncturing his heart, he and his colleague develop a magnetic field generator installed in his chest, which also powers a fearsome suit of armor that allows him to escape from his captors. The other scientist sacrifices himself to buy time to power up the suit. This noble gesture awakens a social conscience in Stark and sets him on his heroic path. However, from this point on, Stark is a slave to the technology that keeps him alive, and his secret prevents him from getting close to anyone else in his life. He is literally the rich playboy with a broken heart. The power of this story appealed not just to male superhero fans but to a new audience of women and girls.

Subsequent writers in comics and film developed the backstory even further. Current canon holds that the iron man with a wounded heart began life as a precocious child who was interested in technology and inventing. Tony Stark's father owned Stark Industries, a prominent US manufacturing firm. As a child, Tony enjoyed playing with and building machines. He graduated with two advanced degrees – electrical engineering and physics – from MIT, by the age of 19, after which he went to "work" for Stark Industries; however, he was more interested in living the rich, spoiled kid, playboy lifestyle than putting his engineering skills to work.

Tony's choices: tradeoffs, utility and irrational actors

While the intent of this chapter is to focus on what happens if superpowers are available to normal people, we want to warm up with some of the basic economic concepts that appear in Iron Man; these include: the trade-offs people face any time they make a choice, utility and the difficulties that economic theory has accounting for non-rational attributes such as hedonism, instinct and serendipity in analyzing those choices. Since those factors tend to play a large part in the decision-making of iconoclastic entrepreneurs, they are helpful in recognizing the issues that might come into play if a real inventor were to develop something like an Iron Man suit.

Economists are fond of saying that all choices involve trade-offs. By way of example, I might decide in the next hour to either read a comic book or watch a movie. I cannot do both simultaneously, so if I read a comic book I must sacrifice watching a movie – that's my trade-off. My time and attention are scarce, so if I use them to do one thing, I must give up something else. That next best option that you do not choose is referred to as an opportunity cost. Thus, the total cost of my choice includes not only what I pay when I select my main activity, but also the value of what I forego by passing up on other opportunities.

Microeconomic theory further holds that actors make their economic choices rationally, with a view toward maximizing utility. If I have chosen to read a comic book, then I must be doing so because I believe that activity yields the maximum utility (in this case, pleasure or information), and whatever I get from reading the comic outweighs the benefits of watching the movie.

While economists presume rationality, Stark's choices (and if we are to be honest, many of our own day-to-day choices) illustrate that people do not always make rational, utility-maximizing decisions. This is often the case in fiction, where poor decisions by various characters help drive the narrative, but it also rings true to life, especially in the cases of driven, idiosyncratic entrepreneurs and inventors. Despite Tony's potential and talent, he often decides to allocate his time to his playboy lifestyle, rather than using his engineering skills and developing the business skills necessary to operate Stark Industries. He focuses on maximizing his immediate pleasure, not future business success, and the costs turn out to be substantial. When his parents died in a car accident two years after his graduation, he was ill-equipped to take the reins of the company and had to rely on others. In some cases, that worked out; in others, there were unintended consequences.

One choice Stark made was to promote his secretary, Pepper Potts, to be his executive assistant.[1] This worked out well, despite being the product of impulse and instinct rather than deliberation. Pepper first appeared in *Tales of Suspense* #45 (Lee & Bernstein, 1963). After Pepper proved to have impressive business knowledge and skills, demonstrated when she noticed and fixed one of his accounting errors, Stark rewarded her with a promotion. Choosing Pepper – someone he could rely upon and trust – as his executive assistant, turned out to be a good choice even if it didn't appear rational and systematic when he made it. While Pepper took care of most of the daily tasks, Stark continued to lead his charmed life, occasionally making appearances at important functions. One was his ill-fated trip to the battle zone that resulted in his becoming Iron Man. Serendipity, both in stories and in the real world of economics, often plays more of a role than theory can account for.

Another consequence of Tony's choice to pursue a life of pleasure rather than business was to leave the management of Stark Industries in the hands of a caretaker CEO, Obadiah Stane. This, as we shall see, did not turn out so well.

Hidden agendas and information asymmetry

A possible problem with developing a superhero suit is that Stark decided to maintain his identity as Iron Man and use the technology benefits of his invention for the good of the public, but, like any good superhero, he opted at first to do so in secret because of the dangers inherent in having his adversaries know who he really was. This gave rise to a situation known in economic theory as information asymmetry: one person knows something that the other party doesn't.

Like irrational behavior, information asymmetry goes against another assumption of classical economics, which is that all parties to a transaction have perfect information to inform their rational, utility maximizing choices. As we have seen, decisions are not always rational, and neither is information always perfect. When information is withheld deliberately, even for good cause, the result is often distorted because the actors misidentify one another's motivations.

Superhero stories provide a good format for illustrating the problems of information asymmetry because the superhero protagonist often conceals his or her real identity. A superhero can act out of personal altruistic motives, higher purpose, obsession, vengeance or dozens of other reasons. Because the public at large does not have important information about the hero's true identity, they don't know those motivations in advance and can't make rational decisions about how to react to a super-powered actor in their midst, at least until the hero establishes a reputation. Likewise, because the people in Tony Stark's life don't know the full story of what happened during his kidnapping or his experiences as Iron Man, many of his actions as a businessman appear arbitrary and inexplicable according to the usual profit-maximizing calculus of capitalism, leading to consternation among his managers and investors. Unsurprisingly, one of the consequences of information asymmetry is less trust among partners, which increases the costs of doing business.

In Iron Man's case, this has important consequences. After his escape from captivity, Tony Stark, and Iron Man with him, began to evolve and see the wider implications of his actions in the world. Stark became a founding member of the Avengers, fighting alongside other superheroes: Thor, Ant-Man, the Wasp, the Hulk and Captain America. Later, Stark became affiliated with the anti-terrorist, super-spy agency S.H.I.E.L.D., which was co-founded by his father. But the major turning point in Stark's life came after he witnessed his weapons killing innocent civilians. That's when he decided to stop producing weapons, and devote resources to creating electronics and computer technology. This preference for gadgets over weaponry became a lasting theme in Iron Man stories. But if you were a shareholder in Stark Industries, not privy to the information and experiences informing Tony Stark's decision, you might well wonder why the company's CEO had decided to discontinue this lucrative line of business.

One person who took exception to this decision was Obadiah Stane, the caretaker CEO who ran the company while Tony was in his irresponsible playboy stage, but got pushed aside when the prodigal son assumed his role at the helm. In this case, Stane's opposition to Stark came down to a management principle known as fiduciary responsibility, where executives in a business are obliged first and foremost to the financial interests of shareholders. As a senior manager tasked with the goal of maximizing profits, Stane could not understand why Stark would abandon the easy money of developing weapons for global governments in favor of a riskier endeavor, providing low-cost alternative energy through his experimental ARC reactor (which also powered the Iron Man armor). Furthermore, Stane had undisclosed personal interests that were aligned with the goals of Stark Industries when it was in the weapons business, but were jeopardized by Stark's decision to move in another direction.

The conflict between Stark, acting out of secret motivations informed by his experiences as Iron Man, and Stane, ostensibly acting in the fiduciary interests of the company's other shareholders but also having hidden personal motives, illustrates another concept that often arises from information asymmetry: the principal-agent problem. Principals are actors with a stake in the outcome of a situation, such as the shareholders of a company. Because they can't be present to oversee every aspect of the operations of the company, they delegate that responsibility to agents: executives like Stane who are paid to make sure shareholder interests are being served. The problem occurs when the incentives for agents and principals are misaligned: that is, when the agent has interests that diverge from those of the principal, or the principals have objectives that they don't share with agents. A lot of poor decisions in business, military operations, government and other complex multiparty transactions occur because of an information asymmetry between agents and principals. Both sides may be acting in good faith, but without full information, suboptimal outcomes often result.

The principal-agent problem aggravated the already tense situation at Stark Industries when Tony fell off the wagon: he resumed his reckless lifestyle, and eventually decided to give up opposing Stane. As a result, when a villain attacked Stark Industries, Stark was too drunk to fight. In a moment of clarity, he revealed his secret identity to his friend, Marine James "Rhodey" Rhodes, who used the Iron Man suit to defeat the villain. Stark fell more deeply into depression, told Rhodey to keep the armor, ignored Stark Industries and drank himself out of his fortune until his assets were frozen. That left Stane free to realize his agenda: he turned on Stark, took over the company and renamed it Stane International. Once again, Rhodey came to the rescue and prevented Stane from keeping the Iron Man technology; Stark maintained control of his invention.

Iron Man's backstory has changed slightly over the years to keep up with the times and as the Iron Man comics have evolved. While the antagonists have changed, the information asymmetry issues remained the same, and so did the problems of proper decision-making in an environment of low information, complicated principal-agent relationships and unclear personal motivations. In the next section, we will explore the tensions arising from those issues in the context of Tony Stark's role as an industrialist and corporate executive.

Tony's a danger to us all: moral hazard

This brings us to the crux of the economic question of this chapter. If a super-powered suit were available, what could possibly go wrong? The first answer to this question revolves around another economic concept that plays a role in superhero stories generally, and Iron Man in particular: moral hazard. Moral hazard arises from a situation where an actor is indemnified from the consequences of making a bad choice, but gets to collect the benefits of a good choice or investment. In short, individuals will alter their behavior regarding how much risk to take because they do not bear the cost if things go awry.

As a rational, utility-maximizing capitalist, if there is no downside, then why not make a big bet? For example, the primary impetus for the financial crisis of the late 2000s was the belief that some financial institutions were too big to fail. Because there were no true consequences for following unwise lending practices, the banks continued to engage in making loans to high-risk individuals. Eventually the sustained lack of consequences encouraged a cascade of risky decisions that increased systemic instability. The result was a near collapse of the financial system as a whole, something far worse than the individual failures of poor investments if they had been allowed to go bad through the ordinary work of markets and regulators. In this case, the downside risk of making bad loans was covered for the financial industry. The result was, predictably, that firms took more risks. High risks mean potentially high reward, and if someone else bears the risk of failure, then it's full steam ahead.

Connecting this to the principal agent problem of the prior section, moral hazards sometimes occur in situations when agents act in a reckless manner, because principals do not hold them accountable. They can also occur when either an agent or a principal is placed in a situation where they are forced to assume more risk than they can reasonably cover: for example, when a superhero puts lives and property at risk in the course of confronting a super-powered threat. We want to trust the superhero, but the community, not the superhero, will bear the consequences of any risks the hero takes. We are unwilling principals; the hero is our unaccountable agent. If pressed, the hero may rationally maximize the chances for his own survival rather than the preservation of innocent life or property. This is the premise for the Marvel comic *Civil War* (Millar and McNiven, 2009).[2] The story begins with some C-list heroes filming their apprehension of a group of escaped villains for a reality television series. It is clear the heroes are nonchalant about the dangers such an encounter might entail. Unfortunately, things spin out of control; one of the villains explodes himself (he can reform so it doesn't bother him) and kills hundreds at a nearby public school. At the funeral, Tony Stark is confronted by the angry mother of one of the victims. She blames Stark for the death of her son. By funding and encouraging the action of heroes, Stark is acting as the unconcerned agent, while the people, the principals, bear the costs. If the population really wants the services provided by heroes though, there might be another way to achieve that end.

Maybe Tony's not so bad: public goods

O'Roark (2017) noted that superheroes provide public goods – goods that many people can use at the same time without limiting the benefits to any of the users, even if they don't pay for them. This is true of Iron Man to be sure. When he saves the day, everyone in New York City and around the world benefits. No one's saving is made less valuable because someone else was also saved. That means Iron Man's actions as non-rival in consumption, a precondition for the provision of a public good. To be a public good though, it must also be true that the hero cannot exclude people from being saved, even if they do not pay. In superhero stories, people are saved regardless of how much they pay for hero services. In fact, people almost never pay superheroes for doing good deeds. Hero work isn't done on a contract basis, primarily because a hero can't (or won't) force someone to pay. The hero cannot not save someone if they don't pay, especially if the threat is an alien invasion of Earth.

However, there are costs and risks associated with the creation of public goods, particularly those that result purely through the initiative of a single actor, without a deliberative process or public participation. In comics and movies, Iron Man has invented his armor and monopolizes its use. He chooses when to step into a situation, but as we just noted, it is the general public who will likely be the ones bearing the unintended consequences of his actions.

Usually, inventors bear risks during the development of a product or an idea. The kinks, along with the risks inherent in the product, are worked out before bringing a creation to market. Additionally, any financial burden accompanying the development fall on the inventor. Because an individual has borne those risks privately, the fruits of that labor belong to the inventor, including the discretion of if, when and how the invention should be brought to market.

Superhero innovation is a bit different. Like most entrepreneurs, Tony Stark must take risks to bring his ideas to fruition. The difference between him and, say, Henry Ford is that Stark's invention (his suit, not the output of Stark Industries) does not arise from a profit motive, but from an altruistic desire to serve the public good. His suit allows him to battle supervillains and aliens – probably a good thing on balance, since ordinary humans are not well equipped for those sorts of challenges. But the ramifications of failure are potentially disastrous, not just for Stark, but for innocent bystanders. Crack the pages of an Iron Man comic or watch any of the movies: the destruction of property caused by these battles is tremendous.

Innovation in the superhero world sometimes has dire implications for many people who are just standing around, minding their own business. In those cases, what is the proper policy approach? Does government have a right to regulate the use of this technology even though it is the property and invention of a private individual, or can they go a step further? Can government take the invention through eminent domain in an attempt to protect the general public, or to scale up the technology for its own use?

Taking Tony's toys away: eminent domain

This question of eminent domain emerged in the *Iron Man 2* movie (Feige and Favreau, 2010). At the end of *Iron Man* (Marvel Studios and Favreau, 2008), Tony Stark revealed himself to the world as the armored avenger, doing away with certain problems of information asymmetry but raising other, thornier issues. Now that everyone knew this brilliant but unpredictable and erratic individual possessed such enormous power, how did that change the relationship between the public (the principal) and the superhero (our agent)? The government, media and the general public pressured Stark to share the trade secrets of his technology with the military. Justin Hammer – CEO of rival Hammer Industries – was in a race to build his own suit of armor and gain his share of the military market. Another character in the movie, a U.S. senator, was eager to subject the Iron Man suit to eminent domain.

This senator used the excuse of Stark's drinking problems to argue that Stark would be more likely to act irresponsibly while using the Iron Man suit. The senator has a Constitutional role as an agent acting on behalf of the public that requires him to find ways to protect the public from the unintended consequences of Stark's actions. He can also claim that the benefits of the suit are a public good, and that as a result, the suit should be under the control of the government, not an individual. And because the senator is a representative of the government, he has a tool to accomplish this goal – eminent domain.

Through the Fifth Amendment to the U.S. Constitution, the government is required to provide just compensation to the owner of private property they wish to use for public use. Air, water and land rights are subject to eminent domain because they are often needed for transportation projects that will benefit a multitude of people. Even so, taking property comes with risks. Property rights are central to the ability of markets to function well (Alchian 2008). Private property rights must be exclusive, transferable and enforceable for individuals to correctly determine the value of private property. If government can simply take property, even with cause, it interferes with the market mechanism.

Eminent domain creates a problem of valuation. In a free market, value is mutually agreed to by buyer and seller. If the seller does not offer a satisfactory price, the buyer can walk away and look for a better offer. But if the buyer – in this case the government – has the legal authority to compel the sale, then the transaction is unlikely to realize full value for the seller.

That asymmetry in the power dynamic can create a moral hazard for the public if the government abuses its authority. There is no downside risk for government in using its eminent domain power unjustly in any single transaction to deprive an individual in the name of the common good. However, over time, if people recognize their property rights are at risk because of the arbitrary or frequent use of eminent domain, what happens to the willingness of individuals to develop valuable private property? Individuals who fear that their inventions will be taken through eminent domain will be less likely to invest time and effort in development of new ideas if they also fear that governments will try to undervalue their investment.

Can the government confiscate the Iron Man suit? By law, personal property and intangible property, like patents, trade secrets and copyrights, may be taken through condemnation proceedings (Mufson 1985). There has been some debate whether the Iron Man suit involved a patent or a trade secret. In the movie, Pepper Potts demanded action from patent attorneys. However, if Stark had patented the information, the government would have had access to the designs through the United States Patent and Trademark Office.

Therefore, the suit might better be considered a trade secret. Stark had the legal right to recourse; the law protects both patents and trade secrets. Although he kept his trade secret, that did not prevent other, more nefarious characters, from copying his design. Patent laws only work for people who are legally playing the game. So, when Rhodey tried to confiscate an Iron Man suit, presumably under military orders, was he breaking the law? Was he working as an agent for the military? What were the intentions of the military? What happens to the free market when the military extends its authority over personal property in this way?

This is a difference between the films and the original comics, which emphasized the importance of inventors being able to profit from their inventions. In *Iron Man 2*, after the senator demanded Stark hand over the Iron Man technology, the government took it from him and turned it over to a rival corporation, who proceeded to fill a defense contract. The U.S. government then pressured Stark to hand over secret specifications of the Iron Man suit.

Is there a rationale to why a government would want to confiscate Stark's designs? We now come full circle and explore the principal-agent problem and moral hazard of Stark's evolving invention.

Does Tony play well with others? Unintended consequences and the challenges of managing disruptive innovation

From its beginnings, Iron Man explored the high-tech world of robotics, computers, cybernetics and other advanced machinery. The armor's gadgets and weapons evolved with the need to solve particular problems, reflecting Stark's inventor/entrepreneur persona. What began as a fantasy concept in the 1960s now struggles to stay a step ahead of fast-moving trends in the real world. That raises not just economic questions but philosophical ones as well.

Meadows (2010) claims that in cases where humans wear the Iron Man suit, and control the machines and weapons with their minds, the line between a human and robot is blurred. More germane to the issue at hand, the more autonomous the suit becomes, the further the principal-agent problem is amplified. Over the years, Stark created suits that could be worn by humans, in addition to remote controlled Iron Man robots. In the movies, these autonomous robots were controlled by Stark's computer system called J.A.R.V.I.S. – Just a Rather Very Intelligent System – named after Edwin Jarvis, the butler who worked for Stark's father.

The role played by J.A.R.V.I.S. – an AI so advanced that it eventually manifested as the android hero The Vision in *Avengers 2* – raises an interesting proposition: who is responsible if the computer is hacked? Is it Stark, who invented the technology and monopolizes its use? Is it the hacker? Or is it the AI itself, which may be complicit in its own corruption, as was the case with Ultron, a Stark-created construct that went off the rails and decided the best way to keep the world safe was to eliminate humans.

This isn't a new problem. No inventor, no matter how farsighted, can foresee every possible use of his or her invention. Inventions often have unintended consequences as the economic systems that grow up around them run counter to the goals for which they were invented. Consider Eli Whitney's cotton gin. Although it was invented to automate the labor-intensive process of separating cotton from the seeds, it ended up increasing the demand for land and slave labor because it made cotton-growing more profitable than ever.

The point is, even ideas that inspire our imagination, like the armor that powers Iron Man, may have some significant drawbacks in the real world. And, thanks to intrepid inventors, we are getting closer and closer to finding out what they might be.

The evolution of Iron Man: from fiction to fact

In 2010, in the book *We, Robot: Skywalker's Hand, Blade Runners, Iron Man, Slutbots, And How Fiction Became Fact*, Mark Meadows predicted that the world probably would not see an Iron Man suit in the next decade, but we would see "something quite different, and probably more lethal. Also more humane" (Meadows, 2010, p. 94). He forecasted these new technologies would be designed for military use and disabled individuals. In the article, he described some early forerunners of a real-life Iron Man-like suit. For example, in 2008, Honda presented a device that could help support body weight, relieve knee stress and increase walking strength. Meadows also discussed the Human Universal Load Carrier (HULC), an exoskeleton created by the Association of the U.S. Army (AUSA) that can help a soldier carry up to 200 pounds.

It appears, however, that technology has developed faster than Meadows predicted. In 2016, various news sources reported on a tweet from Elon Musk, chief executive of Tesla, after he met with U.S. Secretary of Defense Ash Carter. Musk's tweet, "Something about a flying metal suit," led to much online chatter. However, a Department of Defense spokesman said that the closed-door meeting was about the current state of innovation in technology. Various media outlets discussed these developments. For example, in *Popular Mechanics,* Price (2014) asked if Hollywood could teach the Pentagon how to build a real Iron Man suit. In a CNN report, Diamond and Starr (2016) announced a "liquid body armor" under development by scientists at Massachusetts Institute of Technology (MIT). The armor – perhaps inspired by Stark's liquid armor in the *Marvel NOW Initiative* 2013 comics – will transform from liquid to solid. Then, in 2017, a variety of media outlets (c.f. Ernst, 2017) reported that by 2018 the military U.S. Special Operations Command planned to have prototypes of their Tactical Light Operator Suits (TALOS), which include exoskeletons and strength increasing systems. In *Popular Mechanics,* Mizokami (2017) also discussed the TALOS suit, in addition to a "Star Wars" inspired armor being created by Russia.

These inventions, superhero suits come to life, beg for discussions of moral hazards. Moral hazards result from the change in incentives people face. The protection offered by the suit is the incentive change that leads people to act like heroes. Then they act in more dangerous ways and possibly create unintended consequences for everyone else. The moral hazards experienced in comics and movies as a result of the Iron Man suit, could manifest in the real world.

What might happen when the general public decides to create an Iron Man prototype? In 2017, Richard Browning, an inventor and entrepreneur from the United Kingdom, created a YouTube video of himself flying around in his homemade prototype of an Iron Man suit. According to *Wired* (Manthorpe, 2017), the suit cost him 40,000 euros to create and is powered by six small jet engines. The suit includes gadgets including a Sony heads-up display. Browning, who called the suit Daedalus, after the mythological Greek inventor, noted plans for future suit enhancements. Like Stark, in addition to being an inventor, he is also an entrepreneur; he is already developing a business that will include a "Tony Stark lab, garage thing" where he can do flight training for wealthy people.

While Stark kept his trade secret to himself and tried to limit the use of his suit, as much as he could, to people with responsible goals, what happens when the general public is able to buy a suit? Can the average citizen be trusted to engage in ethical behavior?

Average citizens are engaged in superhero-like activities. According to the *Superheroes* documentary in 2011 (James and Barnett, 2011), there are over 300 registered Real Life Superheroes in the United States. Most of these individuals operate like vigilantes, claiming to keep the world safe from criminals and other evildoers. Who should be able to buy a weapon-enhanced Iron Man-like suit with the ability to fly around downtown? If these purchases are not limited, then the general public may bear the costs imposed by the use of the suit by those who cannot control it well.

And what about killer robots, like the autonomous Iron Man suits that are remotely controlled by Stark's computer system J.A.R.V.I.S.? In August 2017, media outlets reported that Elon Musk had something to say about lethal autonomous robotic weapons. On CNN, Pham (2017) reported that Musk is part of a group of 100 robotics and artificial intelligence experts who have proposed calling on the United Nations to impose a ban on autonomous weapons. According to the *Washington Post* (Holley, 2017) a letter, which included signatures from dozens of organizations in nearly 30 countries, discussed weapons of terror and weapons that can be hacked to behave in dangerous ways. Holley (ibid.) also discussed a report that was released following the 2017 AI for Good Global Summit. Based on a speech in the Plenary session, Izumi Nakamitsu (2017), UN High Representative for Disarmament Affairs (UNODA), noted that although technology has been advancing rapidly, regulation has not kept adequate pace. Nakamitsu described how in some global military hot spots, like the demilitarized zone between North and South Korea, "guard robots" are used as surveillance tools. While it has not been enacted, these robots currently have the *capacity* for an autonomous mode.

Just as with a "manned" Iron Man suit, autonomous killer robots may act in ways unintended by their inventors, raising the principal-agent problem and related moral hazards. However, these problems may be exacerbated by the fact that while the "actor" in this case is non-human, the actions impose costs on humans. It's one thing to be dealing with people with nefarious aims, but quite another when we are dealing with robots. These robots, which may only be able to recognize whether or not orders are being followed, do not have any sense of whether the orders cause harm.

Coming soon?

When the lines blur between fact and fiction, and comic book creations appear in real life, we are confronted with real-life decision-making. Economics gives us one way to analyze choices. Within the scope of choice making, economists argue that rational choices are ones for which the benefits exceed the costs. We expect people to understand that choices involve tradeoffs and to weigh those tradeoffs appropriately. As we have seen, however, decision-makers may not always be able to completely identify the benefits and costs associated with their actions. In these cases, we are faced with unintended consequences – external costs that were not taken into account when the original decision was made.

Of course, to make good decisions requires good information, and that isn't always readily available. Information asymmetry can prevent decision makers from choosing well. This is further complicated when agents, purportedly acting for a principal, decide to follow their own agenda. If the agent's interests aren't fully aligned with those of the principal, decisions will be made that are not in the best interest of all.

In the case of superheroes this can be a particularly problematic occurrence. When heroes are indemnified against responsibility for their actions because they are providing public goods, then they may take more risks than are good for society. This moral hazard problem then requires a government solution in order to bring the interests of society and the hero together.

Iron Man is in many respects a morality play. Tony Stark is an innovative genius, but his character flaws leave the world around him prone to suffer the consequences of his excesses; yet, as the character has aged, he has become more socially aware. His role as advocate for the Superhuman Registration Act cemented his status in post-party boy life. However, as we have shown, Iron Man is not just a redemption story. It is a microcosm of the questions real world decision makers must address regarding the advance of technology.

So what happens if an Iron Man suit becomes available in the real world? Economics would say the response is a function of the choices society makes. If society values the safety of individuals, then pressure to regulate the use and the availability of the suit will be great. If society values the contribution of crime deterrence that the superhero provides, then society will choose to be less heavy handed, tacitly encouraging individuals to develop skills in using the suit. Economies based on markets will insist on preserving private property rights to the intellectual property (i.e. the suit). Economies that are more command based will be more inclined to have governments confiscate this type of intellectual property in order to control its use. To wit, is the suit more like military weaponry or a handgun? The answer to that question is an indication of how much government control a society of superheroes might face.

Notes

1 Pepper eventually becomes the CEO of Stark Industries.
2 The movie *Civil War* has a different beginning that is not nearly as conducive to the discussion at hand.

References

Alchian, A. (2008). Property rights. *The Concise Encyclopedia of Economics*. Retrieved from www.econlib.org/library/Enc/PropertyRights.html

Blumenthal, E. (2016, June 9). Elon Musk may or may not actually be Iron Man. *USA Today*. Retrieved from www.usatoday.com/story/tech/2016/06/09/elon-musk-may-may-not-actually-iron-man/85641024/

Diamond, J. and B. Starr. (2016, April 11). U.S. military is on its way to getting its Iron Man. Retrieved from www.cnn.com/2015/10/06/politics/special-operations-iron-man-talos-suit/index.html

Dunn, G. (2010). The Stark madness of technology. In M. White (Ed.), *Iron Man and philosophy: facing the Stark reality* (pp. 7–24). Hoboken, New Jersey: John Wiley & Sons Inc.

Ernst, D. (2017, February 16). SOCOM expects 'Iron Man' suit testing by summer 2018. *Washington Times*. Retrieved from www.washingtontimes.com/news/2017/feb/16/special-operations-command-expects-talos-iron-man-/

Feige, K. (Producer) and J. Favreau (Director). (2010) *Iron Man 2* [Motion Picture].

Fellman, P. (2010). Iron Man: America's cold war champion and charm against the communist menace. *Voces Novae: Chapman University Historical Review* 1(2), 11–22.

Genter, R. (2007). With great power comes great responsibility: Cold war culture and the birth of Marvel Comics. *The Journal of Popular Culture* 40(6), 953–979.

Holley, P. (2017, August 21). Elon Musk calls for ban on killer robots before weapons of terror are unleashed. *Washington Post*. Retrieved from www.washingtonpost.com/news/innovations/wp/2017/08/21/elon-musk-calls-for-ban-on-killer-robots-before-weapons-of-terror-are-unleashed/?utm_term=.46cd782dcaab

James, T. (Producer) and M. Barnett (Director). (2011). *Superheroes* [Motion Picture].

Lee, S. and R. Bernstein. (1963). *Tales of Suspense*, #45. Marvel Comics.

Lee, S. and L. Lieber. (1963). *Tales of Suspense*, #39. Marvel Comics.

Lee, S. and G. Mair. (2002). *Excelsior!: The amazing life of Stan Lee*. New York: Simon & Schuster.

Manthorpe, R. (2017). The real-life Iron Man: watch inventor Richard Browning 'fly' in his jet-powered suit. *Wired*. Retrieved from www.wired.co.uk/article/real-life-iron-man-richard-browning.

Marvel Studios (Producer) and J. Favreau (Director). (2008) *Iron Man* [Motion Picture].

Meadows, M. (2010). *We, Robot: Skywalker's Hand, Blade Runners, Iron Man, Slutbots, and How Fiction Became Fact*. Lanham MD: Roman and Littlefield.

Millar, M. and S. McNiven. (2009). *Civil War*. New York: Marvel Worldwide, Inc.

Mizokami, K. (2017, July 5). Russia unveils 'Star Wars' armor for infantry. *Popular Mechanics*. Retrieved from www.popularmechanics.com/military/weapons/a27173/russia-star-wars-suit-infantry/

Mufson, E. (1985). Jurisdictional limitations on intangible property in eminent domain: Focus on the Indianapolis Colts. *Indiana Law Journal* 60(2). Retrieved from www.repository.law.indiana.edu/cgi/viewcontent.cgi?article=2178&context=ilj

Nakamitsu, I. (2017, June 7). *AI for Global Good Summit Plenary 1: State of Play*. Retrieved from https://s3.amazonaws.com/unoda-web/wp-content/uploads/2017/06/HR-AI-summit-remarks-June-2017.pdf.

O'Roark, B. (2017). Super-economics man! Using superheroes to teach economics, *Journal of Economics Teaching* 2 (1), 51–67. Retrieved from http://downloads.journalofeconomicsteaching.org/2/1/1-4.pdf

Pham, S. (2017). Elon Musk backs call for global ban on killer robots. Retrieved from http://money.cnn.com/2017/08/21/technology/elon-musk-killer-robot-un-ban/index.html

Price, E. (2014, July 11). Can Hollywood teach the Pentagon to build a real Iron Man suit? *Popular Mechanics*. Retrieved from www.popularmechanics.com/military/research/a10846/can-the-military-really-build-iron-man-16975296/

9

THE SHADOW VS. BATMAN

Contrasting approaches to "producing" justice

John R. Swinton

An economic lesson common to just about any introduction to economics class is how producers decide what inputs to use when turning out their goods or services. Like consumers, producers have choices to make in the marketplace after they decide what it is they intend to make. Classroom presentations of these choices often simplify the problem to a decision between two inputs: labor and capital. For example, a rug maker in Afghanistan may find capital hard to come by but workers readily available. A carpet maker in Dalton, Georgia may have plenty of machinery but relatively few people willing to work at minimum wage. Both producers will bring floor covering to the market, just in different ways. While the example may start as an interesting story, neither input is endowed with much character as simplification and homogenization trump nuance and realism in the classroom. Soon the flavor of the story is lost. To be sure, this is done in an attempt to clarify the producer's problem for students new to the subject by simplifying the choice to its barest elements, but the effort to simplify can leave the subject short on punch and a little dry. To expand output the manager of a firm faces the mundane decision of whether to add another worker or instead employ another unit of capital. This is hardly a choice that inspires interest.

Instead, consider the trade-offs involved when super heroes make the same type of decision. To battle villains, heroes need to put some thought into their strategy. In this chapter, I compare the approaches of the Shadow and Batman to fighting crime. Both are heroes who originated just before the advent of what is now considered the Golden Age of comics (1938–1954 according to Misiroglu, 2012). Both characters made their way into popular culture by meting out justice where police officers could not freely operate; however, both approach their avocations in distinctly different ways. The differences between the choices the two vigilantes make are illustrative of the labor/capital choice all producers face, implying that the rudiments of such decisions are universal: even comic book heroes follow the same economic principles the rest of us do.

In the following section I provide a little background information about both characters and their treatment in the various media forms in which they have appeared. While Batman is culturally ubiquitous, it has been a while since the Shadow was a major figure in the popular zeitgeist. Following this introduction, I review the basic economic model of the producer's optimal decision process when it comes to selecting inputs. I then highlight what we might consider our two heroes' production functions. While the Shadow relies heavily on labor to accomplish his "production," Batman leans almost exclusively on capital. The reason is Kent Allard (later Lamont Cranston), the alter ego of the Shadow, has an uncanny ability to surround himself with loyal followers. In contrast, while Bruce Wayne, aka Batman, is endowed with almost unlimited wealth giving him easy access to all the crime-fighting contraptions imaginable, he finds personal relationships difficult. I use the two characters to illustrate that their optimal approaches to fighting crime mirror the decision making of everyday producers.

Two of the oldest American comic book heroes: a little introduction

The Shadow and Batman first appear in the earliest years of comic books. Each character was incredibly successful allowing them a much longer life than most of the early creations who fell by the wayside. The two characters are essentially the same. Both are detectives par excellence, and as such, they are both trying to accomplish the same basic task – fight crime. The differences in their techniques highlight the fact that there is often more than one way to accomplish a goal.[1]

The Shadow

To understand how the character of the Shadow becomes reliant on labor to help him fight crime it is useful to review his history. The Shadow debuted on the radio in 1930 as the narrator for the Street & Smith Detective Story Magazine Hour. The object of the radio broadcast was to advertise the publisher's *Detective Story Magazine* pulp publication. In contrast to comic books, pulp fiction was text-driven which translated well to radio. As the popularity of the Shadow grew, listeners insisted he have his own stories. In 1931, the editors of *Detective Story Magazine* pressed Walter Gibson into service to write stories for *The Shadow* ("A Brief History of the Shadow," n.d.). Both Gibson's pulp stories and the radio broadcasts became incredibly popular, and the radio broadcasts would run (off and on) until 1957 under various sponsorships. The Shadow flourished with radio, and while he has made occasional appearances since 1957, including movies in 1958 and an ill-fated 1994 remake, the Shadow has yet to return to his former glory.

Despite the volume of story lines and interpretations of the Shadow available, fans have only a limited back story from which to draw. Even though one man, Walter Gibson, is responsible for most of what we know about the Shadow's world, the origin story he created was inconsistent. We know the Shadow was a World War I flying ace known as the Black Eagle and an adventurer named Kent

Allard; he served as a master spy for Tsar Nicholas, the last Tsar of Russia, before the Bolshevik Revolution; he amassed a fortune in gold in South America ("The Shadow," 2017) and he has a fondness for the Far East – Tibet in some publications, Shambalah in others.

During his travels, he acquires the ability to "cloud men's minds" which enables him to either go unnoticed as he gathers intelligence or intercede in order to bring villains to justice – all unseen. This trick of the trade also bestows upon him an uncanny ability to hypnotize people. Other than his spy craft, the Shadow appears to have few other powers. He is credited with a nearly photographic memory, the ability to manipulate his voice and abnormal strength ("The Shadow," 2017). He is sometimes credited with the ability to levitate, but under most occasions he is simply good at scaling walls (with the aid of suction cups). His only unusual aid is his pair of fire opal or girasol rings which are said to augment his mental abilities. The first was a gift from Tsar Nicholas for his services prior to the fall of the Romanovs. The second (which is said to be a mate to the first) was recovered in the jungles of South America.

The Shadow's costume is simple: a black trench coat or Inverness coat often depicted as being lined in red, a red scarf that covers all but his eyes and aquiline nose, and a black fedora. Underneath the coat is a black suit. His chosen weapons are equally unassuming but effective: a pair of .45-caliber M1911 semi-automatic pistols or a pair of LAR Grizzly .45-caliber Win Mag pistols ("The Shadow," 2017). As far as equipment is concerned, very little stands out. The Shadow travels in a cab, a limousine or a gyrocopter. Communications are transmitted by way of a private radio tower. For the world of radio and pulp fiction, these suffice. What sets the Shadow apart, however, is his network of agents.

When Allard settled in the US after World War I he assumed other men's identities to gather information or work his way into various criminals' confidences. Primarily, he assumes the identity of Lamont Cranston.[2] In the very first episodes (both print and radio) the Shadow starts building his network of agents. The Shadow prevents Harry Vincent from committing suicide in *Shadow Magazine #1* (Gibson and Wert, 1931). Mr. Vincent then becomes one of the Shadow's more versatile agents. Other agents quickly follow: Moe Shrevnitz, cabbie and limousine driver, who gathers intelligence on the streets; Clyde, the reporter, who feeds leads to the Shadow; Burbank, the switchboard and short-wave radio operator, who gets information to where it needs to be; Jerico Druke, an African American strongman, who provides extra muscle when it is needed; and Margo Lane, the girl friend to Lamont Cranston and one of the few agents to know the Shadow's real identity. This is just the tip of the iceberg. Each adventure calls for new supporting characters.[3]

Typically, the Shadow recruited his agents from the leagues of people he has helped. In this way, he methodically built up a loyal network of willing assistants who were deeply indebted to him. One can think of these agents as being inexpensive inputs to the Shadow's operation. From time to time he also enlists those who were being menaced by particular villains as part of a plan to bring those villains to justice. For those operatives who remained in the Shadow's services, he offered financial compensations while allowing them the freedom to maintain their daily routines until called upon to serve.

Taken as a whole, the Shadow's network of agents proves to be his biggest asset. They ultimately provide the critical elements of his crime-fighting efforts. They gather information and get resources to where they are needed when they are needed. Without his agents, the Shadow would lack the information he needs to fight crime. Either he would have to gather that information on his own, taking up valuable time, or find another line of work.

Batman

Bob Kane and Bill Finger introduced Batman in *Detective Comics* #27 in 1939 (Kane and Finger, 1939). According to Misiroglu (2012), Kane often credited Douglas Fairbank's performance as Zorro and Michelangelo's sketches of flying machines for his take on the Batman look, but undoubtedly Gibson's Shadow also inspired Finger's approach to the stories ("Secret Origins of Batman," 2007). The title was instantly popular and soon came to dominate *Detective Comics*. By 1940, Batman had his own title publication. Batman has been a title character in one form or another continuously ever since.

Over the years, however, the treatment of the Batman character has varied dramatically, both in comics and on screen. In the early editions, Batman was a steely detective who often operated well outside of acceptable police practices and typically alone. Later, the emphasis on Batman's solitary crusade against crime was softened as he became a father figure to his ward, Dick Grayson, better known as Robin. Attempts to humanize Batman's image came to an end in the 1980s as various projects including Frank Miller's *Dark Knight* series returned Batman to his singular devotion to fighting crime.

Like the Shadow, the character of Batman begins his career as more of a detective than crime fighter. Keeping with the pulp stories popular at the time, Batman often dealt harshly with the criminals he did catch. Through *Detective Comics* #33 (Kane, Fox, Finger, and Moldoff, 1939), Batman regularly carried and used guns (Whitbrook, 2014). In fact, until issue #33 there is little to distinguish Batman from other title characters. But *Detective Comics* #33 introduces the beginning of Batman's backstory – Joe Chill's cold-blooded murder of Bruce Wayne's parents before the child's very eyes. From this brief incident, readers gain insight into Batman's often-times grim, single-minded pursuit of the criminal element in Gotham City. Readers also come to understand that, as an orphan, Bruce might prefer to fight crime alone. Other than his childhood trauma, however, the comic books offer little about how Bruce made the transformation from grieving orphan to Batman. In two panels in *Detective Comics* #33, we learn that Bruce devotes his time to honing his mind and body to become an exceptional crime fighter. In the same issue, Bruce decides to take on the persona of the bat to play upon criminals' superstitious nature. Later versions of Batman's origin story in different media outlets play with and expand upon these themes.

One constant in the depictions of Batman over the years is his reliance on state-of-the-art gadgets. Initially, Kane and Finger depicted Batman with a utility belt – a costume feature that survived in one form or another throughout the various manifestations of the caped crusader. In the pouches of the belt were contraptions such as Batarangs (a variation on a boomerang), Bat-ropes, a micro-camera, a tape recorder, gas pellets, acetylene torch, bolas, respirator, first aid kit, pen light, Bat-cuffs and – in the campy 1966 film version – Bat-shark repellent (Daniels, 1999; Greenberger, 2008; Misiroglu, 2012). The main take away is that Batman always has at his fingertips the tools necessary for the job.

The Bat-cave was an early fixture in the Batman world, dating back to the first movie serials. It can be thought of as an extension of Batman's utility belt. While it provides a sanctuary for Batman, it is a place to store his ever-increasing list of crime-fighting tools. First, it housed Batman's many vehicles. The Bat-mobile – made famous in the 1960s television series and radically updated in the 1990s and 2000s – is probably the most iconic vehicle in the comic world. But there are also Bat-copters, Bat-boats, Bat-planes and vehicles of every nature all stored in the cave under Wayne Manor. Batman's crime lab is anchored by the Bat-computer which has always been depicted as beyond state-of-the-art. Batman's many different outfits are also warehoused in the Bat-cave, along with artifacts from many cases, to the point where, eventually, there would have to be an annex to the Bat-cave to hold not just the equipment Batman used but many of the souvenirs from his exploits.

In contrast to Batman's impressive catalog of vehicles, weapons and other aids, his success at working with others is muted. He prefers to work alone and at night. Writing for *The Atlantic,* Warshak (2014) undertakes a psychological analysis of both Batman and Bob Kane. Like his creation, Kane endured a violent childhood trauma. At age 15 he was brutally beaten by a Bronx gang. In Warshak's analysis, Batman is an attempt by Kane to work through his memories of this beating. The result is a character bent on vengeance but a loner, largely unable to connect with other people. An economist with a discerning eye would note that this increases Batman's cost of working with other crime fighters and makes the need for equipment obvious.

A limited number of people help Batman in his efforts. There is, first and foremost, Alfred J. Pennyworth, Bruce Wayne's trusted manservant. Next are various incarnations of Robin. Police Commissioner James Gordon is a sometimes ally and sometimes foe who must constantly struggle with Batman's methodology. In the 1970s Lucius Fox was introduced to ease the burden of creating new crime-fighting gadgets. Nevertheless, most of Batman's (and Bruce Wayne's) relationships are difficult and rarely work out well. Even his attempts to work with other superheroes (such as in the Justice League of America or JLA) rarely last long. This difficulty is highlighted in the JLA *Tower of Babel* story arc where Batman, through a combination of his mistrust of others and hyper-vigilance, puts the lives of the other Justice League members at risks by cataloging their weaknesses (Waid and Scott, 2000). We are left with a character who, backed by an unparalleled arsenal, prefers to grimly stalk his quarries alone through the night.

Basic economic idea: consider productivity and cost

Economic educators confront numerous confounding issues when contemplating how to teach production decisions. There are normally three basic objectives when introducing production: Explain how producers decide how much to produce; explain how producers decide what to charge (if they have the opportunity to select a price); and explain how producers decide upon the best combination of inputs to use when producing their product. The first decision follows a simple rule (at least at an introductory level) – produce up to the point where the additional cost of one more unit of output is equal to the additional revenue it generates. The basic idea is that if the additional benefits of something exceed the additional costs, do it.

The second decision depends upon the type of market the producer inhabits. In a competitive market the price is dictated by the market. In a less than competitive market producers may be able to charge different prices. If a producer is given the opportunity to select price because she has some market power, she will take that into consideration when looking at the additional benefits and costs of producing one more unit of output – too high a price and people will not buy her product, too low a price and she misses out on potential revenue. Of the three issues, the third one, how to produce, is probably the most perplexing for students, and the focus of this chapter.

A simple way to make sense of production is to consider the way a chef views a recipe. There are combinations of various ingredients that, when put together correctly, result in a specific dish. A peanut-butter-and-jelly sandwich is a basic example. It requires bread, peanut butter and jelly. For the producer, the issue may not be the ingredients per se, but rather the method used to combine the ingredients. Another cooking example may be useful: My wife and I both enjoy making chocolate chip cookies. We both follow the instructions on the bag of chocolate chips. My wife, however, prefers to use a fancy KitchenAid stand mixer to combine the ingredients. I prefer to use a fork and some elbow grease. The cookies turn out the same with both approaches so what does it matter how the cookies are prepared?

An economist would point out that the first process is capital intensive (using a stand mixer) while the second is labor intensive (using elbow grease). What draws the economist's focus is the different combination of these two inputs – labor and capital – from which a producer might choose. With an eye toward using resources efficiently, the upshot is that the producer should use the combination of inputs that produces the "biggest bang for the buck," and that isn't the same for every producer.

Why would two producers choose different methods to produce the same thing? There are two key economic insights involved in determining the answer. The first is that the relative productivity of the inputs matters. Productivity is measured by examining how much output changes if one more unit of a particular input changes, holding all other inputs constant. If increasing input A allows either more output to be made or a given amount of output to be made faster as compared to increasing input B, it might be preferable to use input A.[4] Input A is more productive, meaning you get more "bang." The second insight is that the relative cost of the two inputs should be considered. If one input is less expensive than the other it might be preferable to use more of the less expensive input, all other things being equal. This is the "for the buck" concern businesses constantly fret over.

Both ideas, however, should be considered simultaneously. One input may increase output by twice as much as a different input, but it might be outrageously expensive. By putting these two insights together an important principle emerges: Producers (who want to maximize their profits) want to use the inputs that allow them to produce more (or faster) at the least cost. So, if expanding output is desirable, use the input that increases output at the greatest amount per dollar spent. When my wife makes cookies, she finds mixing with a fork tiresome and time consuming. So, she uses the mixer. When I make cookies, I find using a fork just as quick as the mixer but I do not like cleaning the mixer. So, we each choose the approach that gets the job done at the lowest perceived cost.

When we discuss production input choices in a principles of economics class it is, by necessity, a stripped-down version of the choices producers confront between inputs in the real world. Rather than discuss all of the various things that might be required to produce an actual good, we boil the production decision down to two inputs – most often labor and capital. To make matters worse (or better, depending upon your point of view) we tell students that all labor is identical – clones, perhaps. Units of capital are identical as well. Perhaps we can think of units of capital like Lego® blocks that interlock in increasing amounts.

In the simple example of making cookies above, a standup mixer and a fork can both be thought of as capital. Clearly though, we would not think of the mixer as just more of a fork, and, if truth be told, my wife is a better cook than I am and we should not be considered as just different quantities of labor. Of course, this abstraction can take students too far away from what the things they find familiar, so we simplify the analysis to clones and Legos®.

This level of abstraction might make it difficult to drive home an important lesson that arises in discussing how producers choose the correct combination of inputs – different circumstances can lead to different optimal choices. In a world where labor is abundant an approach to production that utilizes more labor and less capital might be best. In a world where labor is scarce but capital is plentiful, an approach to production that utilizes more capital and less labor might be best. Which brings us back to the Shadow's and Batman's approaches to fighting crime.

Vigilante production choices

One can think of both the Shadow and Batman as producers – consider their output as the number of villains they can detain in a night. Like any producer, they both must make decisions concerning how they go about the task of apprehending villains. Besides the individual skills each crime fighter brings to the task, they both make use of the labor of others and capital. Although both Lamont Cranston and Bruce Wayne are depicted as being wealthy individuals, both face different costs of acquiring the labor they use and the capital they use. This difference dictates the least cost approach each vigilante pursues. While there are many striking similarities between the two crime fighters, one aspect about their modus operandi is quite different. The Shadow has chosen a very *labor intensive* approach to fighting crime. This means that he uses a relatively large amount of labor compared to the amount of capital he uses. Batman has chosen a very *capital intensive* approach. Which means he uses a relatively large amount of capital compared to the amount of labor he uses. To be sure, this does not mean that the Shadow does not use any capital and Batman does not use any labor. It only means they use significantly more of one resource rather than the other. To understand why this makes sense (economic sense in addition to expositional sense) it is worth the effort to build an economic model that demonstrates how rational producers make decisions when confronted with input choices.

To visualize the typical trade-off producers face it is useful to graph a set of combinations of labor and capital that yield the same amount of output. Economists call this visual device an "isoquant" ("iso" for the Greek isos meaning equal and "quant" short for quantity). In the context of our comparison of the Shadow and Batman, consider output to be the number of criminals brought to justice in a given amount of time. On the X axis we will place units of labor (or number of agents). On the Y axis we will place capital (or amount of crime fighting tools). Figure 9.1 presents an example of three isoquants that represent three different levels of output (number of criminals caught in a night).

The first key concept to the graph is that there are multiple ways to accomplish the same task. In fact, the reason the isoquants are smooth lines is that I have assumed that small fractions of labor or capital are possible (I can hire labor part-time if I like). A second idea in the representation is that adding more of either input

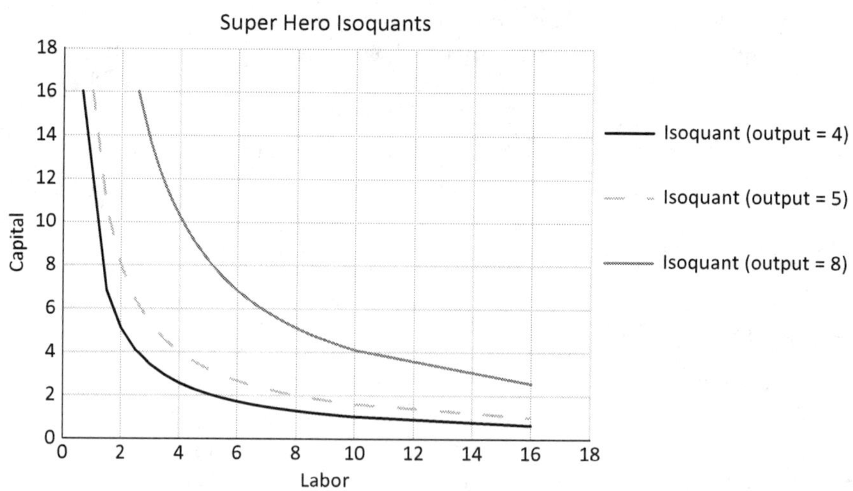

FIGURE 9.1 Superhero isoquants

without taking any away should lead to more output being produced – and result in a new isoquant that is up and to the right of the original one. In Figure 9.1, the black isoquant represents all of the combination of labor and capital that will lead to four villains being caught in a night. It represents the lowest level of output presented in the table. The dark grey isoquant represents all of the combinations of labor and capital that will lead to eight criminals being apprehended in a night. It is the highest level of output presented. Taking any of either input away will lead to less output and result in a new isoquant that is down and to the left of the original one. A third key concept addresses what happens if more of one input is added without adding more of the other. As Batman adds more items to his utility belt the additional usefulness of the item (the number of additional criminals Batman can catch per night) gets smaller. He probably put the most useful items in his belt first and at some point, the weight of the additional items will slow him down.[5] Similarly, as the Shadow adds additional agents there are fewer jobs for them to do as the most important jobs are already taken. This third key observation goes by the name of "diminishing marginal productivity." It is represented in Figure 9.1 as the isoquants getting steeper as more and more capital is used at the expense of less and less labor. The corollary occurs when the isoquants get flatter indicating that more and more labor is used while less and less capital is used. Taken together, these three ideas result in isoquants that have the characteristics of being downward sloping and bending away from the origin.

Information about the relative cost of each input will help us consider which point on the isoquant is best. One way to represent the cost of each input is with a straight line with a slope equal to the negative ratio of the cost of labor divided by the cost of capital. Lines closer to the origin represent lower total cost. Lines further from the origin represent greater total cost. For convenience, economists refer to these lines as "isocost" lines (meaning the various combination of inputs a firm could hire for the same budget). These lines typically represent the financial trade-off the producer faces, but in our superhero example, we can also think of the tradeoff in more general terms. In the world of the Shadow, he finds additional capital more expensive than labor because it is more scarce. In writing *The Shadow* stories Walter Gibson chose to develop characters rather than gadgets. As a result, the Shadow has limited options when it comes to crime fighting capital. Batman finds labor more expensive than capital because he finds it difficult to connect with people. Like Gibson, Kane and Finger made choices that left Batman with relatively few colleagues but plenty of tools to work with.

With our own economic tools available to us, let's consider a hypothetical situation where the Shadow and Batman each would like to apprehend five criminals per evening. For the sake of a simple example imagine they both have access to agents who are of equal quality. They also both have access to capital or crime fighting tools that are equally effective. Due to having access to the same quality inputs, we can present the isoquant for five villains apprehended per night as being the same for the two crime fighters. The first three columns of Table 9.1 present the different combinations of labor (agents) and capital (crime fighting tools) that

TABLE 9.1 Hero production (five villains per night)*

			The Shadow	*Batman*
Output	**Labor (agents)**	**Capital (tools)**	**Total cost**	**Total cost**
5	1	16	\$6,500	\$2,000
5	2	8	\$3,400	\$1,600
5	4	4	\$2,000	\$2,000
5	8	2	\$1,600	\$3,400
5	16	1	\$2,000	\$6,500

* For those interested in the math behind the choice of inputs, I used the production function $Q = 1.25 (L^{0.5})(K^{0.5})$ where Q is number of villains caught per night, L is the amount of labor used and K is the amount of capital used.

will allow either hero to capture five villains. If we look at the point at which either the Shadow or Batman use one agent and 16 crime fighting tools one might notice that it takes only one additional agent to make up for the loss of eight crime fighting tools (labor increases from 1 to 2, and capital decreases from 16 to 8). But as you move down the rows in the table, it takes more and more agents to make up for fewer and fewer crime fighting tools.

For this example, we assume that both heroes have access to equally effective inputs, but we also assume the cost of acquiring the inputs is different. Let's assume that for the Shadow each agent costs him \$100 per evening and each unit of capital costs him \$400 per evening. This is consistent with the observation that the Shadow favors agents over crime fighting capital. Batman, conversely, has to pay \$400 per evening for each agent he hires but only \$100 per evening for each unit of capital he uses. The symmetry serves to keep the example from getting overly complicated. The final two columns in Table 9.1 presents each hero's cost for each potential combination of labor and capital.

The same tradeoff information is presented in Figure 9.2. The dashed line represents an isoquant showing all of the different combinations of labor and capital that will result in the apprehension of five villains per evening. The black line represents an isocost line for the least expensive approach Batman can take to fight crime. The first thing to notice is that it has a slope of −4/1. One can think of the slope in different ways. The slope represents the relative prices Batman must pay to get either additional helpers or additional units of capital. In Batman's case, labor is four times more expensive than capital. Or, because additional agents cost Batman four times more than each crime fighting tool, he must give up four tools to gain one more agent. The second thing to note is that Batman's isocost line touches the isoquant at one point. There is no other point on the isoquant that will allow Batman to capture five criminals in an evening at a lower cost.

From Table 9.1 it is apparent that the least cost combination of inputs for Batman is two agents (perhaps Robin and Commissioner Gordon) and eight crime

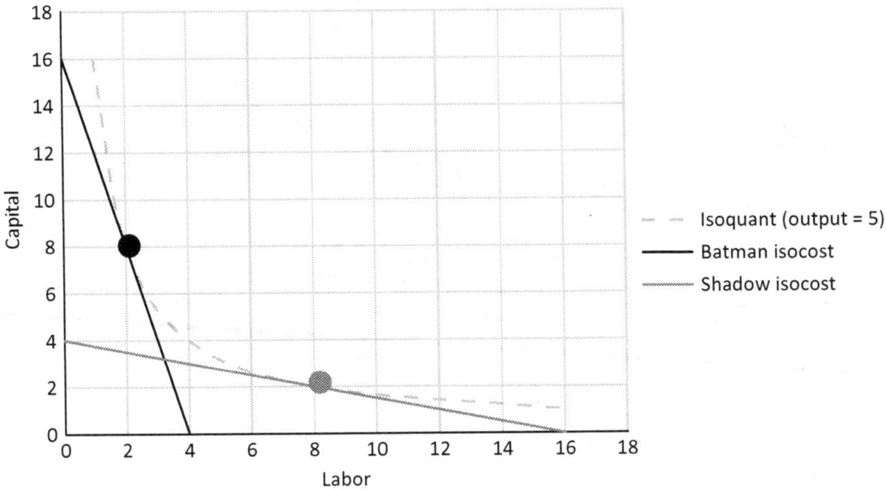

FIGURE 9.2 Superhero isoquant and isocost lines

fighting tools. (This combination is highlighted in Figure 9.2 by the black dot.) The cost to Batman of this combination is $1600 per night.

The Shadow's isocost line is represented by the grey line. It is relatively flat, an indication that labor is less expensive for the Shadow to obtain than capital is. In fact, the slope of the line is −1/4 which means that labor is one-fourth the cost of capital for the Shadow. Again, an examination of Table 9.1 shows that there is a least cost combination of inputs for the Shadow. In his case, eight agents and two crime fighting tools will minimize his cost of capturing five villains in an evening. (This combination is highlighted in Figure 9.2 by the grey dot.) While other combinations of labor and capital will allow the Shadow to continue to apprehend five bad guys per night, no other combination will allow him to do so at lower cost.

Two crime fighters are confronted with the same problem: How to gather resources to fight crime. But because they face different costs of the resources they make different choices. Both approaches are equally effective, and in the simple case presented here, the final overall cost is the same.[6] The situation is identical to the one producers face every day – albeit more dramatic. Just like the two rug makers finding the best way to produce floor coverings in the face of different constraints, super heroes must also make cost-minimizing decisions if they are to be effective in their chosen task.

Only the Shadow knows

Although it is not overwhelmingly difficult to find common examples of producers making different input decisions when confronted either with different costs of inputs or inputs that have different levels of marginal productivity, going outside of the mundane for examples can be rewarding. In this example, I have taken two similar superheroes, the Shadow and Batman, and demonstrated that their approaches to fighting crime follow the same logic we would expect producers to use when determining the cost-minimizing combinations of inputs to employ. The Shadow, who finds labor easier to obtain than capital, utilizes a legion of agents to assist him in his battle against crime but little capital. Batman, although similar in many ways to the Shadow, takes a different approach. Because Batman is typically portrayed as being somewhat of a loner, he has a harder time recruiting collaborators and, therefore, eschews labor. Through Wayne Industries, however, he has almost unlimited access to state-of-the-art crime fighting tools. It should then be no surprise that Batman's approach to crime fighting is dominated by his use of capital.

Notes

1 I apologize in advance if my description is less than encyclopedic. Both characters have endured multiple treatments from multiple writers and artists in multiple media presentations since their original inceptions. As many readers may be aware, the DC universe underwent a complete historical rewrite in the *Crisis on Infinite Earth* series. My goal is to paint pictures of each hero that is true to the overall nature of their characters and highlights one facet of their crime fighting – their choice of inputs.
2 In print, the Shadow convinces the real Lamont Cranston to leave the country. This allows Allard to make use of Cranston's financial resources and gives him access the inner circles of New York society
3 The pulp stories and the comics made more use of the Shadow's agents than the radio broadcasts did as it was difficult to keep different characters' voices sufficiently distinctive over the airwaves.
4 This assumes that all other things are equal. This favorite assumption of economists is essential because if more than one thing in the production process is changing it is difficult to ascribe causation.
5 Technically, if we assume all capital is identical, it is not that the additional item is of any lower quality. There are just fewer opportunities to use it.
6 This result happens to be an artifact of the symmetry of the presentation. Altering the situation so that capital and labor costs differ between the two heroes is certainly possible, but it would needlessly complicate the analysis while bringing us to a similar conclusion.

References

"A Brief History of the Shadow." (n.d.). *The Shadow Master of Darkness*. Retrieved from www.shadowsanctum.net/history/history.html

Daniels, L. (1999). *Batman: The Complete History*. New York: First Chronicle Book.

Gibson, W. and G. Wert. (1931). *The Shadow Magazine*, #1. Smith and Street.

Greenberger, R. (2008). *The Essential Batman Encyclopedia*. New York: Del Ray Books, Random House, Inc.

Kane, B. and B. Finger. (1939). *Detective Comics*, #27. DC Comics.

Kane, B., G. Fox, B. Finger and S. Moldoff. (1939). *Detective Comics*, #33. DC Comics.

Misiroglu, G. (2012) *The Superhero Book (2nd edition): The Ultimate Encyclopedia of Comic-Book Icons and Hollywood Heroes*. Canton, Michigan: Visible Ink Press.

"Secret Origins of Batman." (2007). *Dial B for Blog*. Retrieved from www.dialbforblog.com/archives/389/

"The Shadow." (2017, May 17). *Comic Vine*. Retrieved from https://comicvine.gamespot.com/the-shadow/4005-28923/

Waid, M. and S. Scott. (2000). *Justice League of America*, #46. DC Comics.

Warshak, R. A. (2014, May 6). "Batman's Traumatic Origins" *The Atlantic*. Retrieved from www.theatlantic.com/entertainment/archive/2014/05/batmans-traumatic-origins/361638/

Whitbrook, J. (2014, September 12). "7 Times Batman Has Bent His 'No Gun' Rule." *Gizmodo*: Retrieved from http://gizmodo.com/7-times-batman-has-bent-his-no-guns-rule-1634040693

10

THE AVENGERS VS. THE INCREDIBLE (BUT UNPREDICTABLE) HULK

Amanda Mandzik

In the superhero universe, the Incredible Hulk stands apart as a unique kind of hero. While we frequently think of superheroes valiantly rescuing defenseless bystanders and using their superpowers and wits to outsmart the evil plans of supervillains, the Hulk's role is not so straightforward. His strength and power are undeniable, yet his transformation into a green monster precipitated by uncontrollable anger renders him more beast than man. Nevertheless, when channeled effectively, the Hulk's power is a force to be reckoned with for the good of humanity as a member of the Marvel Comics hero group the Avengers. This chapter will use an economic lens to assess the occupational hazards of teaming up with the Hulk. First, it is clear that the Hulk has a completely different preference set from his human alter ego, the meek Bruce Banner, and therefore must be considered a completely different individual. Recognizing that Banner and the Hulk represent distinct personas, the Avengers must anticipate their expected payoff from including the Hulk on their team despite the uncertainty of the outcome. Ultimately, the Avengers' decision demonstrates their attitude towards risk when weighing the possible payoffs gained from harnessing the Hulk's power versus the very real possibility that the Hulk will cause more destruction to his surroundings, or worse, turn on one of his partners.

The origin of the Hulk

The story of the Incredible Hulk begins in 1962. In the first comic of this new series, creators Jack Kirby and Stan Lee introduce the world to Bruce Banner, a quiet, unassuming yet brilliant scientist working on the development of the gamma bomb (Lee and Kirby, 1962). During a bomb test, Banner notices a young civilian on the test site. He rushes to the aid of the teen, but in the process, Banner exposes himself to gamma radiation when the bomb is detonated. Although he does not die, the accident marks the birth of Banner's other self – the monster. From this time forward, stress or anxiety transforms the previously reserved Banner into an enormous green creature. Various inceptions of the Hulk have appeared within the comics as well as in a 1970s-television show and three big screen incarnations, yet while the versions of the Hulk have varied somewhat in origin story, size and appearance, the propelling theme of the Hulk has always been the unassuming Banner's transformation into the raging monster.

As his original self, Banner is a man of small stature and mild disposition, yet genius-level IQ. As the Hulk, however, he has nearly unmatched strength that only increases as he becomes angrier. Comic book readers have long debated and compared the abilities of superheroes, but the Hulk undoubtedly ranks in the top tier for absolute advantage in strength and power. The Hulk is considered "the world's most powerful human being" and "is about as close to indestructible – in the comics, anyway – as a human being can get" (Kiefer, 2003). Even gods from other realms are no match for the Hulk. With a single punch, the Hulk effortlessly knocks out the villainous god Loki,[1] delighting moviegoers as he comments "Puny god" (in *Marvel's the Avengers* (Weeden, 2012)). His superhuman strength allows him to knock down buildings, long-jump great distances and create shock waves merely by clapping his hands together. Different renderings of the Hulk depict him as between 6 and 15 feet tall, weighing between 330 and 1,500 pounds (Kiefer, 2003). Because of his enormous power, even comic book authors and screenwriters have been reluctant at times to include the Hulk in stories with other superheroes. Screenwriter Christopher Markus explained the absence of the Hulk in *Captain America: Civil War*:

> You put [him] in a fight, it's over quickly. It's like, "Well, we have the Hulk on our side." Oh, fine, then … You've got to kind of choose your roster depending on what kind of fight you want to have.
>
> *(Breznican, 2015)*

While the Hulk prefers to be left alone, frequent antagonistic confrontations provoke his anger and a fight becomes inevitable. In their first encounter, even the villain Loki perceives that "although there is no evil in his heart, mankind fears him because of his awesome strength" (Lee and Kirby, 1963). The Hulk's superhuman power causes the misunderstood Hulk to be continually hunted down by the U.S. military and sought after by superheroes and villains alike to either collaborate with or exploit his capabilities.

Among those superheroes seeking to benefit from the Hulk's overwhelming abilities are the Avengers. First established in 1963, not long after the introduction of the Hulk, the Avengers are a team of superheroes self-appointed as protectors of planet Earth. In the very first issue of the Avengers comic, the founding members of the team, Ant-Man, Iron Man, Thor and the Wasp, work alongside the Hulk to thwart one of Loki's evil plots (thus technically giving the Hulk founding status as a member of the group). However, the other Avengers quickly find that channeling and sustaining the Hulk's help is easier said than done. While the Avengers maintain friendly relations with Dr. Bruce Banner, the Hulk has a mind of his own. Like an animal, the Hulk reacts primarily based on instinct, so an ill-timed irritant can trigger a reversal of the Hulk's productive efforts. Working with the Hulk therefore becomes a study in strategy for the Avengers. In a given situation, they must anticipate the actions of the Hulk based on their understanding of his proclivities and exhibited past behavior in order to achieve the highest possible benefits from their green comrade.

In the discussion that follows, we will explore the complexities of the Hulk as both an individual and as a potential teammate on the Avengers' superhero team. Just as consumers have different yet individually consistent preferences when making purchases, Banner and the Hulk have different preferences regarding the choices that each would make in a given situation. Their diverging preferences reveal that, even though Banner and the Hulk are physically inseparable, they are not the same person. Consequently, the Avengers must acknowledge that decisions made by the Hulk are not necessarily compatible with Banner's intentions to help them. Misjudging the Hulk's expected behavior can mean an even more difficult situation for the Avengers who already have their hands full saving the world. The Avengers ultimately must evaluate their own attitude towards risk and whether the Hulk's incredible power is worth taking the chance that they might rouse his equally ferocious rage.

Bruce Banner vs. the Hulk: two different preference sets

Despite their inextricable physical connection from sharing the same body, Banner and the Hulk have a complicated interpersonal relationship evidenced in both the comics and the movies. After the first-ever Hulk transformation in the original comic, the Hulk sees a picture of Bruce Banner and exclaims, "That face! I – I know that face! But it is weak – soft! I hate it! Take it away! … I'd rather be me, than that puny weakling in the picture!"[2] (Lee and Kirby, 1962, p. 59). When the Hulk turns back into his original self, Banner is appalled by the monster that he mutates into. Following the accident, Banner spends much of his time trying to find a cure for his transformation episodes. In the film *The Incredible Hulk* (Leterrier, 2008), while living on the run, Banner recruits the help of the cellular biologist Dr. Samuel Sterns (known as Mr. Blue). Banner's despair and desperation reaches rock bottom, referenced in both the comics and the movies, as he tries and fails to commit suicide. Alas, he is thwarted by his Hulk-self. Banner explains to the other members of the Avengers team: "You can't [kill me]! I know! I tried!… I got low. I didn't see an end, so I put a bullet in my mouth … and the other guy spit it out!" (Weeden, 2012). Ultimately, Banner describes his Hulk-self as a "brutal, bestial mockery of a human – that creature which fears nothing – which despises reason and worships power" (Lee and Kirby, 1962, p. 63).

In order to understand the predicament of trading the Hulk's power for Banner's reason, we need a tool to reflect the preferences of both personas. In economics,

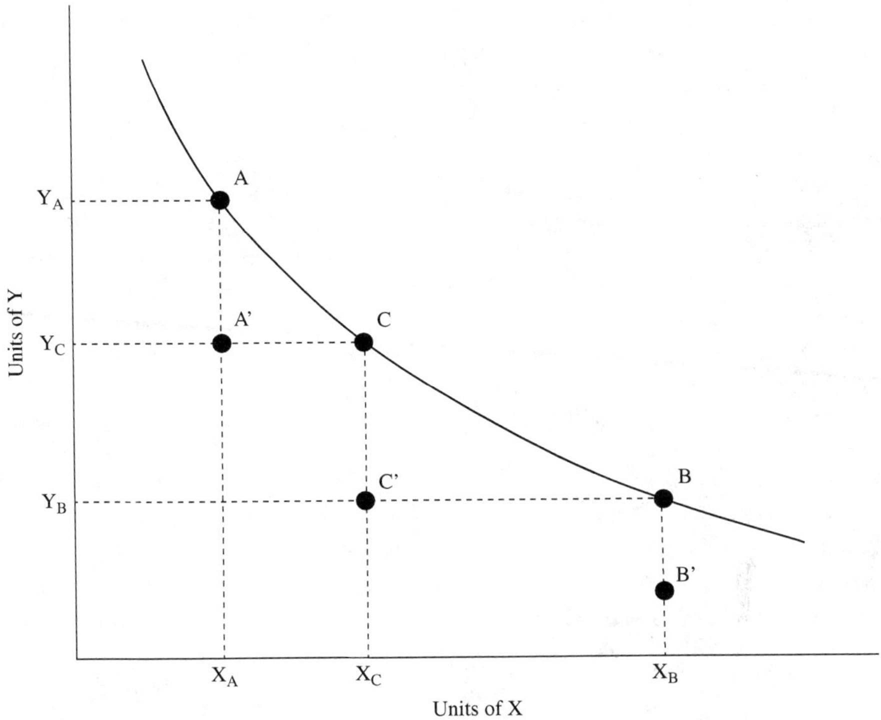

FIGURE 10.1 An indifference curve

we can pull a tool called an indifference curve out of our tool bag. An indifference curve, as shown in Figure 10.1, illustrates various combinations of two goods that would make an individual equally satisfied; we define this satisfaction as the total "utility" for the individual.

If we examine Figure 10.1, we can see that there are several important assumptions that form the basis of our indifference curve model:

1. *Individuals can choose among combinations of the goods.* Each point represents a combination of Good X and Good Y and can be thought of as a "bundle" (Points A, B, C, A', B' and C' all represent different bundles). When comparing one bundle to another, the individual can prefer one bundle to the other or he can be indifferent to the two bundles.
2. *More is better.* We will assume that increasing amounts of either good (X or Y) makes an individual better off. In Figure 10.1, moving from one bundle to another bundle in the "northeast" direction (for example from Point C' to Point C) will provide more utility since the individual will not have less of either good and will have more of at least one of the two goods.
3. *Individuals make their choices consistently.* For example, in Figure 10.1, if an individual reveals that he prefers Point A' to Point B' then shows that he

prefers Point B' to a third alternative Point C', then it must be the case that he prefers Point A' to Point C'. This is an assumption of *rationality*.

4. *Individuals are willing to have less of a good but only in return for compensating amounts of the other good.* The individual can give up some of one good and still be equally satisfied only if he receives more of the other good in proportion to his unique preferences.[3] This is why the individual is indifferent between the points on a given curve. In Figure 10.1, moving from Point A to Point A' would make the individual worse off because he now has the same amount of Good X (X_A) but less of Good Y (moving south from Y_A to Y_C). However, if the individual is compensated for the loss of Y with an increase of Good X from X_A to X_C moving him to Point C, the individual will be equally satisfied here as he was at his original bundle at Point A. We can say that he is indifferent between A and C, both of which are on the same indifference curve.

Every individual has a unique family of indifference curves, known as a preference map (shown in Figure 10.2), where higher curves are preferred to lower curves because they are further in the northeast direction. This means that while the individual in Figure 10.2 is indifferent between Point A and Point B, he would prefer to be at Point C on a higher indifference curve.

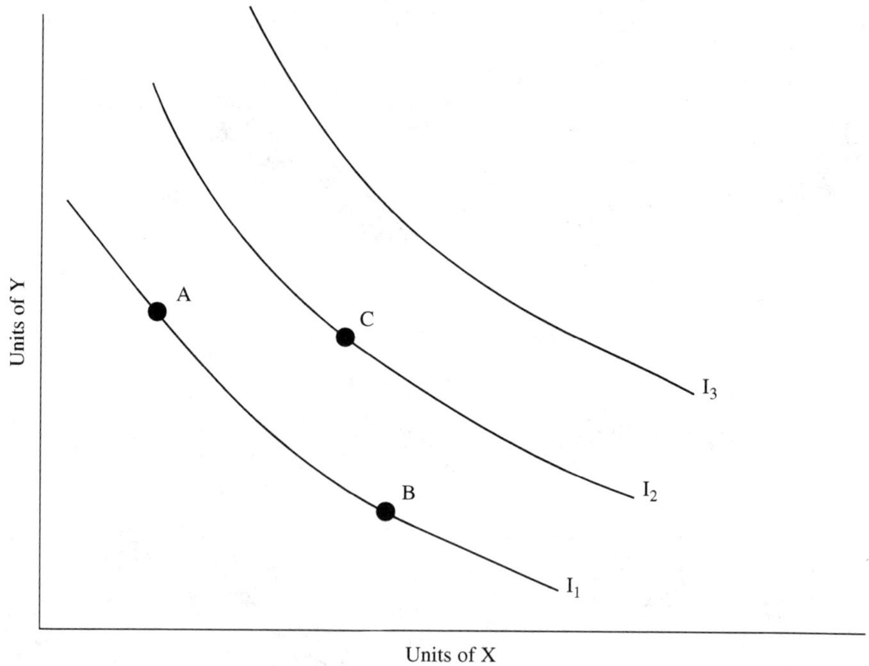

FIGURE 10.2 Preference map: a family of indifference curves

Returning to our case study of Banner and the Hulk, we can analyze different combinations of "power" and "reason" which take the places of Good X and Good Y on the graph's axes. Without a doubt, the Hulk favors power over reason. But the Hulk does not want power exclusively. Throughout the comics and movies, the Hulk does display varying levels of intelligence, although "the Hulk's creators have never been in complete agreement on how smart the Hulk should be" (Kiefer, 2003, p. 120). While we frequently see the Hulk as brutish and not especially bright, he is nevertheless always able to distinguish between good and bad guys. Furthermore, there have been intelligent versions of the Hulk in the comics including his alternate personality Doc Green, and his post-apocalyptic self, The Maestro (Holmes, 2017). Nevertheless, the Hulk's preference map would undoubtedly display his predilection for power over reason. Looking at the Hulk's preference map in Figure 10.3, the indifference curves are close to horizontal. Because the Hulk favors power over reason so heavily, it would take a large quantity of reason for the Hulk to be willing to give up some of his power. On the graph, moving from point A to point B, the Hulk is willing to give up an amount of power – the gap between Power A and Power B – only if he is compensated with a larger amount of reason – the gap between Reason A and Reason B.

On the other hand, Banner values reason over power. Only seconds before the fateful accident that would turn him into the Hulk, Banner states that he "detest[s] men who think with their fists" (Lee and Kirby, 1962, p. 3). As a highly educated

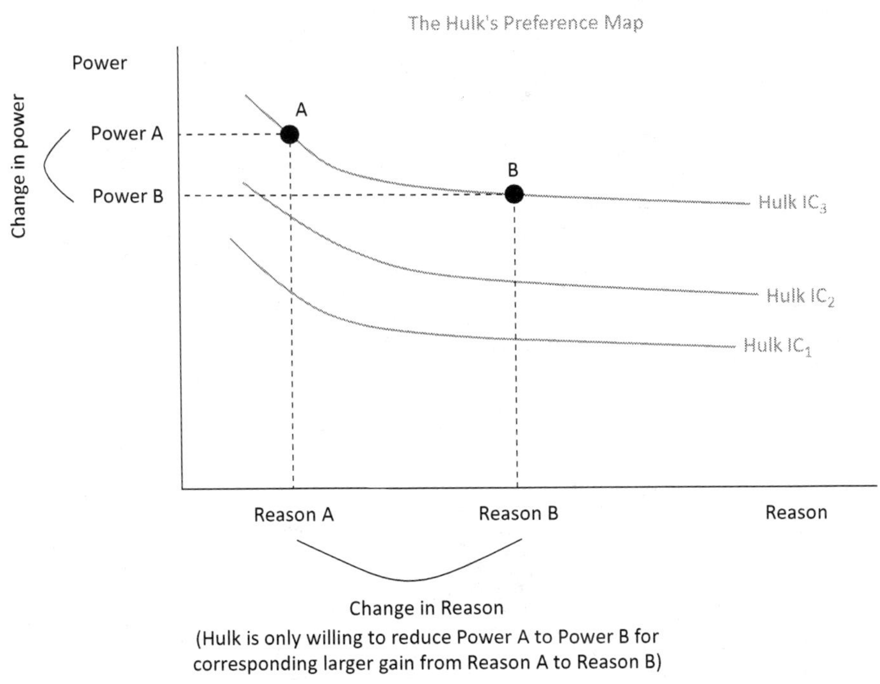

FIGURE 10.3 The Hulk's preference map

and learned scientist, Banner does not want to be defined by the violent eruptions for which the Hulk is known. In his mind, the Hulk is a monstrosity that defies the natural state of humanity. But Banner is not entirely opposed to power. Even before the initial accident, he was helping to develop a gamma bomb, and he later willingly helps the Avenger team by "lending" his Hulk self to fight on the team. Examining his preference map (Figure 10.4), we see that Banner is willing to give up a large amount of power to obtain a small amount of reason (Moving from point A to point B).

For both Banner and the Hulk, some mix of reason and power is optimal based on their unique preference maps. However, if we map both sets of curves simultaneously, we see that the curves would intersect (Figure 10.5).

Returning to our initial assumptions about indifference curves, this is a violation of rationality if we consider Banner and the Hulk to be a single individual. Each indifference curve represents combinations of power and reason that would provide equal satisfaction for Banner and the Hulk. In other words, they should be indifferent to the distinct bundles along a given curve. Furthermore, utility increases as the indifference curves move in the northeast direction because this indicates that there is more of both power and reason. If Hulk and Banner are truly one individual then, examining Figure 10.6, this individual should be indifferent between point C and D (on Banner's indifference curve) and indifferent between point C and E (on the Hulk's indifference curve). However, point E would be preferred to point D as this combination contains more of both power and reason.

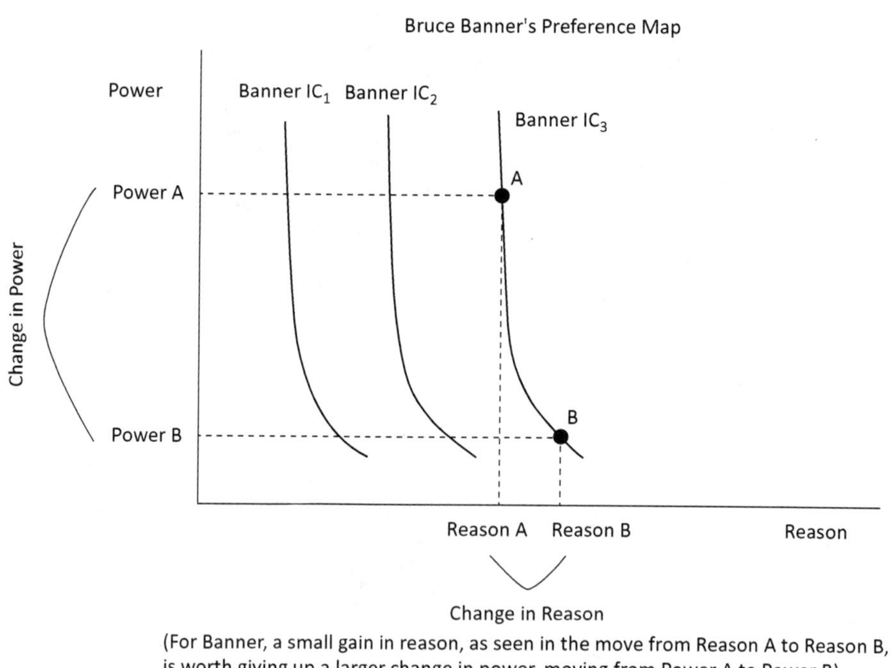

FIGURE 10.4 Bruce Banner's preference map

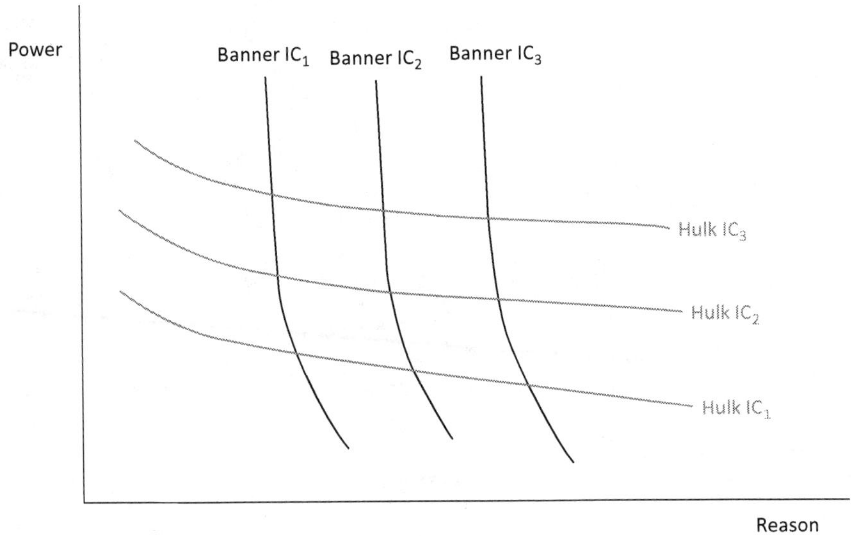

FIGURE 10.5 Banner and the Hulk's preferences mapped simultaneously

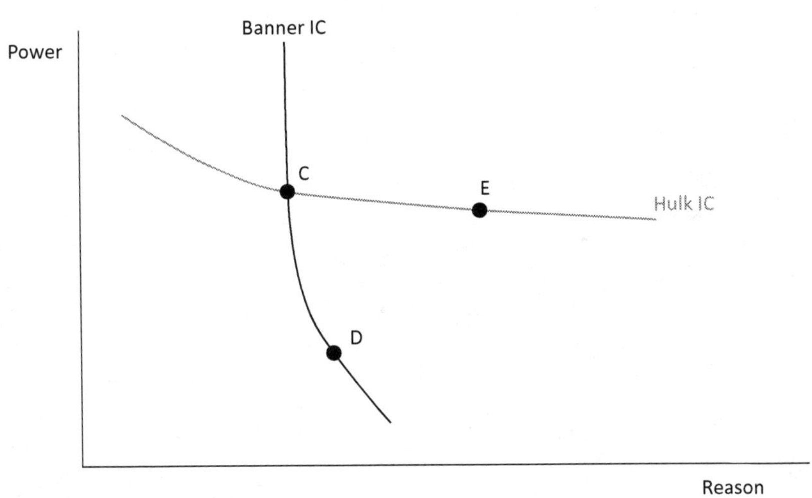

FIGURE 10.6 Violation of rationality: overlapping indifference curves

This presents the problem of inconsistent preferences thereby violating our notion of rationality. Therefore, we must treat this single "body" as two individual economic agents – Banner and the Hulk.

Making this distinction is important before proceeding to analyze the strategy that unfolds in the Hulk comics or movies. We must consider the rationale for the behaviors adopted by Bruce Banner and the Hulk separately, since they are not one and the same. In turn, in the next section, we will be able to apply these expected preferences made by Banner and the Hulk to decision-making situations with the members of the Avengers superhero team.

The Hulk vs. the Avengers: moving preferences into game theory situations

When the Avengers superhero team assembled for the first time in 1963, the Hulk was one of the founding members. Ironically, but perhaps fittingly, for most of the first edition of this comic the Hulk battles against his future teammates after the villain Loki falsely impugns him as the cause of a train wreck. The Hulk takes a break from the team in the very next issue, however, when he recognizes his volatility is a source of concern for the other Avengers.

Without a doubt, strategy is a hallmark of every superhero story. Superheroes and villains each must consider the consequences of different choices that they make based on their expected payoffs. In economics, game theory is the study of strategy in which an economic agent attempts to maximize his own well-being while anticipating and reacting to the actions of others. We can analyze the strategies of the Avengers team and the Hulk by creating a decision tree. A decision tree is a graph or flow-chart where each player makes a decision in alternating turns. Read from left to right, within the decision tree each player faces a decision node, or the point where a decision must be made and the tree branches into potential outcomes. In sequence, the players choose among these options establishing a specific path ultimately leading to a conclusion. The end result of a particular combination of choices is shown at the end of each possible path of branches.

In the hypothetical decision tree shown in Figure 10.7, we can consider the choices for the Avengers, Bruce Banner and the Hulk. The decision tree begins as the Avengers make the first move in choosing whether or not to call in Bruce Banner. Without the Hulk's assistance, they will be limited to the fighting power of the remaining team-members. In the 2012 *Avengers* film, we see the Avengers making this first move as Natasha Romanoff seeks out Banner in Calcutta, India to invite him to join the team (Weeden, 2012). However, because of the conflict between the Hulk and Banner described in the previous section, procuring Banner's help is not a straightforward assignment nor is anticipating his response.

Throughout the comics and movies, Banner, who prefers "reason" to "power," is not always willing to help the Avengers. When Banner transforms into the Hulk, he "can't control it"; at best, he might be able to "guide it, aim it in the right direction" (Leterrier, 2008). Knowing his capabilities and his proclivity to cause utter destruction as the Hulk, Banner leaves the team on different occasions and spends much of his time in seclusion to avoid unwanted and uncontrollable altercations as the Hulk. He therefore faces the decision to accept or decline the Avenger's invitation as the second player in the decision tree.

If Banner chooses to provide his assistance as the Hulk, the Hulk in turn will choose one of two actions: cooperate or defect.[4] When the Hulk cooperates, the

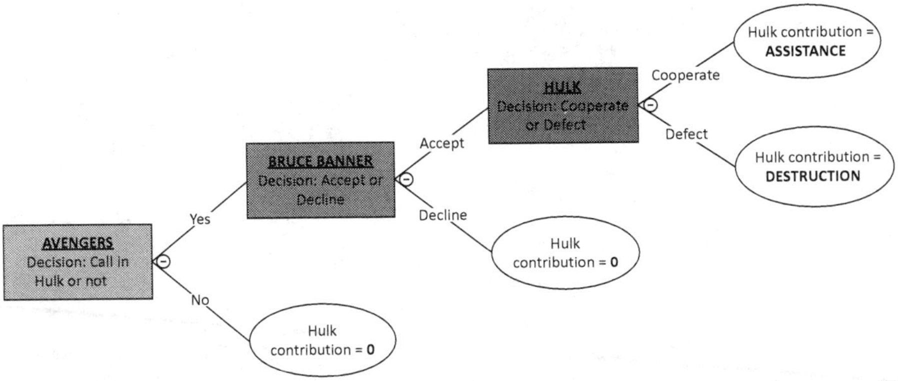

FIGURE 10.7 Decision tree for the Avengers: include the Hulk or not?

Avengers team is better off than if they did not call in the Hulk, and the fighting power of the Avengers increases by the contribution of the Hulk's force against the current villain. This is clear when the Avengers face an alien invasion of New York City in *Marvel's the Avengers* (Weeden, 2012). The Hulk shows himself to be an incredible asset to the team taking on the aliens, overpowering their leader Loki and rescuing teammate Iron Man as he falls from the sky. On the other hand, in the case that the Hulk chooses to defect, the Hulk may actually turn on the team-members and fight them. In this case, the Avengers are worse off than if they did not call in the Hulk in the first place. Not only must the Avengers fight the original villain, but they must also simultaneously fend off the defecting Hulk. Before the attack on New York City, the Avengers face this other side of the Hulk when an attack on the team's Helicarrier[5] sparks the Hulk's fury causing him to turn on his friends Romanoff and Thor.

If the Hulk is going to be included on the team, what determines if he will cooperate or defect? Knowing the danger of the Hulk when he is hostile to the team, the Avengers can, to an extent, arrange the conditions and environment of the fight to avoid the possibility that the Hulk will turn on them. Banner himself notes that the confined nature of the Helicarrier does not provide an optimal setting in the event of a Hulk transformation. However, even if bad-Hulk inducing situations are avoided, there is always the possibility that some unforeseen factor will set off the Hulk causing him to lose control, clearly illustrating his strong preference of power to reason. For example, while the Hulk is aiding the Avengers in *Age of Ultron*, the Scarlet Witch unexpectedly gains mind control of the Hulk, only to send him into such a rage that he wreaks havoc on a South African city and battles his own teammate Iron Man (Weeden, 2015). Therefore, it is important to consider the probability that the Hulk will or will not turn on the team in different scenarios.

Given that the Avengers are able to accurately predict the odds of the Hulk's decisions throughout this decision tree, then their actual choice to call in the Hulk (or not) can be classified as either a risk-averse, risk-loving or risk-neutral decision. We evaluate these decisions in the following section.

The Hulk: friend or foe to the Avengers?

Clearly, while the Hulk may be the Avengers' most valuable asset, at the same time, he is undeniably their biggest liability. Actor Mark Ruffalo, who plays Bruce Banner in the Marvel movies, explains the unstable role of the Hulk on the Avengers, "He's like the teammate none of them are sure they want on their team. He's a loose cannon. It's like, 'Just throw a grenade in the middle of the group and let's hope it turns out well!'" (Nevets, 2011).

While the Avengers realize the immense potential of utilizing the Hulk's power for their team, they also acknowledge the damage that can follow if his power is misdirected. The Hulk has taken on all the members of the Avengers at various times throughout the comic history of the team. Moreover, innocent bystanders are frequently put at risk in the ensuing confrontations. Even when the Hulk is cooperating with the team, his sheer size and power is likely to cause damage to his surroundings as was seen in the alien invasion of New York.

A cost-benefit analysis can help the Avengers to evaluate if pursuing the Hulk for their team will be a valuable use of their time, resources and effort. Using hypothetical values, we can estimate the expected "payoffs" for the Avengers from choosing to include the Hulk on their team. A positive payoff for the Avengers would result from the Hulk helping to defeat a villain, whereas a negative payoff for the team would mean the Hulk causes relatively more harm than good by fighting with teammates, damaging the surroundings and generally sidetracking the mission.

There are two components that we need to calculate the Avengers' expected payoff from including Hulk. These are: 1) the utility that the Avengers receive from all possible outcomes of the invitation, and 2) the probability of each of those respective outcomes occurring. Looking first at the Avengers' utility requires us to understand the nature of how individuals, and specifically the Avengers, accrue higher levels of satisfaction. We have already encountered the term "utility" in the discussion on indifference curves, but we will expand on that definition here. Utility for an individual can be illustrated in a graph known as a utility function where increasing consumption of the good as shown on the X-axis will result in changing levels of utility for that individual as shown on the Y-axis. However, increasing consumption of a good will not necessarily affect the level of utility at the same rate or in the same way. A very important concept in economics is how things change from the consuming *one additional unit*. Additional units are known as margins. Thus, the marginal utility is the satisfaction you get from consuming one more unit of something, and it is the *marginal* utility that distinguishes the shape of the utility function. Consider two possibilities: *diminishing* marginal utility and *increasing* marginal utility. Diminishing marginal utility is described in the following example and shown in Panel (A) of Figure 10.8. For the average consumer, eating one slice of pizza when hungry is very satisfying. The next slice may be delicious, but not quite as good as the initial piece. By the third slice, the individual may enjoy the taste but might begin feeling stuffed or prefer to save room for dessert.

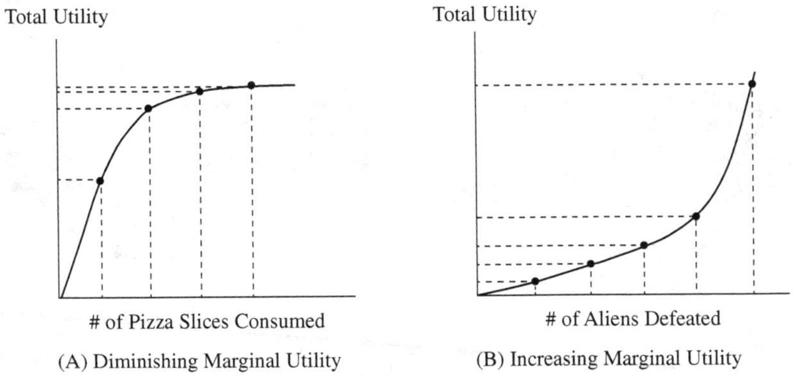

FIGURE 10.8 Utility functions: diminishing marginal utility and increasing marginal utility

This demonstration of diminishing marginal utility is illustrated as a concave utility curve that increases but gets flatter and flatter as more of a good is consumed and could even start to fall if the individual ate too much and became sick from the pizza.

On the other hand, it is also possible to experience increasing marginal utility. This is illustrated with the example of superheroes in their battle against evil forces (see Panel (B) of Figure 10.8). During an alien invasion, defeating one alien may be beneficial, but defeating the next one is even more satisfying because it means the city is closer to being safe from attack. As the Avengers defeat more and more aliens, their total utility increases at an increasing rate giving the graph its convex shape.

Since we are using fictional characters from comics, it is difficult to pin down a precise utility function, but we can use our own hypothetical values for our example.

Once we know the utility received from a particular outcome, to calculate a payoff, we multiply the probability that the Hulk makes the decision to cooperate or defect by the utility associated with each respective decision, and then add them together. This creates a weighted average of the outcomes of each possible decision.[6] In a simple example, suppose the Avengers receive a relatively high payoff if the Hulk joins the team and cooperates (utility = 500) while the Avengers receive a disutility (utility = −100) if the Hulk turns on them. The expected payoff for the Avengers will be dependent on the probability of making each decision in the tree shown in Figure 10.7. If there is a 50–50 chance that the Hulk will cooperate or defect, and if Banner agrees to unleash the Hulk, the expected payoff for the Avengers is: (0.5 × 500) + (0.5 × (-100)) = 200. Suppose, instead, that the payoff from the Hulk's assistance is smaller (utility = 100) than the possible outcome if the Hulk were to defect (utility = −500). Given the same probabilities, the expected payoff for the team would be (0.5 × 100) + (0.5 × (-500)) = −200. These two possibilities are shown in Figure 10.9. In this case, the possible damage caused by the Hulk weighs more heavily than the possible good that he could do.

If the Avengers calculated the above payoffs for the unpredictable Hulk's decision, would they choose to include him on the team? While the expected payoff is negative in the second scenario as a result of the weighted average, there is still a

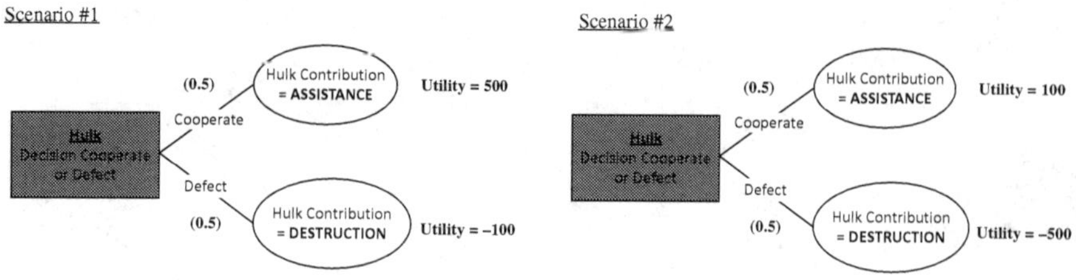

Expected Payoff: 0.5 × 500 + 0.5 × (–100) = 200
[a]

Expected Payoff: 0.5 × 100 + 0.5 × (–500) = –200
[b]

FIGURE 10.9 Two hypothetical payoffs for the Avengers after the Hulk joins the team

50% probability that the Hulk will help. Thus, the inclusion of the Hulk on the Avenger's team becomes a question of the other members' perception of the risk involved and their attitude towards risk. In economics, the degree of an individual's risk aversion defines the extent of hesitation with which he or she will agree to terms with an unknown payoff as opposed to terms with a known payoff that is potentially lower. If the Avengers are risk-averse, then they prefer a more certain or guaranteed outcome from *not* soliciting the Hulk's help over the uncertain outcome associated with calling in the Hulk. On the other hand, if the Avengers are risk-loving, then they are willing to take on uncertain outcomes associated with the Hulk knowing that while it is possible that there will be more net destruction with the Hulk, there is also a chance that they will be more effective with the Hulk's help. Finally, if the Avengers are risk-neutral, then they are willing to include the Hulk when his expected damage is equal to his expected assistance to the team, or in other words, their expected payoff is zero.

They're superheroes, they like risk

In the real world, firms and individuals are unlikely to engage in repeatedly risky behavior for high-stakes situations since it does not pay off for them in the long run. Diminishing marginal utility causes many individuals to "play it safe" with a certain outcome. Once diminishing marginal utility set in, the individual is trying to obtain an additional unit which yields a relatively smaller increase in utility when compared to the addition of previous units of the good. Therefore, the risk associated with this additional unit is not worth what the individual might potentially lose. On the other hand, because we revealed that superheroes actually experience increasing marginal utility in some cases, then superheroes might be risk-loving. This is apparent in the graph of the Avengers' convex utility function and in the following scenario shown in Figure 10.10.

Suppose there are five aliens attacking Earth. Without the Hulk's help, the Avengers can defeat three aliens providing a certain utility of U_3 (measured along the Y-axis). When the Hulk is on the team, but turns against his teammates, the Avengers can only defeat one alien (as measured along the X-axis) since they are

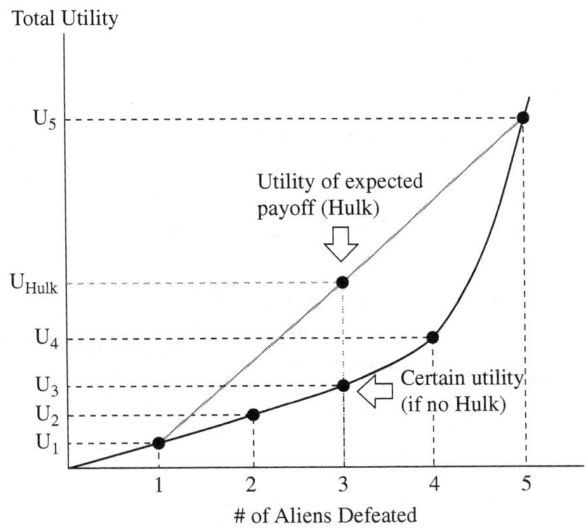

FIGURE 10.10 The convex shape of the Avengers' utility function shows that they are risk-loving

busy trying to fend off the Hulk too. Thus, they receive a utility of only U_1. On the other hand, the Avengers can defeat all five aliens when the Hulk is a cooperative part of the team so that their total utility will be U_5. With a 50% chance that the Hulk will cooperate, the expected payoff from having the Hulk on the team is equal to $(0.5 \times U_1) + (0.5 \times U_5)$, shown on the graph at U_{Hulk}. Because of the convex shape of the graph, the Avengers will receive more utility by gambling with the Hulk instead of playing it safe without the Hulk's assistance ($U_{Hulk} > U_3$).

Even for the average individual, it may pay to play the odds in certain instances. This may occur if a failing business is dealing with circumstances that indicate there is one shot that it may avoid going out of business if it gets lucky. Unlike businesses, however, superheroes are more likely to come across such desperate situations on a regular basis – they *are* responsible for saving the world, after all. For example, during the battle for New York City, Iron Man is able to intercept an approaching nuclear missile and flies it towards a portal opening in outer space (Weeden, 2012). Despite Captain America's warning that this plan is a "one way trip," Iron Man continues without hesitation. If superheroes are accustomed to choosing the "go for broke" strategy, then risks involved with recruiting the Hulk may seem acceptable considering his potential to help.

Furthermore, superheroes typically do not have to bear the full consequences of being wrong about a decision. Whether the superheroes win or lose, it is the local residents who are left to clean up the aftermath of a superhero altercation. This lack of accountability is yet another reason why calling in the Hulk may look like an appealing option for the Avengers.[7]

As a team, the Avengers do choose to employ the Hulk frequently, but not without taking precautions. Over time, the Avengers develop different ways to mitigate the risk of working with the Hulk. In the *Avengers* film, Nick Fury admits to Loki that the containment cell in which he is being held was "built for something a lot stronger than [him]" alluding to the reality that it was intended to hold the Hulk if he were to lose control (Weeden, 2012). Tony Stark additionally takes precautions for a Hulk gone rogue. On more than one occasion in the comics and the movies, Stark designs and operates variations of a specially-engineered "Hulkbuster" suit capable of battle with a green adversary (Kaminski and Hopgood, 1963; Weeden, 2015). These steps, taken in an attempt to control or repress the Hulk, require physical resources, time and effort that could be spent on their other heroic activities, but the Avengers nevertheless see this as a valuable undertaking for the end result of benefiting from the Hulk's power on their team.

Interestingly, even Bruce Banner joins in the efforts to rein in and subdue his other self. As a side story in the film *Age of Ultron* (Weeden, 2015), Banner collaborates with Stark to create "VERONICA," a satellite-run apparatus designed to house the Hulkbuster suit and other gear for putting down a raging Hulk. This "worst-case measure" represents Banner's intentions to help the Avengers, feelings which are not always shared by the Hulk given their contrasting preference sets.

Hulk smash! – but we're willing to take that chance

Although the Hulk may appear to be a simple and brutish character notorious only for his epic tantrums, the Hulk is actually a much more complex superhero involved in complicated relationships with his Banner-self as well as his fellow Avenger teammates. The inner relationship between the alter egos of Banner and the Hulk is defined by a continual struggle to maximize each side's utility based on their preferred allocations of power and reason. While their indifference curves illustrate the dichotomy between the two sides, Banner and Hulk nevertheless need each other for their shared body. In relating to others, the Hulk's association with the Avengers is one of uncertainty. While the Avengers hope to procure the power of an agreeable Hulk, they must prepare for the possibility that the Hulk can turn on them at any time with potentially disastrous ramifications. Consequently, employing the Hulk comes with risk that the Avengers must accept. Lucky for comic fans, the Avengers have a history of being risk-loving, allowing Hulk enthusiasts to see their favorite green monster in action.

Notes

1 In the Marvel comics, Loki is a god originating from Jotunheim, one of the distant planets making up what is known as the Nine Realms. King Odin, from the neighboring realm of Asgard, rescues Loki as a baby from abandonment and raises him alongside his own son Thor. Despite his adoption into the royal family of Asgard, Loki conspires against his family in multiple attempts to seize the throne for himself. Loki becomes a constant rival to Thor and a powerful villain for much of the Marvel universe, including planet Earth.

2 Although most people know the Hulk as a more reticent behemoth uttering only short, simplistic comments (i.e., "Hulk is the strongest one there is" and "Hulk smash!"), the original Hulk in the comics was much more loquacious.
3 This relationship of exchange is known as the *marginal rate of substitution*, which is also the slope of that individual's indifference curve.
4 There is some debate about the extent to which the Hulk is able to control himself and make decisions. However, in a final scene of *Avengers: Age of Ultron* (Weedon, 2015), we see the Hulk riding off in a jet and choosing to shut off communication with Black Widow when she requests that he take the jet out of stealth mode. This implies that the Hulk has full control of his faculties to decide not to be a part of the team for a while. For the purposes of our example, we do assume that the Hulk is able to intentionally choose to help or not – albeit, this will be based on his Hulk preferences of power over reason.
5 In the Marvel comics, a Helicarrier is analogous to a modern-day aircraft carrier. The main difference is that it can fly. It is the comics after all.
6 A weighted average is an average of a set of numbers where not all values are equally likely to occur. As a result, the numbers in the set are weighted based on their relative importance, or their probability of occurring.
7 Interestingly, the issue of the Avengers' liability and accountability is tackled in the film *Captain America: Civil War* (Russo, 2016). After the Avengers are publicly involved in an incident in Lagos, Nigeria which results in the death of humanitarian workers, the United Nations proposes the Sokovia Accords as a means of regulating and overlooking superhero activity. In the comics, the situation is a bit different, but the premise of making superheroes more accountable is the same.

References

Breznican, A. (2015, December 3). "Spider-man: 'Captain America: Civil War' role revealed." *Entertainment Weekly*. Retrieved from: http://ew.com/article/2015/12/03/spider-man-captain-america-civil-war/

Holmes, A. (2017, August 5). "Thor 3 may make this major change to the Hulk." *Cinema Blend*. Retrieved from: www.cinemablend.com/new/Thor-3-May-Make-Major-Change-Hulk-101707.html.

Leterrier, L. (Director). (2008). *The Incredible Hulk*. [Motion Picture].

Kaminski, L. and K. Hopgood. (1963). *Iron Man*, #304. Marvel Comics.

Kiefer, K. (2003). *The Hulk: Marvel Encyclopedia*. Vol. 3. New York: Marvel Comics.

Lee, S. and J. Kirby (1962). *The Incredible Hulk*, #1. Marvel Comics.

Lee, S. and J. Kirby. (1963). *The Avengers*, #1. Marvel Comics.

Nevets, S. (2011, May 27). "The Avengers' news: Mark Ruffalo on Hulk, relationship with Tony Stark." *The Global Dispatch*. Retrieved from: www.theglobaldispatch.com/the-avengers-news-ruffalo-on-hulk-58181/

Russo, A. (Director). (2016). *Captain America: Civil War*. [Motion Picture].

Weeden, J. (Director). (2012). *The Avengers* [Motion Picture].

Weeden, J. (Director). (2015). *Avengers: Age of Ultron* [Motion Picture].

INDEX

A Nation Under Our Feet 73, 75
Action Comics 81, 85
Alfred Pennyworth 16, 19, 21–23, 115
Amazing Spider-Man, The 40, 44, 46
Amazons, Amazonian 33–35
American Slavery, American Freedom 76
Ant-Man aka Hank Pym 44–45, 101, 125
Aphrodite 34
Aquaman 27
Arab Spring 71
Aunt May 38–40, 42–45
Avengers 41, 44, 52, 60–62, 65, 67, 75, 77, 101, 124–126, 130, 132, 133, 134–138
Avengers 52, 60, 132–133, 138
Avengers 2 106
Avengers: Age of Ultron 60, 133, 138

bat-shark repellent 115
batarang 19, 115
batcave 15, 18–20, 115
batcomputer 19, 23, 115
batfamily 22
Batgirl 22
Batman aka Bruce Wayne 8, 15–23, 91, 111–112, 114–115, 117
Batman Begins 17
batmobile 19, 21–23, 115
batplane 18–19
Batwoman 22
Becker, Gary 41
behavioral economics 57–58
Black Panther 65–68, 73–77
black swan 10
blood diamonds 71
Botswana 65, 72
Browning, Richard 107
Busiek, Kurt 11

capitalist system, market system 4, 88–89, 92, 109
Captain America aka Steve Rogers 3, 51–63, 65, 67, 77, 101, 137
Captain America: The First Avenger 51–53, 56, 58
Captain America: Winter Soldier 52, 57
Captain Marvel aka Shazam 5
Civil War 46, 47, 52, 60–61, 65, 69, 77, 103, 125
Coase, Ronald 84
Coates, Ta-Nehisi 73
colonialism, colonialization 66, 77
command system 88–89, 91–92, 109
Communist party 91
comparative advantage 23, 89
competitive market 116
compound return 52–54
corruption 69–70, 72, 82–83, 85–86
creative destruction 56

Daily Bugle, The 40, 43, 46
Daily Planet, The 81
Dark Knight 18–19
Dark Knight 17, 21, 91, 114
decreasing marginal utility 134–136
demand and supply 34
democracy 72–77, 83–84

Detective Comics 15, 114
dictator 68, 71, 74, 76, 81, 87–88, 90, 92
Dictator's Handbook, The 74
diminishing marginal productivity 119
Ditko, Steve 39
division of labor 70, 77
Doc Green 129
Doctor Doom 67, 75
Doctor Manhattan 8, 10

Eclipse Comics 5, 8
economic development 77
economic growth 51, 57, 63, 71, 82–83, 85
economic systems 88–89
Ellis, Warren 11
Elite, The 88
Elseworlds 91
eminent domain 104–105
Ethiopia 69–70
externalities 39, 45, 47, 59–60

Fantastic Four 3, 19, 40, 42, 66–67
Fantastic Four 65
feminist 25–28, 35
feminist economics 26, 29, 31, 35
fiduciary responsibility 101
Finger, Bill 114–115, 119
Forbes 15
Ford, Henry 104
free-rider 61
Frost, Robert 18
Fukuyama, Francis 84

game theory 132
Gibbons, Dave 8, 10
Gibson, Walter 112, 114, 119
Gotham 15–23 114
Green Arrow aka Oliver Queen 3, 17
Green Goblin 44–45
Gross Domestic Product (GDP) 29–31, 67, 70
Gwen Stacey 38, 45

habituation 59
Harold Alnut 21
hedonic adaptation 59
Hercules 34–35
Heroes for Hire 41
Hippolyta 28, 34
Howard Stark 53, 56
Hulk, the Incredible aka Bruce Banner 47, 65, 101, 124, 126, 129–132, 135–138
human capital 38, 41–42
Human Torch 42
Hume, David 74
Hydra 51–52, 58, 60

If Women Counted 29
incentives 62, 73, 107
income inequality 73, 88
increasing marginal utility 134–135
Incredible Hulk, The 126
indifference curve 127–130, 134, 138
inflation 52, 54, 63
information asymmetry 98, 100–102, 104, 108
institutions 51, 72, 80–83, 85–86, 89, 93
intellectual property 97, 109
internalize 47, 61–62
international trade 68
Iron Fist aka Danny Rand 17, 41
Iron Man 17, 104
Iron Man 2 104–105
Iron Man aka Tony Stark 3, 17, 41, 44–47, 52, 60, 62, 65, 97–109, 125, 133, 137–138
isocost 119–121
isoquant 118–120

J. Jonah Jameson 46
J.A.R.V.I.S. 106, 108
James "Rhodey" Rhodes 102, 105
James Gordon 115, 120
Jason Todd 22
Jobs, Steve 42
Joker 21
Jonathan Bates aka Kid Miracleman 6, 9
Justice League 19, 28, 115

Kane, Bob 114–115, 119
Kenya 69–70
Khama, Seretse 72
Kingdom Come 87
Kirby, Jack 65–66, 98, 124
Krypton 80–81
Ku Klux Klan 67

labor/capital choice 111
Lee, Stan 39, 65–66, 98, 124
Lex Luthor 87, 90
living wage 32
Locke, John 75
Lois Lane 87, 89–90
Loki 125, 132–133, 138
Lucius Fox 21, 115

marginal productivity 121
Mars 32, 35

Marston, William Moulton aka Charles Moulton 26–27, 31
Marston, Elizabeth 27–28
Mary Jane Watson 38, 44–45
Miller, Frank 114
minimum wage 33
Miracleman 7, 9
Miracleman aka Marvelman 1, 5–6, 10
money 7
Moore, Alan 1–3, 8, 10–11
moral hazard 98, 102, 105, 107–109
Morgan, Edmund 76
Morrison, Grant 11
Mr. Fantastic aka Reed Richards 41, 44, 67–68
Ms. Magazine 25, 33, 35
Musk, Elon 97, 107–108

Natasha Romanov 132–133
natural resource curse 65, 68, 70–71
Nazi 5, 34, 51, 58
negative externality 46–47, 61–62
New York City 41–42, 46, 66, 103, 133–134, 137
Nick Fury 52, 57–58, 60, 138
Nobel Prize 29, 81–82, 84–85
North, Douglas 81

Obediah Stane 100–102
Of the First Principles of Government 74
opportunity cost 18, 21, 23, 38, 47, 99

Pa Kent 81, 90
Peggy Carter 58
Penguin 21
Pepper Potts 100
positive externality 45–47, 61–62
Power Man aka Luke Cage 41, 46
preference map 128, 130
principal-agent problem 98, 101–102, 105–106, 108
production function 112
productivity 68, 116
property rights, private property 71, 73, 83–85, 87, 105, 109
public choice 52
public goods 52, 59–60, 62, 72–73, 75, 103–104, 109
Punisher, The 40

Radio Shack 42, 56
risk aversion 136, 138
rivalry 59
Robin aka Dick Grayson aka Nightwing 16, 22–23, 114–115, 120, 24n3
Ruffalo, Mark 134
Rule of 70 53

S.H.I.E.L.D. 41, 52, 60, 101
Sanger, Margaret 27
Scarcity 16- 18, 21, 23, 29, 51
Scarlet Witch 133
Scenario Planning 9–11
Schumpeter, Joseph 56
Sen, Amartya 29
Series E Savings Bonds aka Defense or War Bonds 53
Sese Seko, Mobutu 71
Shadow aka Lamont Cranston aka Kent Allard 111–113, 117
Shuster, Joe 82, 86
Siegel, Jerry 82, 86
Smith, Adam 59, 69
Sokovia Accords 52, 60–62
Solow Robert 82
specialization 23, 68, 77
Spider-Man aka Peter Parker 3, 38–47, 89
Spoiler Alert 21
Squirrel Girl 43
Stalin, Joseph 91
Steinem, Gloria 25, 33
Steve Trevor 28, 34
Sudan 69–70
Superhero Registration Act 47, 109
Superman aka Clark Kent aka Kal-El 3, 8, 80–82, 85–93
Superman: Red Son 91–92
Swamp Thing 8

TALOS 97, 107
T'Challa 67, 76–77
Thanos 45, 75
Themescarya aka Paradise Island 26, 34–35
Theory of Moral Sentiments 59
Thing 42, 68
third party 39, 60–62
Thor 65, 101, 125, 133
Tim Drake 22
trade offs 23, 98–99, 108, 111

Uganda 69–70
Ultron 10
Uncle Ben 39–41, 45
United Nations 108
utility 38, 42–43, 47, 58, 90, 98- 100, 102, 127, 130, 134–136, 138
utility function 134–135

V for Vendetta 1, 4–5, 7
vibranium 66, 68, 73, 76

Wakanda, Wakandan, Wakandans 61, 65–70, 72–73, 75–77
Waring, Marilyn 29
Warrior 4–5, 8
Warsaw Pact 91
Wasp 101, 125
Watchmen 1, 7, 8, 10
Wayne Enterprises aka Wayne Industries 15, 17, 19, 20, 21, 23, 122
Wayne Manor 15, 17, 18, 19, 20, 21, 115
Wealth of Nations 59
Whitney, Eli 106
Winter Soldier aka Bucky Barnes 51, 65, 77
Women and the New Race 27
Women's Lib issue 33
Wonder Woman aka Diana Prince 25–35
World War I 112–113
World War II, Second World War 26, 28, 32, 51, 53, 72, 80,

Zeus 28